Edward Harrison Barker

Two summers in Guyenne: A chronicle of the wayside and waterside

Edward Harrison Barker

Two summers in Guyenne: A chronicle of the wayside and waterside

ISBN/EAN: 9783337142995

Printed in Europe, USA, Canada, Australia, Japan

Cover: Foto ©Andreas Hilbeck / pixelio.de

More available books at **www.hansebooks.com**

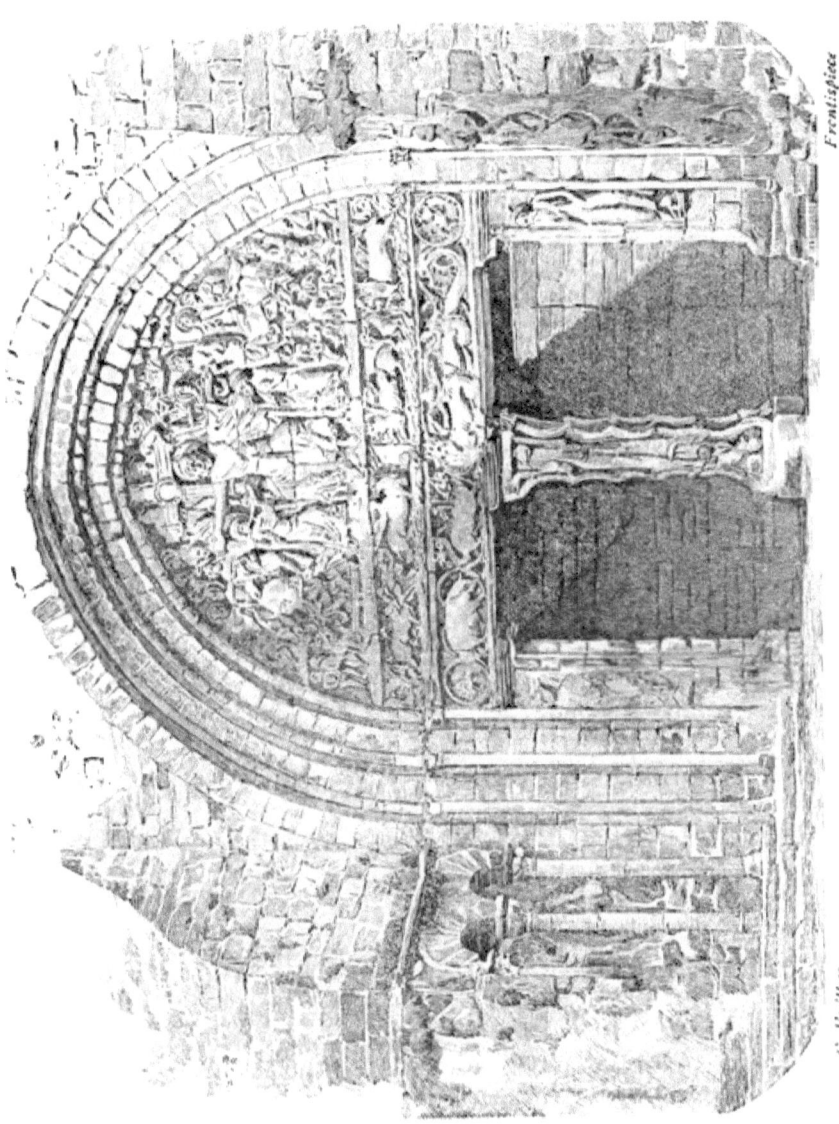

DOORWAY OF THE ABBEY CHURCH AT BEAULIEU (CORRÈZE).

Two Summers in Guyenne

A Chronicle of the Wayside and Waterside

BY

EDWARD HARRISON BARKER
AUTHOR OF
'WAYFARING IN FRANCE,' 'WANDERINGS BY SOUTHERN WATERS,' ETC

WITH MAP AND ILLUSTRATIONS

LONDON
RICHARD BENTLEY AND SON
Publishers in Ordinary to Her Majesty the Queen
1894
[All rights reserved]

PREFACE.

Of the four summers which the writer of this 'Chronicle of the Wayside and Waterside' spent by Aquitanian rivers, the greater part of two provided the impressions that were used in 'Wanderings by Southern Waters.' Although the earlier pages of the present work, describing the wild district of the Upper Dordogne, through which the author passed into Guyenne, belong, in the order of time, to the beginning of his scheme of travel in Aquitaine, the summers of 1892 and 1893, spent chiefly in Périgord and the Bordelais, furnished the matter of which this volume is mainly composed. Hence the title that has been given to it.

It may be thought that there is not a sufficient separation of interest, geographically speaking, between the tracts of country described in the two books. The author regrets that it is not possible to convey in a few words an idea of the extent of the old English Duchy of Aquitaine as it was defined by the Treaty of Brétigny. Still less easy would it be to deal rapidly with its physical contrasts, its relics of the past, and its historical associations. Surely no writer could pretend to have exhausted the interest of such a subject even in two volumes.

Before the final expulsion of the English, Aquitaine was gradually taking the name of Guyenne; but when this designation came to be definitively applied, at the time of the Renaissance, Gascony was not included in it, nor were Poitou, Saintonge, Angoumois and Limousin. Even when thus restricted in its meaning, Guyenne still represented a very considerable part of France, including as it did the regions or sub-provinces known as the Bordelais, Périgord, the Agenais, the Rouergue, and the Quercy.

If the author's work during the fifteen years that he has been living in France has served to make the people, the scenery, and the antiquities of this ever-fascinating country somewhat better known to those who speak the English language, he believes that it is to his favourite mode of travelling that such good fortune must be largely attributed. His faring on foot has caused him to see much that he would otherwise have never seen; it has also widened his knowledge of his fellow-men, and has helped him to control prejudices which are not to be entirely overcome, but ever remain an insidious snare to the traveller and student of manners.

E. H. B.

PARIS, *May*, 1894.

CONTENTS

	PAGE
THE UPPER DORDOGNE	1
ACROSS THE MOORS OF THE CORRÈZE	29
IN THE VISCOUNTY OF TURENNE	66
IN UPPER PÉRIGORD	88
IN THE VALLEY OF THE VÉZÈRE	151
IN THE VALLEY OF THE ISLE	180
FROM PÉRIGUEUX TO RIBERAC (BY BRANTÔME)	218
THE DESERT OF THE DOUBLE	244
A CANOE VOYAGE ON THE DRONNE	281
BY THE LOWER DORDOGNE	322
BY THE GARONNE	378

LIST OF ILLUSTRATIONS

	PAGE
DOORWAY OF THE ABBEY CHURCH AT BEAULIEU (CORRÈZE)	*Frontispiece*
A BIT OF AUVERGNE	1
THE DORDOGNE AT LA BOURBOULE	3
A MOORLAND WIDOW	15
THE VALLEY OF THE RUE	28
A WOMAN OF THE CORRÈZE	29
A PEASANT OF THE MOORS	34
PLOUGHING THE MOOR	53
A GORGE IN THE CORRÈZE	55
TURENNE	66
A PEASANT OF THE CAUSSE	76
CHÂTEAU DE FÉNELON	96
RETURNING FROM THE FIELDS	100
BEYNAC	109
CLOISTERS OF THE ABBEY OF CADOUIN	143
CHÂTEAU DE BIRON: THE LODGE	146
TRUFFLE-HUNTERS	151
CHÂTEAU DES EYZIES	154
CHÂTEAU DE HAUTEFORT	179
A HOUSE AT PÉRIGUEUX	180
THE TOUR DE VÉSONE	214
THE 'NORMAN GATE' AT PÉRIGUEUX	216

LIST OF ILLUSTRATIONS

	PAGE
THE DRONNE AT BOURDEILLES	218
THE ABBEY OF BRANTÔME	222
CHÂTEAU DE BOURDEILLES	226
THE DRONNE AT COUTRAS	281
A STREET AT ST. ÉMILION	322
CHÂTEAU DE MONTAIGNE	329
MONOLITHIC CHURCH AND DETACHED TOWER AT ST. ÉMILION	364
CONVENT OF THE CORDELIERS AT ST. ÉMILION	367
TOUR DE L'HORLOGE AT LIBOURNE	374
THE HILL OF FRONSAC	376
BAZAS	381
INTERIOR OF THE CHÂTEAU DE VILLANDRAUT	385
THE GARONNE	387
CHÂTEAU DE MONTESQUIEU	400
THE GARONNE AT BORDEAUX	406
THE PALAIS GALLIEN AT BORDEAUX	407

THE UPPER DORDOGNE.

A BIT OF AUVERGNE.

I HAD left the volcanic mountains of Auvergne and had passed through Mont-Dore and La Bourboule, following the course of the Dordogne that flowed through the valley with the bounding spirits of a young mountaineer descending for the first time towards the great plains where the large towns and cities lie with all their fancied wonders and untasted charm. But these towns and cities were afar off. The young Dordogne had a very long journey to make before reaching the plains of Périgord. Nearly the whole of this distance the stream would have to thread its way through deep-cut gorges and ravines, where the dense forest reaches down to the stony channel, save where the walls of rock rising hundreds of feet on either side are too steep for vegetation. Above the forest and the rock is the desert moor, horrible to the peasant, but to the lover of nature beautiful when seen in its dress of purple heather and golden broom.

I had not been long on the road this day, when I saw coming towards me an equipage more picturesquely interesting than any I had ever met in the Champs-Elysées. It was a ramshackle little cart laden with sacks and a couple of children, and drawn by a pair of shaggy sheep-dogs. Cords served for harness. A man was running by the side, and it was as much as he could do to keep up with the animals. This use of dogs is considered cruel in England, but it often keeps them out of mischief, and I have never seen one in harness that looked unhappy. Traces must help a dog to grow in his own esteem, and to work out his ideal of the high destiny reserved for him; or why does he, when tied under a cart to which a larger quadruped is harnessed, invariably try to persuade himself and others that he is pulling the load up the hill, and that the horse or donkey is an impostor?

The width of the Mont-Dore valley decreased rapidly, and I entered the gorge of the Dordogne,

where basaltic rocks were thrown up in savage
grandeur, vividly contrasting with which were bands

THE DORDOGNE AT LA BOURBOULE.

and patches of meadow, brilliantly green. Yellow
spikes of agrimony and the fine pink flowers of the

musk-mallow mingled with the wiry broom and the waving bracken about the rocks.

It was September, but the summer heat had returned, and when the road passed through a beech-wood the shade was welcome. Here over the mossy ground rambled the enchanter's nightshade, still carrying its frail white flowers, which really have a weird appearance in the twilight of the woods. The plant has not been called *circe* without a reason. Under the beeches there were raspberry canes with some fruit still left upon them. After leaving the wood, the scene became more wild and craggy. The basalt, bare and sombre, or sparsely flecked with sedums, their stalks and fleshy leaves now very red, rose sheer from the middle of the narrow valley, adown which the stream sped like fleeing Arethusa, now turning to the right, now to the left, foaming over rocks or sparkling like the facets of countless gems between margins of living green.

Then I left the valley in order to pass through the village of St. Sauve on the right-hand hill. There was little there worth seeing besides a very ancient Romanesque archway, or, as some think, detached portico leading to the church.

Many of the women of St. Sauve wore the black cap or bonnet of Mont-Dore, which hangs to the shoulders. It is a hideous coiffure, but an interesting relic of the past. The prototype of it was worn by the châtelaines of the twelfth century. Then, however, it had a certain stateliness which it lacks now. It is only to be seen in a very small district.

I consulted some of the people of St. Sauve respecting my plan of following the Dordogne through its gorges. They did not laugh at me, but they looked at me in a way which meant that if better brains had not been given to them than to me their case would be indeed unfortunate. I was advised to see a cobbler who was considered an authority on the byways of the district. I found him sitting by the open window of his little shop driving hob-nails into a pair of Sunday boots. When I told him what I had made up my mind to do, he shook his head, and, laying down his work, said:

'You will never do it. There are rocks, and rocks, and rocks. Even the fishermen, who go where anybody can go, do not try to follow the Dordogne very far. There are ravines — and ravines. *Bon Dieu!* And the forest! You will be lost! You will be devoured!'

To be devoured would be the climax of misfortune. I wished to know what animals would be likely to stop my wayfaring in this effectual manner.

'Are there wolves?'

'No; none have been seen for years.'

'Are there boars?'

'Yes, plenty of them.'

'But boars,' I said, 'are not likely to interfere with me.'

'That is true,' replied the local wiseacre, 'so long as you keep walking; but if you fall down a rock—ah!'

'I would not care to have you for a companion, with all your local knowledge,' I thought, as I thanked the cobbler and turned down a very stony path towards the Dordogne. It is always prudent to follow the advice of those who are better informed than yourself; but it is much more amusing—for awhile—to go your own way. I had lunched, and was prepared to battle with the desert for several hours. It was now past mid-day, and notwithstanding the altitude, the heat was very great. But for the discomfort that we endure from the sun's rays we are more than amply compensated by the pleasure that the recollection brings us in winter, when the north wind is moaning through the sunless woods and the dreary fog hangs over the cities. When I again reached the Dordogne there was no longer any road, but only a rough path through high bracken, heather and broom. Snakes rustled as I passed, and hid themselves among the stones. The cobbler had forgotten to include these with the dangers to be encountered. To my mind they were much more to be dreaded than the boars, for these stony solitudes swarm with adders, of which the most venomous kind is the red viper, or *aspic*. Its bite has often proved mortal.

The path entered the forest which covers the steep sides of the ever-winding gorge of the Dordogne for many leagues, only broken where the rocks are so nearly vertical that no soil has ever formed upon them, except in the little crevices and upon the ledges, where the hellebore, the sedum, the broom, and other unambitious plants which love sterility flourish where the foot of man has never trod.

The rocks were now of gneiss and mica-schist, and the mica was so abundant as to cause many a crag and heap of shale to glitter in the sun, as though there had been a mighty shattering of mirrors here into little particles which had fallen upon everything. There was, however, no lack of contrast. To the shining rocks and the fierce sunshine, which seemed to concentrate its fire wherever it fell in the open spaces of the deep gorge, succeeded the ancient forest and its cool shade; but the darkly-lying shadows were ever broken with patches of sunlit turf. Pines and firs reached almost to the water's edge, and the great age of some of them was a proof of the little value placed upon timber in a spot so inaccessible. One fir had an enormous bole fantastically branched like that of an English elm, and on its mossy bark was a spot such as the hand might cover, fired by a wandering beam, that awoke recollections of the dream-haunted woods before the illusion of their endlessness was lost.

The afternoon was not far spent, when I began to feel a growing confidence in the value of the cobbler's information, and a decreasing belief in my own powers. It became more and more difficult, then quite impossible, to keep along the bank of the stream. What is understood by a bank disappeared, and in its stead were rocks, bare and glittering, on which the lizards basked, or ran in safety, because they were at home, but which I could only pass by a flank movement. To struggle up a steep hill, over slipping shale-like stones, or through an undergrowth of holly and brambles, then to scramble down and to climb again, repeating the exercise every few hundred yards, may have a hygienic charm for those who are tormented by the dread of obesity, but to other mortals it is too suggestive of a holiday in purgatory.

Having gone on in this fashion for some distance, I lay down, streaming from every pore, and panting like a hunted hare beside a little rill that slid singing between margins of moss, amid Circe's white flowers and purple flashes of cranesbill. Here I examined my scratches and the state of things generally. The result of my reflections was to admit that the cobbler was right, that these ravines of the Upper Dordogne were practically impassable, and that the only rational way of following the river would be to keep sometimes on the hills and sometimes in the gorge, as the unforeseen might determine. Hitherto, I had not troubled to inquire where I should pass the night, and this consideration alone would have compelled me to depart from my fantastic scheme. After La Bourboule there is not a village or hamlet in the valley of the Dordogne for a distance of at least thirty miles, allowing for the winding of the stream.

After a hard climb I reached the plateau, where I saw before me a wide moor completely covered with bracken and broom. Here I looked at the map, and decided to make towards a village called Messeix, lying to the east in a fork formed by the Dordogne and its tributary the Chavannon. Going by the compass at first, I presently struck a road leading across the moor in the right direction. I passed through two wretched hamlets, in neither of which was there an auberge where I could relieve my thirst. At the second one a cottage was pointed out to me where I was told a woman sold wine. When, after sinking deep in mud, I found her amidst a group of hovels, and the preliminary salutation was given, the following conversation passed between us:

'They tell me you sell wine.'
'They tell you wrong—I don't.'
'Do you sell milk, then?'
'No; I have no beasts.'

As I was going away she kindly explained that she only kept enough wine for herself. I had evidently not impressed her favourably. Although I think water a dangerous drink in France, except where it can be received directly from the hand of Nature, far from human dwellings, I was obliged to beg some in this place, and run the risk of carrying away unfriendly microbes.

Having left the hovels behind me, the country became less barren or more cultivated. There were fields of rye, buckwheat, and potatoes, but always near them lay the undulating moor, gilded over with the flowers of a dwarf broom. It was evening when I descended into a wide valley from which came the chime of cattle-bells, mingled with the barking of dogs and the voices of children, who were driving the animals slowly homeward. There were green meadows below me, over which was a yellow gleam from the fading afterglow of sunset, and in the air was that odour which, rising from grassy valleys at the close of day, even in regions burnt by the southern summer, makes the wandering Englishman fancy that some wayfaring wind has come laden with the breath of his native land. Suddenly turning a corner, I so startled a little peasant girl sitting on a bank in the early twilight with a flock of goats about her, that she opened her mouth and stared at me as though Croquemitaine had really shown himself at last. The goats stopped eating, and fixed upon me their eyes like glass marbles; they, too, thought that I could be no good.

I hoped that the village of Messeix was in this valley; but no, I had to cross it and climb the opposite hill. On the other side I found the place that I had fixed upon for my night quarters.

Very small and very poor, it lies in a region where the land generally is so barren that but a small part of it has been ever broken by the plough; where the summers are hot and dry, and the winters long and cruel. Although in the watershed of the Gironde, it touches Auvergne, and its altitude makes it partake very much of the Auvergnat climate, which, with the exception of the favoured Limagne Valley, is harsh, to an extent that has caused many a visitor to flee from Mont-Dore in the month of August. In the deep gorges of the Dordogne and its tributaries, the snow rarely lies more than a few days upon the ground, whereas upon the wind-swept plateau above the scanty population have to contend with the rigours of that French Siberia which may be said to commence here on the west, and to extend eastward over the whole mass of metamorphic and igneous rocks, which is termed the great central plateau of France, although it lies far south of the true centre of the country.

At the first auberge where I applied for a night's lodging, an elderly woman with a mournful face declined to take me in, and gave no reason. When I had left, she came after me and said, with her eyes full of tears :

'I have a great trouble in the house, that is why I sent you away.'

I understood what she meant ; somebody dear to her was dying. A man who was listening said his brother-in-law, the baker, was also an innkeeper, and he offered to take me to the auberge. I gladly consented, for I was fearful of being obliged to tramp on to some other place. Presently I was in a large, low room, which was both kitchen and baker's shop. On shelves were great wheel-shaped loaves (they are called *miches* in the provinces), some about two feet in diameter, made chiefly of rye with a little wheaten flour. Filled sacks were ranged along the wall. In a deep recess were the kneading-trough, and the oven, now cold. The broad rural hearth, with its wood-fire and sooty chimney, the great pot for the family soup hanging to a chain, took up a large share of the remaining space. I sat upon a rickety chair beside a long table that had seen much service, but was capable of seeing a great deal more, for it had been made so as to outlast generations of men. Bare-footed children ran about upon the black floor, and a thin, gaunt young woman, who wore very short petticoats, which revealed legs not unlike those of the table, busied herself with the fire and the pot. She was the sister of the children, and had been left in charge of the house while her father and mother were on a journey. She accepted me as a lodger, but for awhile she was painfully taciturn. This, however, her scanty knowledge of French, and the fact that a stranger even of the class of small commercial travellers was a rare bird in the village, fully accounted for. The place was not cheerful, but as I listened to the crickets about the hearth, and watched the flames leap up and lick the black pot, my spirits rose. Presently the church bell sounded, dong, dong, dong.

'Why are they tolling the bell?' I asked.

'Because,' replied the gaunt young woman, 'a man has died in the village.'

By pressing her to speak, she explained that while a corpse lay unburied the bell was tolled three times in the day—early in the morning, at mid-day, and at nightfall. The conversation was in darkness, save such light as the fire gave. It was not until the soup was ready that the lamp was lighted. Then the young woman, addressing me abruptly, said:

'Cut up your bread for your soup.'

I did as I was told, for I always try to accommodate myself to local customs, and never resent the rough manners of well-intentioned people. The bread was not quite black, but it was very dark from the amount of rye that was in it. The soup was water flavoured with a suggestion of fat bacon, whatever vegetables happened to be in the way, and salt. This fluid, poured over bread—when the latter is not boiled with it—is the chief sustenance of the French peasant. It was all that the family now had for their evening meal, and in five minutes everyone had finished. They drank no wine; it was too expensive for them, the nearest vineyard being far away. A bottle, however, was placed before me, but the quality was such that I soon left it. To get some meat for me the village had to be scoured, and the result was a veal cutlet.

I was not encouraged to sit up late. As the

eldest daughter of the inn showed me my night quarters, she said :

'Your room is not beautiful, but the bed is clean.'

This was quite true. The room, in accordance with a very frequent arrangement in these rural auberges, was not used exclusively for sleeping purposes, but also for the entertainment of guests, especially on fair and market days, when space is precious. There was a table with a bench for the use of drinkers. There were, moreover, three beds, but I was careful to ascertain that none would be occupied except by myself. I would sooner have slept on a bundle of hay in the loft than have had an unknown person snoring in the same room with me. One has always some prejudice to overcome. The bed was not soft, and the hempen sheets were as coarse as canvas, but these trifles did not trouble me. I listened to the song of the crickets on the hearth downstairs until drowsiness beckoned sleep and consciousness of the present lost its way in sylvan labyrinths by the Dordogne.

At six o'clock the next morning I was walking about the village, and I entered the little church, already filled with people. It was Sunday, and this early mass was to be a funeral one. The man for whom the bell was tolled last night was soon brought in, the coffin swathed in a common sheet. It was borne up the nave towards the catafalque, the rough carpentry of which showed how poor the

A MOORLAND WIDOW.

parish was. Following closely was an old and bent woman with her head wrapped in a black shawl. She had hardly gone a few steps, when her grief burst out into the most dismal wailing I had ever heard, and throughout the service her melancholy cries made other women cover their faces, and tears start from the eyes of hard-featured, weather-beaten men.

Most of the women present wore the very ugly headgear which is the most common of all in Auvergne and the Corrèze, namely, a white cap covered by a straw bonnet something of the coal-scuttle pattern. There were many communicants at this six o'clock mass, and what struck me as being the reverse of what one might suppose the right order of things, was that the women advanced in life wore white veils as they knelt at the altar rails, while those worn by the young, whose troubles were still to come, were black. These veils were carried in the hand during the earlier part of the rite. Throughout a very wide region of Southern France the custom prevails. The church belonged to different ages. Upon the exterior of the Romanesque apse were uncouth carvings in relief of strange animal figures. They were more like lions than any other beasts, but their outlines were such as children might have drawn.

I returned to the inn. The baker had come back, and was preparing to heat his oven with dry broom. I learned that he had not only to bake the bread that he sold, but also the coarser rye loaves which were brought in by those who had their own flour, but no oven. Three francs was the charge for my dinner, bed, and breakfast. The score settled and civilities exchanged, I walked out of Messeix, expecting to strike the valley of the Dordogne not very far to the south. The landscape was again that of the moorland. On each side of the long, dusty line called a road spread the brown turf, spangled with the pea-flowers of the broom or stained purple with heather. There were no trees, but two wooden crosses standing against the gray sky looked as high as lofty pines. I met little bands of peasants hurrying to church, and I reached the village of Savennes just before the *grand' messe*. Many people were sitting or standing outside the church—even sitting on the cemetery wall. When the bell stopped and they entered, literally like a flock of sheep into a fold, all could not find room inside, so the late-comers sat upon the ground in the doorway, or as near as they could get to it. As the people inside knelt or stood, so did they who had been left, not out in the cold, but in the heat, for the sun had broken through the mist, and the weather was sultry. As I walked round the church I found women sitting with open books and rosaries in their hands near the apse, amidst the yarrow and mulleins of forgotten grave mounds. They were following the service by the open window. I lingered about the cemetery reading the quaint inscriptions and noting the poor emblems upon wooden crosses not yet decayed, picking here and there a wild flower, and watching the butterflies and bees until the old priest, who was singing the mass in a voice broken by time, having called upon his people to 'lift up their hearts,' they answered: '*Habemus ad Dominum.*'

I had a simple lunch at a small inn in this village, where I was watched with much curiosity by an old man in a blouse with a stiff shirt-collar rising to his ears, and a nightcap with tassel upon his head. The widow who kept the inn had a son who offered to walk with me as far as some chapel in the gorge of the Chavannon. We were not long in reaching the gorge, the view of which from the edge of the plateau was superbly savage. Descending a very rugged path through the forest that covered the sides of the deep fissure, save where the stark rock refused to be clothed, we came to a small chapel, centuries old, under a natural wall of gneiss, but deep in the shade of overhanging boughs. It was dedicated to St. John the Baptist, and on St. John's Day mass was said in it, and the spot was the scene of a pilgrimage. Outside was a half-decayed moss-green wooden platform on which the priest stood while he preached to the assembled pilgrims. The young man left me, and I went on alone into the more sombre depths of the gorge, where I reached the single line of railway that runs here through some of the wildest scenery in France. I kept on the edge of it, where walking, although very rough, was easier than on the steep side of the split that had here taken place in the earth's crust. Upon the narrow stony strip of comparatively level ground the sun's rays fell with concentrated ardour, and along it was a brilliant bloom of late summer flowers—of camomile, St. John's wort, purple loosestrife, hemp-agrimony and lamium. At almost every step there was a rustle of a lizard or a snake. The melancholy cry of the hawk was the only sound of bird-life. Near rocks of dazzling mica-schist was a miserable hut with a patch of buckwheat reaching to the stream. A man standing amidst the white flowers of the late-sown crop said, in answer to my questioning, that I could not possibly reach the village of Port-Dieu without walking upon the line and through the tunnels.

When I had left him about fifty yards behind, his curiosity proved more than he could bear in silence; so he called out to me, in the bad French that is spoken hereabouts by those who use it only as the language of strangers: '*Quel métier que vous faites?*'

I waved my hand in reply and left him to his conjectures.

On I went, now over the glittering stones, now wading through the pink flowers of saponaria, then in a mimic forest of tall angelica by the water's edge, until I realized that the peasant's information was sound—that it was impossible to walk through this gorge except upon the railway.

Presently the rocks rose in front of me and the line disappeared into the darkness of a tunnel. I did not like the idea of entering this black hole, for I had brought no candle with me, but the prospect of climbing the rocks was still more forbidding. It proved to be a short and straight tunnel with daylight shining at the farther end. After this came another short one, but the third was much longer and had a curve; consequently I was soon in total darkness. The only danger to be feared was a passing train, so I felt with my stick for the wires between the rock and the metals, and crept along by them. From being broiled by the sun ten minutes before I was now shivering from the cold. I longed to see again the flowers basking under the warm sky, and to hear the grasshoppers' happy song. By-and-by I saw the blessed light flashing at the end of the black bore. When I came out again into the sunshine, I was following, not the Chavannon, but the Dordogne.

The gorge widened into a valley, where there were scattered cottages, cows, sheep, and goats. Here I found a fair road on the western side of the river, in the department of the Corrèze, and being now free of mind, I loitered on the way, picking strawberries and watching the lizards. It was dark when, descending again to the level of the Dordogne, I sought a lodging in the little village of Port-Dieu. I stopped at a cottage inn, where an old man soon set to work at the wood-fire and cooked me a dinner of eggs and bacon and fried potatoes. He was a rough cook, but one very anxious to please. The room where I passed the night had a long table in it, and benches. There was no blanket on the bed, only a sheet and a heavy patchwork quilt. Ah, yes, there was something else, carefully laid upon the quilt. This was a linen bag without an opening, which, when spread out, tapered towards the ends. Had I not known something about the old-fashioned nightcap, I should have puzzled a long time before discovering what I was expected to do with this object. The matter is simple to those who know that the cap is formed by turning one of the ends in. There were mosquitoes in the room, but they sang me to sleep, and if they amused themselves at my expense afterwards, I was quite unconscious of it.

The murmur of the rushing Dordogne mingled not unpleasantly with the impressions of dreams as I awoke. I got up and opened the small worm-eaten window-frame. High thatched roofs, not many yards in front, were covered with moss, which the morning rays, striking obliquely, painted the heavenly green of Beatrice's mantle. Down the narrow road goats were passing, followed by a sun-burnt girl with a barge-like wooden shoe at the end of each of her bare brown legs. The pure, life-giving air that entered by the window made the blood glow with a better warmth than that of sparkling wine. I soon went outside to see something of the place which I had entered in the darkness.

I found that the village was built partly in the bottom of the gorge and partly on one of its craggy sides. Closely hemmed in by rocks and high hills overgrown with forest was a bright and fertile little valley, with abundance of pear and walnut trees, luxuriant cottage-gardens, and little fields by the flashing torrent, where shocks of lately-cut buckwheat stood with their heads together waiting for the warm September hours to ripen their black grain.

Many of the houses were half hidden in leafy bowers. I threaded my way between these towards some ivy-draped fragments of an ancient priory upon a mass of rock much overgrown with brambles glistening with blackberries and briars decked with coral-red hips. Before descending to the road and beginning the day's journey I indulged for a little while the musing mood of the solitary wanderer in the grassy burying-ground on the edge of the cliff.

I started for Bort ere the intensely blue sky began to pale before the increasing brilliancy of the sun. The road ran along the bottom of the deep valley, where there was change of scene with every curve of the Dordogne. A field of maize showed how different was the climate here from that of the bleak plateau above the deep rift in the rocks. I stopped beside a little runnel that came down from the wooded heights to pick some flowers of yellow balsam, and while there my eye fell upon a splendid green lizard basking in the sun. Here was another proof of the warm temperature of the valley, notwithstanding its altitude. As I went on I skirted long fields of buckwheat upon the slope, but reaching only a little way upwards. The white waxen flowers had turned, or were turning, rusty; but what a variety of beautiful colour was on the stems and leaves! Greens and yellows passed into carmine, purple, and burnt sienna. A field of ripening buckwheat has a charm of warm colour that gladdens the eye, especially when the morning or evening sunshine is upon it. But this glow of many tints was a sure sign of approaching autumn; so, too, were the reddened stalks of persicaria, filling the dry ditches by the wayside.

The valley narrowed, and upon its rocky sides was many a patch of purple heather—little gardens for the wild bees, but not for man. Neither peasant nor local Nimrod ever sets his foot there. Still higher, the outlines of the topmost crags were drawn hard against the sky, for there was no vapour in the air. Verily, the ground seemed quite alive with brown lizards darting along at my approach and raising little clouds of dust, whilst blue-winged grasshoppers—which, perhaps, would be more correctly described as locusts—crossed and recrossed the road in one flight. In the midst of such beautiful scenery, and with such happy creatures for companions, I felt no wish to hurry. Moreover, the blackberries sometimes tempted me to loiter. If they are unwholesome, as French peasants often maintain, I ought to have been dead long ago. Strange that this prejudice should be so general in France with regard to the fruit of so harmless a tribe. But these same peasants gather the leaves of the bramble to make a decoction for sore throat. I passed a cottage that had a vine-trellis, the first I had seen on this side of the Auvergne mountains, and it was half surrounded by a forest of beans in full flower on very high sticks. In a sunny space was a row of thatched beehives.

After walking some eight miles, I was not unwilling to take advantage of a village inn. Here I had a meal of bacon and eggs, haricots, cheese and walnuts, with some rather rough Limousin wine. I soon became aware that there was something amiss in the rustic auberge, and catching a dim glimpse of a figure lying in a bed in a small room adjoining, I asked the young woman who waited upon me if anybody was ill there. 'Yes,' she replied dolefully. Then I learnt from her that her father, struck with apoplexy, was lying in a state that was hopeless. There is no escaping the mournfulness of life. When our minds are least clouded the shadow of death suddenly stands between us and the sunshine. I was in no mood to linger at the table.

What a relief to be out again in the sunshine and the light air, to see the Dordogne flashing through meadows where women were haymaking with bare feet!

It was early in the afternoon when I entered the small but active town of Bort. The burg is only interesting by its exceedingly picturesque situation on the right bank of the Dordogne, under a very high hill, capped by a basaltic table, which is flanked towards the town, or rather a little to the south of it, by a long row of stupendous columns of basalt, known as the *Orgues de Bort*, from their resemblance at a distance to organ-pipes. The basalt here is of a reddish yellow. The table, with its igneous crystallizations, lies upon the metamorphic rock.

I decided to climb to the summit of the prodigious organ-pipes, and to look at the world from that remarkable point of view. For the greater part of the distance the way lay up a tiresome winding road on the side of the hill. A woman, who was tying buckwheat into sheaves, said the distance was 'three small quarters of an hour.' It would have been simpler arithmetic to have said 'half an hour,' but the peasant thinks it safer not to be more explicit than he or she can help. Experience has taught me that 'three-quarters of an hour,' whether they are called little or not, mean an hour or more, and that 'five quarters of an hour' mean an hour and a half, or even two hours. I passed a team of bullocks descending from the moor with loads of dry broom for the bakers, headed by a little old man in a great felt hat, with a long goad in his hand, with which he tickled up the yoked beasts occasionally, not because they needed it, but from force of habit. This goad, by-the-bye, is a slender stick about six feet long, with a short nail at one end, so fastened that the point is turned outwards. A bullock is not goaded from behind, but from the front between the shoulder-blades, and it generally suffices for the animal to see a man in front of him with a stick. Instead of drawing back, as might be supposed, he steps forward at his best pace. Cows and bulls are harnessed to the wain and plough as well as oxen; they have all to work for their living. English cattle are allowed to grow fat in idleness, and their troubles do not begin until the time comes for them to be eaten. It is otherwise in France.

On the banks were fragrant, mauve-coloured pinks, with ragged petals; but at the foot of the *Orgues* was a rocky waste, where little grew besides the sombre holly and fetid hellebore.

The view from the top of the cliff made me fully realize the wildness, the sterility, the desolation of nature in this region. Beyond the valley far beneath me where the Dordogne lay, a glittering thread, was the department of the Cantal. The whole southern and eastern prospect was broken up by innumerable savage, heath-covered or rocky hills, with little green valleys or dense woods filling the hollows, the southern horizon being closed by the wavy blue line of the Cantal mountains. To the north-east the sky-line was marked by the Mont-Dore range, with the highest peak of Auvergne, the Puy de Sancy, clearly visible against the lighter blue of the cloudless air. The feeling that prevailed throughout this wide expanse of country was solemn sternness.

I returned to Bort, and as there were still about two hours of light left, I crossed the river and went in search of the cascades, two or three miles from the town, formed by the Rue in its wild impatience to meet the Dordogne. When I was skirting the buckwheat fields of the valley in the calm open country, there was a sweet and tender glow of evening sunshine upon the purple-tinted sheaves standing with their heads together. The Titan-strewn rocks felt it likewise with all their heather and broom. There was no husbandman in the plain, no song of the solitary goat-girl, no creak of the plough, no twitter even of a bird. It was not yet the hour when Virgil says every field is silent, but the repose of nature had commenced.

The dusk was falling when I reached a silk-mill by the side of the Rue, and passed up the deep gorge full of shadows, led by the sound of roaring waters. A narrow path winding under high rocks of porphyritic gneiss brought me to the cascade called the Saut de la Saule, where the river, divided into two branches by a vast block, leaps fifteen or twenty feet into a deep basin to whirl and boil with fury, then dashes onward down the stony channel, to leap again into the air and fall into another basin.

I reached a rock in the channel by means of a tree that had been laid between it and the bank, and stood in the midst of the seething, broken torrent, from which arose that saddening odour which water in wild commotion gives forth when daylight is

THE VALLEY OF THE RUE.

dying and the darkened trees stand like mourning plumes. On either hand the forest-covered sides of the ravine and their savage crags seemed to reach higher as they grew darker. Where was I? There was a tree hard by that looked very like the infernal elm beneath whose leaves the vain dreams cluster; but it was probably an oak.

ACROSS THE MOORS OF THE CORRÈZE.

A WOMAN OF THE CORRÈZE.

THE night being passed at Bort, the next morning I continued my journey by the Dordogne. Again the sky was cloudless. I kept on the right bank of the river—the Limousin side, leaving the Cantal to some future day, that may never come. A little beyond the spot where the Dordogne and the Rue met and embraced uproariously, the path entered a narrow lane bordered by tall hedges chiefly of hazel and briar overclimbed by wild clematis—well termed the traveller's joy, for it is a beautiful plant that reminds many a wanderer of his far-away home.

Then I passed under precipitous naked rocks, with the river on the other hand, skirted by low bushes of twiggy willow that looked like tamarisk from a distance. The sun was now hot, and the ground was again all astir with lizards. Looking upon the path just in front of me, I brought myself to a sudden stop. Had I advanced a step or two more I could hardly have failed to tread upon a serpent that lay dozing in the sun just in my way. I was glad that I did not do so, for I recognised it, by its olive skin with reddish patches, as the dreaded *aspic*, or red viper. There it lay stretched out its full length, about a foot and a half, either asleep or enjoying the morning sun so much that it was in no humour to move. I do not kill snakes indiscriminately, like the peasants whenever they get the chance, but this one being dangerous, I resolved that it should never take another sun-bath. After being roused by a blow, the creature did not attempt to run, but did battle bravely, fiercely striking at the stick.

The path I had been following with so much confidence dwindled away and was lost. Again the gorge became a deep rift in the rocks, which left no margin on which one could walk. The only way to follow the windings of the stream would have been to wade or swim. Once more I had to own myself beaten by natural obstacles. The Dordogne is a river that cannot be followed throughout its savage wildernesses, except perhaps in a light flat-bottomed boat, and then not without serious difficulties. Anglers might have splendid sport here until they broke their necks, for the trout abound where the shadow of a man seldom or never falls. In the neighbourhood of towns and large villages the fishing is often spoilt by the casting-net.

Having realized the situation, I turned my back to the stream and commenced climbing the steep side of the gorge, choosing a spot where it was well wooded, for the sake of the foothold. For some distance the ground was green with moss and wood-sorrel; but the tug-of-war came when the vast banks of loose stones—hot, bare, and shale-like—were reached. On gaining the plateau, I threw myself down upon the heather and looked at the scene below. The mingling of rock, forest, and stream was superbly desolate. Even the naked steeps of slate-coloured broken stone had an impressive grandeur of their own.

Leaving the Dordogne with the intention of cutting off a wide bend and meeting it again the next day or the day after, I struck across the half-cultivated open country, hoping soon to find a village; for I had spent much time in the gorge and made very little progress, while the sun had moved nearly up to the centre of his arc. The rays fell fiercely, and there was no shade upon the plateau. There was a road, but it was abominable. Only tramps understand the luxury of walking upon a good road.

I came to a hamlet that looked very miserable. The daily toil had scattered the men afield, and only a few women were to be seen. Not one of them wore a stocking, nor even a wooden shoe. Some to whom I spoke did not understand me; those who understood told me that there was no inn in the place—that there was no one who could give me a meal. One of them must have thought that I was begging my way, or was exceedingly hard up, for she said: 'Ah! mon pauvre ami, vous êtes dans un malheureux pays.'

Continuing, I came to a village which was not shown on my map. Here I learnt there was a single auberge, which was also the tobacco shop and grocery of the place. It was kept by an old man who lived alone. This inn was a cottage without any sign over it. I tried the door, but it was locked, and nobody responded to the noise I made. It took me half an hour to find the solitary at the farther end of the village. He returned with me, and, opening the door, we both entered the only room of the cottage. It was shop, bedroom, and kitchen. There was a bed against the wall, and near the window was a small stock of tobacco, snuff, and groceries all mixed up. My host's back was much bent and his face deeply furrowed. He wore a shirt with a high collar, and a blue waistcoat. He was an honest, kindly man, and seemed to take pleasure in doing what he could for me apart from the thought of gaining by it.

In the way of food he had only eggs, bread, cheese, and butter. It was decided that he should fry some eggs. He lighted some sticks upon the hearth, and there was soon a good blaze; then he laid his great frying-pan upon it, resting the long handle upon a chair. While the butter was melting, he opened a trap-door in the floor and went down a ladder into his cellar. Presently he reappeared with a litre of wine, and having set this before me, he proceeded to crack the eggs and empty them into the frying-pan. As a cook he had no pretensions, but he knew how to fry eggs. When my meal was ready, and he had placed everything before me upon the bare board, he sat at a little distance eating a dry old crust with a piece of goat cheese. This was his lunch. I insisted upon his sharing the wine with me, and this little attention made him thoroughly confiding and cheery.

He was left a widower, he told me, with four children, at the age of thirty-eight, and he would not take a second wife because, his father having done so, he remembered the trials and tribulations of his own childhood which came of his having 'a mother who was not a mother.' He said to himself, ' My children shall not run the risk of going through what I went through.' He toiled on alone, brought up his family himself, added to his bit of land in course of years, and acquired other property. His children were now all settled in life, and he had given them everything he had except the cottage in which he

A PEASANT OF THE MOORS.

lived. I was struck by the strong virtue of this illiterate peasant, who had evidently no notion of his own value, and who would not have told the simple story of his life passed amidst the moors of the Corrèze had I not drawn it from him.

As I watched the old man, prematurely bent by labour, eating his hard crust, cheerful and contented, after giving to others the fruit of his many years of toil, I thought, 'If man were nothing but an animal, such a life would be not only absurd, but impossible.' Another glass of wine made my host and cook still more talkative. He told me that not long ago he had walked from this village to Tulle, distant about thirty-five miles, to see a soldier son who was to pass through the place with his regiment. He started at three in the morning and arrived at five in the afternoon, but was only able to exchange a few words with his son. They could not even 'break a crust' together. The old man then turned his face towards his village, and walked the whole night.

'I hope your son would walk as far to see you,' I said, with a little scepticism in my mind.

This is what he replied, almost word for word:

'Ah! children do not do for their parents what their parents do for them. The commandment says, " Honour your father and your mother "—not honour your children. Nevertheless, it is the parents who deny themselves the most. As soon as your children are married they generally forget you.

Perhaps if I had married again I should be happier now. All the same, I am contented. I can keep myself. When I am no longer able to take care of myself, my children must do something for me.'

I confess that I was sorry when the time came for me to leave this old man, knowing well that I should never see again his rugged face and his kind eyes twinkling under their shaggy brows. Perhaps he, too, had some such regret, for we had had a long talk, and he may have tired out all his other listeners, especially those of his own family. When a man has grown old and is near the end, it would often be better for him to go out into the wilderness and talk to the rocks and trees than to repeat the stories of his life upon his own hearth-stone. Before I left the peasant fetched a bottle, which he only brought out on rare occasions, and insisted upon my drinking a parting glass with him.

I passed through another hamlet where there was a high wooden cross. There were walnut-trees, and men were knocking down the nuts. The women here wore wide-brimmed black straw hats over white caps. I soon left these figures behind, and was alone in a birch-wood, where there were many yellow leaves between me and the blue sky. Then I met the road to Neuvic, and following it came to the Artaud, a tributary of the Dordogne, threading its way through deep ravines, amidst wild rocks, dark woods, and bracken-covered steeps. The road crossed the ravine upon a bridge of three arches.

The scene was one to raise the mind above common things. The stream rushed madly down the rocky chasm with a mighty roar, now losing itself in the leafy vaults of overhanging trees, now reappearing like a torrent of fire where the glorious lustre of the September sun struck it and mingled with it.

As I ascended the opposite hill a still deeper ravine came into view, wooded down to the water and all in dark shadow, except a rocky ridge facing the sinking sun and bathed in warm light.

When the top of the hill had been reached, an old man, who wore a large and very weather-beaten felt hat, was sitting on the step of a wayside cross with a flock of geese feeding around him. Next I passed a bare-footed *cantonnier* breaking stones, and he told me that if I made haste I might reach Neuvic before dark. On the outskirts of a village— Roche-le-Peyroux—a wandering tinker and his boy were at work by the side of the road with fire and bellows, and I felt a trampish or romantic desire to stay with them awhile in the cheerful glow; but thinking of the coming night, I smothered the impulse.

Upon the moor which I was now traversing was a very old stone cross, upon which the figure of the Saviour was rudely carved in relief. The form was so uncouth as to be scarcely human. The head was half as wide again as the space across the shoulders, and the hands were nearly as large as the head. How many centuries ago did Christian piety raise this rough image of its hope upon the moors amidst the purple heather and the yellow broom?

The road crossed another stream not far from the spot where it fell into the Dordogne. There was a wooded quietude here, with an odour of fresh grass and water that enticed me to linger; but the evening light in the tops of the trees and the twittering of the birds settling amongst the leaves for the night spurred me on. I had walked many miles since the morning, but had made very little way according to the map, so full of deception is this wild Limousin country to the wanderer who does not know it. I had still some eight miles to walk before reaching Neuvic.

There was a little mill at the bottom of the grassy valley, but it seemed deserted by all living creatures save a dog. This rather large and shaggy animal seized the rare opportunity that was now offered him for a little excitement. Not satisfied with barking at me furiously from his own ground, he followed me about a mile up the hill I had now to climb, but without venturing very near. At length I thought I had had enough of his company, so at the next bend in the road I came to a stand beside a heap of stones that a *cantonnier* had neatly piled up in geometrical pattern. There I waited, and the animal came on gaily, little expecting to find himself suddenly at close quarters with me. Just as he turned the corner he raised a howl that said he was both surprised and shocked. Skipping with great agility, he avoided the next stone, and the expression of his face told me that he was already feeling very home-sick. He turned tail as quick as he could, and used very bad dog-language as the stones followed him down the hill. As a rule, dogs lose all their courage when they are out of sight of their own homes, unless someone whom they know well is near at hand to give them confidence in themselves.

I am again upon the moor. There is a deep silence over the heather, for the last bees have left the pink and purple bells. But there is still a wan glow in the air, which gives a sad beauty to the quiet, mournful land. A boy is returning with some cattle after spending the day upon the heath, and he sings as he thinks of his poor home, the blazing sticks on the hearth, the soup, the buckwheat cake, or the potatoes. Through a mask of silver birches I see a solemn ruddy light as of a funeral-torch in the far western sky. The breath of evening is made sweeter by the odour wafted from some distant fresh-cut grass or broom that has been drying in the September sun. A field-cricket, waking up, breaks the silence with its shrill cry that is quickly taken up by others near at hand and far away in the dusk. The light and colour of the day are now gone, but there is one beautiful star flashing in front of me like a lamp of the sanctuary when the vaulted minster is filled with shadow.

The rest of the walk to Neuvic was by night. The first auberge I entered in this small town of some three thousand inhabitants was a little too rough even for me. The family were at dinner, or at supper, as they would say, eating upon the bare board, without plates, potatoes boiled in their skins. I do not doubt there were hollows cut in the table to serve instead of plates, for this primitive contrivance still lingers in the wildest parts of the Limousin. In answer to my inquiry as to bed accommodation, I was told that I should have to sleep in the same room with others, probably the whole family. I had sufficient taste for civilization left to decline the proposed arrangement, and went in search of another inn.

Happily there was one, and of a better sort. It was thoroughly rustic, but there was not the squalor I had just encountered. In the kitchen, paved with small pebbles, two months' accumulation of used linen had been pressed down in an old wine-cask, and boiling water was now being poured upon it through a cloth covered with a layer of wood ashes. In these rural places the washing-day is usually once in two or three months. This simplifies matters, but it needs a considerable stock of linen, which, by-the-bye, peasants generally possess. The wash-house odour that arose from the *lessive* was not grateful, but I tried to accommodate myself to it. On the floor was a baby swaddled up, and tightly fitted into a small wooden cradle on huge rockers—a cradle that might have served for scores of babies, and been none the worse for wear. Although the fire on the hearth looked tempting, the proximity of the wine-cask and the linen that was being purified with potash made me glad to hear that my meal would be served in another room.

Considering the region, the dinner was not a bad one. I had soup, veal, eggs, and a fair wine. I had also a companion, but would rather have been without him. He was a young man, whose appearance gained by the contrast of a dusty wayfarer's, and he gave himself airs accordingly. I set him down as a petty functionary of the place, and a *pensionnaire* of the auberge. All the time I was with him his mind was exceedingly restless as to my intentions and business in those parts, and such explanations as I gave him to appease his insatiable curiosity and awkwardly-veiled suspicion evidently left him unsatisfied.

The next morning the hostess brought out her police register for me to enter my name, nationality, age, profession, destination, etc. I had no doubt that my acquaintance of the night before had reminded her of this little formality in order that he might afterwards see what I had written. All innkeepers in France are liable to a fine if they do not make every traveller who passes the night with them leave this record of himself for inspection, but the formality is much more often omitted than observed. I have not been able to overcome my English dislike of the practice, which is annoying and useless, like much more that belongs to the French administrative system.

By daylight I found Neuvic to be a cheerful, pleasant little town, with a venerable-looking old church, apparently of the twelfth century. It is entered by a cavernous portal under a very massive low tower, but the interior shows little of interest. What struck me, however, as something quite uncommon was a small altar in the centre of the nave just below the sanctuary. Upon it was an image of the Virgin, which a boy told me had been found in a neighbouring wood about a century ago.

On leaving Neuvic I noticed a woman carrying to the baker's a large dish of edible *boleti*, known to the French as *cèpes*. This excellent fungus during the late summer and autumn is a very important article of food in France wherever there are extensive chestnut-woods. The orange mushroom is also much eaten in the same regions, for it likewise loves the chestnut forest; but it may be mistaken by those who do not know the signs for its relative, the crimson-capped fly-agaric, one of the most deadly of cryptogams.

After seeing the dish of *cèpes*, I was not surprised to find many chestnut-trees along the road that I now took to St. Pantaléon. The country was less barren than that which I had passed over the day before. Although there was much heather, broom and furze, trees and pasture broke the monotony of the moorland. Here was the better Limousin landscape — every knoll and mamelon covered with heather and other moor-plants, woods and meadows in the dells and dips. The numerous clumps of silver birches, and the gorse arrayed in its new flowers of bright gold, added to the charm of the sunlit scene.

To me the weather was all the more delightful by being very warm, for I had run away from winter on the Auvergne mountains. The whirring noise of the grasshoppers as they flew across the road, and the tremulous sheen of their wings, coloured like blooming lavender, brought back to me the best recollections of other wayfaring days in the warm South, when all these things were new, and the sight feasted upon them with the eagerness of bees that suck the first flowers of spring.

I passed a little field of buckwheat that had been cut some days and had fully ripened. A woman was threshing out the grain with a flail upon a spread canvas, surrounded by a circle of purple-tinted cones, the sheaves leaning together. Now the wide level moor returned, but Nature was not quite the same here as she had been before. The vast expanse was dotted over with dark little juniper bushes. These were covered with berries which nobody seemed to think worth the picking. Rock-cist flourished, starring the turf all over with its yellow discs. This moor was an absolute desert.

Long I walked without seeing another human being. At length I met a woman carrying a distaff, and tried to get into conversation with her, but it was impossible; she could not speak a word of French, and I knew nothing of her Limousin patois.

By steadfastly following the road, I came to the village of St. Pantaléon, on the brow of a hill overlooking the Luxège, and stopped at a wayside inn. It was a poor auberge; but there was an air of reaching toward some ideal of superior life and softened manners that made itself felt in small ways not to be described with any certainty, but none the less real. The innkeeper, who was also a peasant-farmer, possessed the doubtful blessing of a mind that rose above what the logic of his existence, sternly bound to a plot of grudging soil and the petty needs of still poorer neighbours, demanded of it. He was blessed or afflicted with that hunger of knowledge and refinement which lifts and casts down, rejoices and saddens. He knew that such ambition with regard to himself was vain, that it was his destiny to live out his days on the edge of a moor in the Corrèze, and that it was his duty to thank Heaven that he was sheltered and had sufficient food, fuel, and clothing for himself and his family: all this he knew, and he accepted his lot bravely. But the fire was only damped down; it glowed in its hidden heart, and strove for a vent. It was not lighted without a purpose. The peasant had a son, to whom the flame had been passed on;

for he aimed at the priesthood. This has ever been a refuge of ambitious minds that cannot rise by any other means above the dulness of the peasant's life, which is the more endurable the more the man is able to place himself upon the animal level of his plodding ox. The son was being educated in a seminary, but he was now home for the holidays. Presently he appeared. He was a youth of about nineteen, wearing a blouse like any other peasant. There was certainly nothing in his appearance to indicate that he was destined for the cure of souls. The proud father said : ' He is in philosophy.' The young man had a twinkle in his eye that might have been philosophical. Neither of them had a suspicion of the vanity concealed in the high-sounding phrase.

But I am forgetting to say anything about what was more important to me than aught else at that time. I had to eat and drink in order to look at nature with an admiring eye, note the interwoven aims and motives and troubled duties of human life ; to be ' in philosophy ' after my own humble fashion. My meal was chiefly of fried eggs and ham, the latter nearly as hard as leather. I ate in a small room where there was a bed with a red curtain. No knife was given me, for in these out-of-the-way inns you are expected to carry your knife in your pocket, which a century ago was the case in most of the French hostelries. In the remotely rural districts the ways of life have changed very slightly in a hundred years. But if the knife was overlooked, the white napkin and small tablecloth were remembered. While talking with the *aubergiste* over the coffee—there was really some coffee here that was not made either from acorns or beans—he told me, as an example of the low rate of wages in the district, that a road-mender, who worked in all weathers, was paid forty francs a month. In the whole commune there were only two or three persons who had wine in their houses. He lent me his two sons—the *séminariste* and his young brother —to walk with me as far as the Luxège, and put me on the path to La Fage, at which village I proposed to pass the night.

As we left, a grand expanse of chestnut forest came into view, following the hills that bordered the curved line of the Luxège. The little river, like all the tributaries of the upper Dordogne, runs at the bottom of a deep gorge. Standing upon the brink of it, I perceived that I was about to enter another sylvan solitude of enchanting beauty. The dense forest descended the abrupt escarpments to the channel and hid the stream, and over the leafy masses was that play of sunshine, shadow, and thin vapour which I had so often watched in a dreamily joyous mood lying at the foot of some pine in the Vosges.

About half-way down the gorge was a ruinous Romanesque chapel upon a rock, the polygonal apse being on the very edge of a precipice. At each exterior angle of the imperfect polygon was a column with a cubiform capital. The interior was all dilapidated; the floor of the sanctuary had fallen in, but the altar-stone—a block of granite—remained in its place. This chapel belonged to a priory. Little is left of the adjoining monastery except some subterranean vaults and the gaping oven of the ruined bakery; all ferny, mossy, given up to the faun and the dryad. The upper masonry was carried away years ago to build a chapel upon the hill. A bit of green slope, where the sunbeams wantoned with yellow mulleins, wild carrot, and bracken, was the cemetery, as a few stone crosses almost buried in the soil plainly told. These crosses doubtless mark the graves of nameless priors. And the dust of the humble monk and serving brother, where is that? Every plant draws from it something that it needs to fulfil its purpose. It is as good for the nightshade as for the violet; flowers that are rank and deadly, and others that are sweet and innocent, strive for the right of clasping with their hungry roots the dust of men.

The innkeeper's sons left me by an abandoned mill on the other side of the stream, which was crossed by a rough wooden bridge. Ascending the opposite hill by a narrow path in the shadow of chestnuts and beeches, and fringed with gorse and heather, I passed another deserted house, the roof of which had fallen in. The gorge was getting very shadowy when I reached the tableland above it. I saw the small town of Laplau in the plain away to the left, but my path did not lie through it, for I preferred the wilder country towards La Fage. When I passed a little lake in a hollow, half surrounded by firs, the slanting rays were diving into its liquid stillness, over which the motionless trees bent gazing at their likeness.

When the sun left me I was upon a hilly waste, amid darkening bushes of holly and juniper, tall bracken, heather, and gorse. The spirit of desolation threw out broad wings under the fading sky; but from afar towards the west, whither I was going, came through the dusk the shine and twinkle of many fires that had been lighted by the peasants upon their patches of reclaimed desert. They flashed to me the sentiment of the autumn fields, of hopeful husbandry, of laying up for the winter, and preparation for harvests that would be gathered under next year's sun.

Tired and hungry, I reached La Fage in the darkness. The village looked very poor and dreary; but I had been told that it contained a 'good hotel,' and I set about looking for it. It turned out to be a rather large but exceedingly rough auberge. On opening the door I saw a great kitchen with pebbled floor, lighted only by the glow of embers on the hearth. The figure of a woman standing in the chimney opening was lit up by the glare. I walked towards her, and asked her if she could give me lodging. After scanning me very acutely for some seconds, she replied, 'Yes.' She was puzzled, if not startled, by the apparition in front of her; but having thrown down my pack and taken a seat in the chimney-corner like a familiar of the house, I talked to her about the comfort of being in such a place after a long walk in so wild a district as hers, and succeeded in making her quite genial. She was the mayor's wife, but she was not too proud to cook for me after lighting a flickering oil-lamp. While I was waiting for my meal peasants came in, and had theirs at the bare tables, of which there were several in the great kitchen. Their soup was ladled out from the immense black pot that hung over the fire, and the noise they made as they fell to it was very grating to the nerves. But the wanderer in the chimney-corner had no business to be there, unless he was prepared to accept all that was customary without wincing. My own dinner commenced with some of this soup, which was like hot dishwater with slices of bread thrown into it. The bit of boiled veal that followed was an improvement, although anything but a captivating dish. Goat-cheese, hard and salt, and with a flavour that left no doubt as to the source from which it came, made up the frugal fare. I returned to the chimney-corner and smoked in silence, now peering up the sooty cavern where the wind moaned, and now watching the clear-obscure effects of the dimly-lighted room. Presently a trap stopped outside, and in walked the aubergiste, accompanied by a sprightly little man who I afterwards learnt was a pedlar.

Monsieur le maire was not exactly a polished gentleman; he took no notice of me after the first searching glance. He made an unpleasant impression, but this wore off when I found that he was a well-meaning man, who had not cultivated fine manners. Why should he have cultivated what would have been of little or no use to him? These rural functionaries are just like the people with whom they live. The young *séminariste* told me an amusing story of a mayor of St. Pantaléon, who had had a very narrow escape of being caught by gendarmes when upon a poaching expedition. '*Tout le monde est braconnier ici*,' added my informant with a sincerity that was very pleasing. Of course, he was a poacher himself when reposing from his theological and philosophical studies. I thought none the worse of him for that. After all, poaching in France generally means nothing more immoral than neglecting to take out a gun license, and to respect the President's decrees with regard to the months that are open and those that are not.

On my way to bed I saw in a corner of the staircase a spinning-wheel of the pattern known throughout Europe. I was told that it had not been used for many years. The distaff and spindle which are to be seen on Egyptian monuments are still employed by thousands of French peasant-women, but the wheel invented in the sixteenth century is rarely used now, unless it be by Martha in the opera.

The next morning I made friends with the pedlar, who was about to start upon my road, and who offered to give me a lift in his trap as far as La Roche Canillac. Meanwhile, he had unpacked all his samples of cloth with a view to doing a little business with the mayor. This personage, however, was not allowed to have much voice in the matter; it was his spouse who represented his interests in the bargaining battle that was now waged with deafening din and much apparent ferocity for three-quarters of an hour. The little pedlar was used to this kind of thing, and was quite prepared for the fray. When the lady offered him, after much depreciatory fingering of the chosen material, two-thirds of what he asked for the stuff that was to be made into a pair of winter trousers for the mayor, he spun round and jumped like a peg-top just escaped from the string. Then he raged and swore, said he was being mocked at, dabbed his hat on his head, and made a pretence of gathering up his samples and rushing off. The mayor watched the scene with a quiet smirk on his face: he knew that he would somehow get the trousers. I have no doubt that he did have them, but I walked out instead of waiting to see the end of the battle. When I returned, the haggling was over, the hostess and the pedlar were on the most affable terms, and there was not a sign of the recent storm.

Presently the pedlar, myself, and the innkeeper's son—a young man who had received his education elsewhere, and had learnt much that did not chime in with his present surroundings—were in a light cart, drawn by a lively horse, speeding along the road over the moors. Here and there, near the village, were small fields of buckwheat in the midst of the heather and bracken. My companions explained that each commune was surrounded by a considerable extent of moorland that belonged to it, and that any native of the commune had the right of selecting a piece, which became his absolute property after he had cleared it and brought it under cultivation; thus anyone could have what land he wanted in reason for nothing. Quite an Arcadian state of things this, were not the conditions of nature such as to chill the ambition to acquire such freeholds. Three years of back-breaking labour are needed before the land is fit to be put to some profitable purpose. And then what does it yield? Buckwheat, and perhaps potatoes. Although the peasants have the faculty of extending their landed property in the manner described, the consideration of means generally stands in the way. They cannot afford to work and wait three years. Their existence is truly wretched, and if it were not for the luxuriant chestnut-woods, which cover the sides of the narrow valleys or gorges with which the barren plateau is deeply seamed every few miles, the population of the region would be more scanty than it is, for the chestnut goes far to sustain the people through the worst months of the year.

The plough used upon these moors, on the *causses* of the Quercy, and in some other districts where the barrenness of the soil has kept the inhabitants for centuries imprisoned within the circle of their old routine, is one of the simplest that the world has known. It differs but slightly from the one figured in the most ancient of Egyptian hieroglyphs, and is really the same as that which was used in Gaul under the Romans. Indeed, it has

PLOUGHING THE MOOR.

not the improvements that the Romans introduced. Two poles forming an obtuse angle is the rough shape of it. The wedge-like share is a continuation of the pole that is held by the ploughman. Often on the *causses*, where loose stones are inseparably mixed with the soil, the entire plough is of wood.

We passed through the village of Marcillac, near the head of one of the valleys. The soil was much more fertile here, and a maize field was a sign that the climate was warmer. There were, moreover, pleasant gardens with fruit-trees and flowers. Oleanders were blooming outside some of the houses. But we had no sooner risen upon the plateau again than the moor returned, and for seven or eight miles it continued unbroken. The ground was slightly undulating, and amongst the gorse and heather were scattered innumerable juniper bushes.

On approaching La Roche Canillac the road descended into a very deep valley by so many turns and windings that I was thankful to be in the pedlar's cart, especially as the mid-day sun smote with torrid strength. But the scenery was of exquisite beauty, and this valley will remain in my memory as one of the most charming I have ever seen. Luxuriant woods, flashing water, savage rocks, emerald-green patches of meadow, little mills by the riverside—I should add nothing to the picture by saying more. Upon the rocky hillside was the burg of five hundred inhabitants. My companions took me to an old auberge whose exterior was not promising, but which was, nevertheless, well supplied with food, and had a good cellar. The meal served there was the best that had fallen to my lot for several days. The sun had lost all the ardour of mid-day when I took leave of the pedlar and the mayor's son. I went away thinking that I might travel far without finding two more kindly, honest fellows.

A GORGE IN THE CORRÈZE.

I had hoped to reach Argentat by the Dordogne that night, but I had stayed too long at the inn for the plan to be practicable; so I set off down the gorge of the tributary with the intention of taking my luck at a village called St. Bazile. I was soon in the shade of the chestnut forest, where boars were said to be plentiful. As time went on, the scenery became more solemn and awe-inspiring. Pines that looked very gloomy in the late afternoon mingled with the chestnuts, while black rocks, faintly flushed with heather towards the sky, reared their jagged outlines above the sombre foliage. All the while the water in the gorge moaned or roared. It was growing very dusk when the walls on either hand rose like the sides of a pit.

I was beginning to ask myself in no cheerful mood whether the map had not deceived me as to the whereabouts of St. Bazile, when, to my relief, I heard a church bell ringing not very far down the stream. It was the angelus. How often has this clear, solemn, heart-touching, and consoling sound been to me what a familiar beacon is to the doubting mariner! Only wanderers in desolate places know the sentiment that it carries through the evening air. More welcome than ever before did it seem in this black gorge. I pushed on, and presently the gloomy walls widened out. Turning a bend of the torrent, I stood in a glow of ruddy light that streamed from the yawning mouth of an open-air oven that had recently been filled with dry broom and kindled for the night's baking. Here was a fresh delight, for there is nothing more cheering, more full of homely sentiment in the dusk, than the view of such a blazing oven.

This, then, was the village of St. Bazile de la Roche, to give its full name. It could scarcely have boasted a hundred houses. There was one miserable little inn, kept by a widow. There I had to pass the night, unless I preferred a cave or a mossy bed under a tree. The poor woman managed to find a piece of veal, which she cooked for me. It seemed to be my lot now to eat no meat but veal. As I sat down to this dish and a bottle of wine, two men at another table were eating boiled potatoes, without plates, and drinking water. The contrast made me uncomfortable. There is some reason in the selfishness that avoids the sights and sounds and all suggestions of other people's poverty and pain; but those who take such base care of themselves never know human life. I could not offer these men wine without running the risk of a refusal, but it was different with regard to a little hump-backed postman who came in to gossip. Half a litre of wine that, at my wish, was set before him made him exceedingly cheerful. He told me that he walked about twenty miles a day on the hill-sides and in the ravines, and I suppose his pay was the same as that of other rural postmen in France— from £28 to £32 a year. The inhabitants of St. Bazile, he said, were all very poor, their chief food being potatoes and chestnuts. Before the vines a little further down the valley were destroyed by the phylloxera and mildew, the people were much better off. Then there was plenty of wine in the cellars, but now St. Bazile was a village of water-drinkers. He spoke of the neighbouring parish of Servières, where, at the annual pilgrimage, women go barefoot from one rock to the other on which the chapel stands.

Before placing myself between the canvas-like sheets, I opened the lattice window of my meagrely-furnished room. The only distinguishable voice of the night was that of the stream quarrelling with its rocky bed just below. Before me was the high black wall of hill and forest, above the ragged line of which flashed the swarming stars.

The angelus sounded again at four in the morning. Before seven I was out in the open air. I saw the curé go up into the tower of his small church, and ring the bell for his own mass. He was probably too poor to pay a sacristan. A little later he was in the pulpit catechising the children, and preaching to the older parishioners between whiles. A boy and then a girl would stand up, and in answer to questions put to them would recite in an unintelligible gabble the catechism they had learnt. If one of them lost the thread and suddenly lapsed into a speechless confusion of ideas, the curé pointed the finger of reprobation at the unfortunate little wretch, and made him or her—especially him—feel the enormity of having a bad memory. While waving his arm in a moment of rhetorical excitement, he let his book fall upon an old woman's head. '*Voilà ce que c'est de faire des gestes !*' said he with a smile that was almost a discreet grin. The children were delighted, and everybody laughed, including the poor old soul, who had seated herself under the pulpit so that she might hear well.

It was evident that the people of St. Bazile quite understood their curé, and that he was just the one for them. He was a strong man, over sixty years of age, and he spoke with a rich southern accent. Under his sacerdotal earnestness there was a sense of humour ever ready to take a little revenge for a life of sacrifice. There are many such priests in France.

I had no sooner walked out of this village, on my way to Argentat, than I became aware that the Girondin climate was beginning to make itself felt. The influence of the plains was overcoming that of the highlands. The warm rocky slopes on each side of the valley were covered with vines—alas! dead or dying. There was no hope for them. On the level of the river were fields of maize, now ripening, and irrigated meadows intensely green. There were beehives, fifteen or twenty together on the sunny slopes, and as I went on, the signs of human industry and ease increasing, I saw petunias climbing over cottage doors. There was a steep descent to Argentat. The town lay in a wide valley by the

Dordogne, in the midst of maize and buckwheat fields and green meadows, the surrounding hillsides being covered here with chestnut woods, and there with vines. I met a woman returning from market with melons in her basket. Truly I had come into a different climate. At the small town, made pretty by the number of its vine trellises, I lunched. The inn where I stopped is not worth describing; but it gave me a dish of gudgeons caught in the Dordogne that deserved to be remembered.

I did not remain long at Argentat, for I was determined to reach Beaulieu that night. A little out of the town some girls whom I passed on the road looked very suspiciously at me out of the corners of their eyes, and reminded me that another whom I had met that morning higher up the valley took to her heels at the sight of me. An old woman who had lived long enough to overcome such timidity, asked me if I was a *marchand*, by which she meant pedlar—the old question to which I have grown weary of replying. About a mile from the town I found the Dordogne again. It had grown to quite a fine river since I last saw it in the ravines below Bort. Many an eager affluent had rushed into it, both on the Corrèze and the Cantal side. Here most of the grass was dried up, and the freshness of the highlands was gone. Still the valley was shut in by steep cliffs. Brambles climbed about the rocks, where the broom also flourished, although tangled with its parasite, the dodder. Looking up the crags, I recognised a wild fig-tree—the first I had seen on this southward journey.

The valley became again so narrow that the road was cut into the escarped side of the cliff, for the river ran close under it. A woman with bare legs and bare chest—really half naked—trudged by with a heavy bundle of maize upon her head, followed by a couple of red-haired children, their perfectly-shaped little legs browned by the sun and powdered with dust. How beautiful are the limbs of these peasant children, however disfigured by toil and the inherited physical blight of hardship their mother's form may be! With each fresh generation, Nature seems to make an effort to go back to her ideal type; but destiny is strong. Old and new causes working together are often more than a match for that most marvellous force in all animal and vegetable life— the love of symmetry.

Resting upon a bed of peppermint, blue with flowers, under an old wall, whose stones were half hidden by celandine and roving briony; loitering dreamily upon a wide waste of sunlit pebbles, watching the flashing rapids of the river where it awoke from its calm sleep to battle with the rocks which had resisted incalculable ages of washing, the hours glided by so stealthily that it was evening when I reached a village which was still eight miles or more from Beaulieu.

Turning into an inn, I fell into conversation with a postman, who made me the offer of his company during the remainder of the journey. I readily assented, and gave him a glass of absinthe—his favourite drink—before leaving. He did not need it, for, as he confessed, he had been clinking glasses with unusual zeal that day. He was a very droll fellow, a striking type of the Southerner, whom it was difficult to look at with a serious face, and whom no one with any sense of humour could really dislike, notwithstanding his immense vanity and his immeasurable impudence. He had a thick black beard, a long, sharp nose, dark eyes full of mischievous mirth, and cheeks the colour of red wine. He wore a stiff new blouse with a red collar—the badge of his office—and a straw hat like a beehive. The whole of the way to Beaulieu his tongue was not still a minute. He told me stories of his bravery and his love adventures with a most amusing accent and intonation. The Rabelaisian expressions, which give such a peculiar flavour to the conversation of the 'people' in Southern France, rolled off his tongue with a sonority that could hardly have been excelled at Nimes or Tarascon. His swagger, his gestures, and his elocutionary power were amazing. He would stop walking, and, placing his stick— which he called his *trique*—under his arm, would speak in a tragic stage-whisper; then, clutching his *trique* and flourishing it over his head, he would burst out into a roar of laughter that made the dogs bark in the scattered farms for miles around. Once, when we were passing under high rocks, he shouted with such a terrible voice that he brought some loose stones rattling down upon the road so close to us that my head, as well as his own, nearly paid the penalty for thus exasperating the peaceful night. This was either the effect of vibration or of the sudden movement of some bird or other creature that he had startled far above us.

Among other things of which this amusing man talked to me was a visit of archæologists, among whom were a number of Englishmen, to Beaulieu.

'If you had only seen them,' he said, 'outside the church, all with their noses lifted in the air! *Grand Dieu!* What noses!'

Long before we reached Beaulieu I had had more than enough of the wild spirits of my comic postman. On entering the town he insisted upon taking me to a hotel which he said he could recommend to me with as much confidence as if I were his brother. Then he left me; but I had not seen the last of him. He presently returned, while I was enjoying the luxury of a quiet and well-served little dinner. Seating himself in front of me without waiting for an invitation, he helped himself with his fingers to a dish of baked *cêpes*, which I in consequence relinquished, but with a complete absence of goodwill. There was no getting rid of him, short of telling him plainly to go, and this I could not do after having accepted his companionship on the road. He devoured all the mushrooms, expressing his astonishment between whiles that I did not like them. '*J'aime bien les champignons*,' he kept on repeating. '*Ça me va le soir. Ce n'est pas lourd.*' When the dessert was brought in, he picked out the only ripe peach in the dish, and having poured another glass of wine down his really terrible throat, he declared that it had given him great pleasure to make my acquaintance, and left me with the hope that I should sleep well, and would not forget the Beaulieu postman. I assured him, with perfect sincerity, that I should never forget him.

When daylight returned I found Beaulieu a pleasant little town lying under hills covered with chestnut woods, and at a short distance from the Dordogne. Its name, however, was probably given to it on account of the fertility of the soil in this bit of valley, where the cliffs that enclose the Dordogne on each side fall back, and, by allowing a rich alluvium to settle in the plain, give the husbandmen a chance of growing something more profitable than buckwheat.

Beaulieu was once the seat of a powerful Benedictine abbey. The original monastery was founded in 858 by Charles le Chauve, who placed it under his protection. Although the territory was included in the viscounty of Turenne, the Viscount Raymond II., before he went crusading, made over his suzerain rights with regard to the abbey and its dependencies to the abbots, who thus became temporal lords. There is nothing left of the monastery; but much of the abbey church, which dates from the twelfth and thirteenth centuries, has been fortunately preserved. The interior is not remarkable, but the large and elaborate bas-relief of the Last Judgment which fills the tympanum of the portal is considered the most precious example of mediæval sculpture in the Bas-Limousin. The face of the Saviour, expressive of something above all human passions and motives, shows a really Godlike combination of serenity and severity. The fantastic spirit of the age is well set forth in the tortured forms of the horrid reptiles and fabulous beasts carved in relief upon the massive lintel, and filling also the broad border at the base of the tympanum. The same spirit finds even stronger expression in the demon figure, so grotesquely long-drawn out, carved upon the scalloped pillar that supports the lintel. The abbey was pillaged by the Huguenots, who lit a fire in the choir, which destroyed much of the woodwork. Notwithstanding the religious wars and the revolutionary convulsions of the eighteenth century, the church has preserved some of its ancient treasure, of which the most precious object is a silver statue of the Virgin of very curious workmanship, dating from the twelfth century.

TURENNE.

IN THE VISCOUNTY OF TURENNE.

WHAT gives us the zest to wander until the hour comes when we must fain be content to sit in the porch, thankful if the evening sun shines warmly, is the fascination of the unknown. As children, did we not long to get at the horizon's verge, to touch the painted clouds of the morning or of the sunset— ay, and to grasp with our outstretched hands that reached such a little way the blood-red glory of the sun itself? The garden, with its glowing tulips and its roses haunted by gilded beetles, became too small to satisfy the mind of infancy fresh from the infinite. Surely, I thought, when I was again in the open country beyond Beaulieu, I must have carried something of my childhood on with me, for me to go wandering over these hot hills exposing myself to sunstroke, weariness, and thirst for the sake of the unknown.

The road at first led up vine-covered slopes towards the west, where the waysides were blue with the flowers of the wild chicory. A priest astride upon a rough old cob passed me, his hitched-up *soutane* showing his gaitered legs. The French rural priests are generally rubicund, but this one was cadaverous. He would have looked like Death on horseback, swathed in a black mantle, but for the dangling gaitered legs, which spoilt the solemn effect. A very curious figure did he cut upon his shaggy, ambling steed. On the top of the hill was a village, in the midst of which stood a little old Gothic church with a gable-belfry, and hard by was a half-timber house, its porch aglow with climbing petunias.

Beyond this village was a deep valley, the sides of which were covered with chestnut-trees. On ascending the opposite hill, I took a by-path through a steep wood, thinking to cut off a long turn of the hot and dusty road. It led me into difficulties and bewilderment. The path disappeared, but I went on. After climbing rocks densely overgrown with brambles, which left their daggers in my skin, I reached the top of the hill, and saw before me a desert of disintegrated rock or drift dotted over with low juniper bushes. Although it was the middle of September, the sun blazed above me with the ardour of July, and the rays were thrown back by the bare stones, on which there was not a trace of moss, nor even lichen. These arid rocky places, so characteristic of Southern France, have a poetry of their own that to me is ever enticing. I love the stony wastes and their dazzling sun-glitter. There I find something that approaches companionship in the prickly juniper, the narcotic hellebore, and the acrid spurge. And these plants likewise love the places where the world has remained unchanged by man. The heat, however, was too great for me to linger upon this shadeless hill, where every stone was warm, and the reflected glare was almost as blinding as that of the sun itself, which seemed so near.

Having crossed another valley, after much casting about, I found the highroad again. The altitude was considerable here, so that the view embraced a wide expanse of the Corrèze and the department of the Lot, which I was approaching. The scene was everything that an English landscape is not. No soft verdure, no hedgerows setting memory astir with pictures of the flowering may and the pink, clambering dog-rose gemmed with dew; no lustrous meadow crossed by shadows thrown by ancient dreaming elms; no flash from the briskly-flowing brook: no, nothing of this, but in its place a parched and rugged land of hills or knolls, stony, wasteful, where for countless ages the juniper, the broom, the gorse, and the heather have disputed the sovereignty, the intervening valleys, timidly cultivated, producing little else but rye and buckwheat, and the deep gorges sombre with overhanging trees.

This road was so tedious, so hot and dusty, that, after walking a few miles upon it, I lost patience altogether with what seemed to be its unreasonable windings, and again made an effort to strike across country by means of by-paths, in order to reach the spot where, according to the map and compass, I thought Vayrac ought to be. I came to a seventeenth century country-house, large enough to be termed a château, but now the dwelling of some peasant-farmer. It was a dilapidated, apparently owl-haunted building, with a dovecote tower overgrown with ivy, and was half surrounded by a wall, whose tottering, ornamental pinnacles told a story of comparative grandeur that had come to grief in this remote spot. The farmer had been winnowing his corn outside, and the narrow lane was ankle-deep with chaff. The only human being that I could find here was a wild-looking girl, with a bush of hair on her head, who made me understand, half in French, half in patois, that I should never reach Vayrac by the way I was going. She sent me off in another direction. I walked on, I know not how many miles, without coming to any village or wayside auberge, over a shadeless plain in the department of the Lot. There was no water; consequently not a bird was to be seen or heard. But there were myriads of flies, and too many hornets for my comfort, for some of them followed me with impertinent curiosity.

I confess that I do not like hornets. When I see them, they remind me of the story of a donkey told me by a man in these parts. He in his youth saw an unlucky ass that, quietly browsing, unconscious of indiscretion, disturbed a hornets' nest. Suddenly the animal showed symptoms of unusual excitement, which became rapidly more violent, until, after some amazing antics, first on his front-legs and then on his hind-legs, he rolled over on his back, and kicked violently at the sky. His master knew what had happened, but stood lamenting afar off, not daring to go to the rescue. In a short time the poor donkey ceased kicking, and swelled up in a manner horrible to behold.

All nature now appeared to be baking. Even the blackberries, which I ate by the handful to slake my raging thirst, were warm. A long, straight road that I thought would never end brought me at length to Vayrac, where there was a good inn. Oh, the luxury of rest at last in a shaded room, with the companionship of a jug of frothing beer just brought up from the cool cellar!

*   *   *   *   *

Months passed before I continued from this point my journey on foot. The spring had come, and the face of nature was wondrously changed. Over the valley that I had seen before so parched had spread the soft verdure of young grass; hedges of quince were all abloom, and at their roots the stitchwort mingled its white starry flowers with the matchless blue of the Germander speedwell, so dear to English eyes. The roadsides were bright with daisies and the gold of the ill-appreciated dandelion.

A lane from Vayrac led up to the escarped sides of the Puy d'Issolu—the Uxellodunum of the Cadurci, according to Napoleon III. and others who have made Cæsar's battlefields in Gaul their study. It was April, and from near and afar came the warbling of nightingales. They moved amongst the new leaves of almost every shrub and tree. A very abrupt ascent through thickets brought me to the tableland, where the turf was flashed with splendid flowers of the purple orchis. From the waste land the sombre junipers rose like scattered cypresses in a cemetery.

If this was not the site of Uxellodunum, we may pretty safely believe it to have been that of some important *oppidum* of the Gauls. A circumvallation there could never have been in a strict sense, for where the plateau rests upon high calcareous walls there was no need of a fortification. But elsewhere, where the position was accessible from the valley, it was protected by a strong wall. On the northern side this rampart can be followed for a considerable distance without a break. In one spot the soil which has collected about it has been dug away, leaving the masonry bare. It is not composed of loose stones of various sizes, like that of the Celtic city at Murcens, but of small flat stones neatly laid together, with layers of mortar between; a circumstance that sets one conjecturing and doubting. The wall appears to have been six or eight feet thick. The line of it now only rises very slightly above the edge of the plateau.

I met a peasant who owned the highest part of the tableland, and who managed to grow crops upon it. Near his cottage he pointed out the remains of an ancient structure, which he called the fort. The masonry was of the same character as that of the wall. Near to it were fragments of ancient pottery and tiles, which he had dug out of the ground. The tiles were very heavy and flat, with turned-up edges, so that they could hang one to another. There were holes, too, for the nails which held them to the roof. Thrown on one side were human bones, which had from time to time been turned up by the plough. The peasant told me that his father, while digging rather deeply, had found a skeleton wearing a bracelet and part of a helmet. A visitor to the Puy d'Issolu, many years ago, was allowed to take these remains away, together with a quantity of iron arrow-heads, on his promise to come back and pay 600 francs for them. He never came back.

The view from the Puy takes in an immense expanse of the solemn Limousin country. To the south is the stone-strewn Quercy, while to the north and east is the still wilder Corrèze. On the west lie the forests of Black Périgord. Looking to the east, I saw the mountains of Auvergne, the Mont Dore range rising beyond the Corrèze against the blue sky, as white as the sugar towers and pinnacles upon a bride-cake. Here it was warm, like June weather in England; there winter still reigned upon the snowy hills. Standing against the north-western horizon were the high towers of the vast feudal fortress of the Viscounts of Turenne. It was there that Madame de Condé, escaping from Mazarin, planned the rising of Guyenne in 1648. I could only distinguish the towers, but I knew that a little below them was the small mediæval town of Turenne, which grew up under the protection of the Viscounts, who for centuries were virtually the sovereign princes of this region. No lover of the picturesque would waste his time by going there.

Descending from the tableland on the southern side, where the rocks form a steep little gorge, I came to the stream from which the besieged Cadurci are supposed to have drawn their water-supply, until it was cut off by Cæsar. Looking at the spot, it is easy to understand how it all happened. The natural fortress, selected with so much judgment by the Cadurci, was almost unassailable. To help them, they had the cover of the wood that still fills the gorge, but which was probably much denser then than it is now. From his tower of ten stages, which commanded the fountain, Cæsar continually harassed with darts, thrown by the *tormenta*, those who came to the spring; and he, moreover, tells us that he caused a gallery to be tunnelled to the fountain-head, and thus drew off the water, to the utter astonishment and despair of the Cadurci, who perceived in this disaster the intervention of the gods. A tunnel such as he describes exists, and the stream flows through it. At a point some distance higher, the sound of gurgling water can be distinctly heard beneath the stones; and it was here probably where the stream originally broke out, and where the inhabitants of the *oppidum* came with their vessels. Napoleon III. had the subterranean gallery cleared, and its artificial character was proved by the discovery that massive beams of wood, of which there were some remains, had been used to prevent the soil from falling in upon the workers. It has now been nearly filled up again by the calcareous deposit of the water. The river mentioned by Cæsar as the one that flowed in the valley beneath Uxellodunum* is a small tributary of the Dordogne, called the Tourmente. This is assuming the Puy d'Issolu to have been Uxellodunum. The most convincing material proof that the two places are the same was furnished by the discovery of the tunnel; but some strong corroborative evidence is to be found in local names. The word *puy* affords no clue, for it simply means a high place. In the dialect of the Viscounty of Turenne the Puy d'Issolu is pronounced *Lo Pé dé Cholu*. In the word Issolu or Cholu, we may have something of the Celtic word, which was Latinized

---

* 'Flumen infimam vallam lividebat quæ totum pœne montem cingebat, in quo positum erat præruptum undique oppidum Uxellodunum.'—'De Bello Gallico,' Lib. VIII.

by Cæsar after his custom ; but this verbal similarity would not in itself go far to prove the identity of the height near Vayrac with the position defended by Drappes and Lucterius. Lying in the Corrèze at no great distance from the Dordogne is the town of Ussel—a name that approaches much more nearly the sound of Uxellodunum. But an educated native of Vayrac, whom I chanced to meet months after my visit to the Puy d'Issolu, furnished me with some local testimony which appears to be of value in connection with a subject that has given rise to so much controversy. The stream where it issues near the base of the rocky height has been known in the neighbourhood from time immemorial as 'Lo foun Conino'—Conino's Fountain. Conino is a natural Romance corruption of Caninius, the name of Cæsar's lieutenant who in the first instance directed the siege of Uxellodunum. The French name for the stream at the bottom of the valley already mentioned is derived from the Romance one, Lo Tourmento. Now, as Cæsar made so much use of *tormenta* as engines of war, to prevent the besieged Cadurci from drawing water, something may easily have occurred to associate the stream with one of these machines. It is to be observed, however, that there are other streams in France to which the name Tourmente has been given, and of which the explanation is much more simple.

How solemnly still seemed this spectre-haunted spot in the quiet evening ! There was the groaning murmur of the stream flowing down its subterranean passage, and there was the low and fitful warble of

A PEASANT OF THE CAUSSE.

a nightingale; but this was all. Who, passing by here without foreknowledge, would suppose that on

this bit of desert the great struggle between Rome
and Gaul was brought to a close? What a wonderful
thing is a book, that it should preserve age after age,
with undiminished reality, all the torment, anguish,
and passion of a siege, and give a human interest
to rocks and streams, which without such aid would
tell us nothing of the horrid tumult that raged over
and around them! Now I can see the half-naked
Gauls rolling down their barrels of flaming pitch
upon the Roman engineers, and hear that great
clamour of the besiegers and the besieged of which
Cæsar speaks. Above were the Celtic heroes
defending their last rock with the obstinacy of
despair, and ready to accept death in any form but
that of thirst; and here were the veteran legionaries
exposing themselves day after day to the burning
pitch, the stones, and the arrows of the defenders,
with that disciplined courage and unwavering resolve
to conquer which made Rome the mistress of the
world. But the most terrible scene must have been
that in which the Gaulish warriors, after their surrender, had their hands cut off. What frightful
business was that, and what a heap of hands must
have been buried somewhere, either upon the tableland or in the valley! A deep-ploughing peasant
may long since have come upon an extraordinary
collection of little bones, and been much puzzled by
them. And poor Drappes, who, after his capture,
refused to eat, and died from starvation; he must
have been buried somewhere near. But Nature says

nothing about all these things; she covers up the traces of human ferocity with her new leaves and moss, and smiles there as tenderly as upon children's graves.

I passed the night at St. Denis, a modern place brought into existence by the line to Toulouse. At the auberge the evening was enlivened by dancing. Two maids of the inn found partners in a couple of rustic youths, and a young soldier *en congé* provided the music by whistling, or imitating the hurdy-gurdy with his mouth. For it was the *bourrée* that was danced.

The next morning I was on the road to Martel, with nightingales and blackcaps singing all around from blossoming quince and hawthorn and copses filled with a gold-green glimmer, until I reached the bare upland country. Upon the barren *causse*, besides the short turf, the gray ribs of rock, and scattered stones, little was to be seen but dark little junipers, tall broom, not yet in flower, hellebore, with bright tufts of new leaves and evil-looking green blossoms edged with dull purple, and the numberless gilded umbels of the spurge, which in springtime lend such beauty to the Southern desert. In the dips and little dingles there were stunted oaks with the brown foliage, that had been beaten by the winter winds in vain, still clinging to them, but which every breath of western breeze now scattered, because the buds were swelling and the unborn leaves were asking to come forth. At wide distances above the undulating, sterile land a farmhouse would appear, with high-pitched tiled roof, and a pigeon-house rising like a tower at one end. The stranger marvels to see such substantially-built houses in the midst of such sterility; but he finds the explanation when he has time to consider that there are so many stones lying about that, where it is possible to plough, the peasant heaps them up in his field, or makes walls that are little wanted. Having reached the top of a knoll, I saw beneath me many old tiled roofs whose lines ran at all angles, and above these rose the massive walls of a half-fortified church, and various towers or fragments of towers. I was looking at Martel.

According to legend and local history, Charles Martel, after defeating the Saracens near this spot, caused a church to be built on a piece of fertile land a few miles from the battlefield, and dedicated it to St. Maur. A town grew around church and monastery, and was named Martel in honour of the founder. In the early days of the Crusades, when princes and barons rivalled one another in virtuous zeal, a Viscount of Turenne decreed that inhabitants of Martel who were convicted of sinning against the marriage tie should be dragged naked through the town. The charter that contains this enactment treats of villeinage also, and orders that whoever has a man for sale within the limits of the viscounty shall fix the price, and shall not change it afterwards.

The marriage of Eleanor of Aquitaine and Henry Plantagenet brought the English to Martel in the twelfth century; but it does not appear that they obtained or cared to keep anything like a permanent grip on the place until the fourteenth century. Inasmuch, however, as Henry Short-Mantle, the rebellious son of Henry II., met with no resistance at Martel when he came thither, after pillaging the sanctuary of Roc-Amadour in 1183, it may be concluded that English influence was already established there. In the market-place is a house a portion of which was once included in a building that has now nearly disappeared, but which is known to every inhabitant as the 'palace of Henry II.' On the first floor, communicating with a spiral staircase, is a room paved with small pebbles. On one side is a broad chimney-place, just such as we see now all through Guyenne, even in the towns. According to the tradition preserved by the family to whom the house belongs, it was in one of the chimney-corners of this room that Prince Henry sat on the evening of the day that he left Roc-Amadour. It is uncertain, however, whether the Prince went to Martel immediately after the sacrilege, or after a pilgrimage that he made to the sanctuary to atone for his crime, when he was suffering from the disease that killed him. There is a local legend that he was followed by two monks, who contrived to put poison into his goblet; but whether he was poisoned or died of dysentery at Martel, as the chroniclers maintain, is a detail of small importance. That he did die here, and very repentantly, on a bed of ashes, and held up by the Bishop of Cahors, is a historical fact.

An indubitable testimony of the English occupation of Martel is the heraldic leopard of the Plantagenets. I found it carved in stone among the ruins of King Henry's palace, and hard by I saw it again upon a rusty fireplate that had been thrown into a corner. There is not a native of Martel who is not ready to talk of *le léopard anglais*.

The English were never loved by the Martellois. The people of this district are strong in their attachments, and perhaps even stronger in their animosities and prejudices. Without doubt the English did not treat them with marked tenderness; but there was very little human kindness in the Middle Ages, and the French, or the races which now compose France, left nothing to be invented in the arts of cruelty and oppression in the wars that they waged among themselves before they learnt, or were forced to learn, that it was to their interest to hold together and form one nation. Moreover, the greater number of the so-called English who kept a considerable part of Aquitaine in continual terror for three centuries were natives of the soil.

All the men of Martel who could carry arms joined the forces of King John, who was defeated by the Black Prince at Poitiers. The consuls of Martel had to pay heavy ransoms for their fellow-townsmen who fell into the hands of the English. Notwithstanding the disaster at Poitiers, the Martellois closed their gates and prepared for a siege, after having obtained from the Viscount a company of crossbow-men to help them in the defence. But an English garrison was soon established at Montvallent, only a few miles off, and this fact seems to have demoralized the Martellois, who, after enduring a few assaults, surrendered the town. The longest period of unbroken English possession of Martel appears to have occurred after this surrender. It is probable that the Sénéchaussée, which now exists under the name of the Hôtel de Ville, was commenced about this time, although the King of England must have been represented in the town by his seneschal long before. By the treaty passed between Henry III. and Reymond VI. of Turenne in 1223, it was stipulated that the Viscount should pay homage to Henry, but that the English officers should exercise no jurisdiction in the viscounty, except in the town of Martel, where the King could hold his assizes with the consent of the Viscount. It was, moreover, provided that in the event of resistance on the part of his fiefs, the Viscount could apply to the English seneschal at Martel for armed assistance. The burghers were in the enjoyment of their political franchises from the year 1256. They had town councillors, who elected four consuls every four years, who represented the borough in the États Vicomtains—an assembly composed of the principal landholders and dignitaries of the viscounty. The more they tasted freedom the more the burghers felt disposed to quarrel with the Viscount. In 1355 they sent a deputation to the Pope at Avignon begging him to ask their lord if it was his wish that the town should retain its privileges. The minutes of the municipal meeting, at which this decision was come to, are in existence, and they show how the Romance language was written at Martel in those days:

'Item fo ordenat que Moss. Aymar de Bessa et P. Karti ano a Vinho far reverensa al papa per nom de la vila eque l'hi recomendo la vila. E quelh fasso supplicacio quelh plas·a far am los vescomte se bot que nos garde nostres previleges.'

This ancient town has suffered grievously from that spirit of demolition which was so active during the first half of the present century, but which in France has been somewhat checked by the Commission of Historic Monuments. There are people who can remember when the town was surrounded by two walls; now only a few remnants of the fortifications remain. The church is exceedingly interesting. There are details indicating a very early origin—they may possibly have come down from the foundation; but the structure in the main belongs to the twelfth and fifteenth centuries. The east end—the oldest portion—has more the character of a stronghold than of a church. It has no apse, and the terminating wall, which is carried far above the roof, has a row of machicolations, and the massive buttresses by which it is flanked are really towers pierced with loopholes. At the foot of the wall is a deep pool of water, which serves as the horse-pond for the town; but it may originally have been part of a moat.

In the tympanum of the twelfth-century portal is one of those bas-reliefs representing the Last Judgment upon which the artistic ambition of the early Gothic period appears to have been chiefly directed in this region.

The fourteenth-century Sénéchaussée, with its embattled belfry, its little turrets or bartizans hanging high at the angles of the wall, its dim old court, with a deep well in the centre, speaks with a ghostly voice of ancient Martel. This building, after the English left, was the residence of the seneschals of the Viscounts of Turenne down to the Revolution. In two of the rooms are chimney-pieces very artistically carved in oak.

Notwithstanding all the demolition that has gone on, bits of picturesque antiquity meet the eye everywhere in the old English town. Now it is a half-ruinous watch-tower, now the Gothic doorway of a thirteenth-century house, now a gateway that has lost its tower, but whose wounds are covered with yellow wallflowers in spring; now a turret running up an entire front, with little windows looking out upon the quiet street, or some high-pitched roof curving inward under the weight of years and tiles.

The inn where I put up was like a hostelry of romance. Entering by a broad archway, I passed along a passage vaulted and groined, where corbel-heads grimaced from dim corners; climbed a staircase broad enough for a palace, and, having reached the landing, saw a great room with hearth and chimney to match, massive old furniture, pots and pans of highly-polished copper, and a hostess stout and cheery, who welcomed me as though I were an old friend, and not a wanderer to whom food and shelter were to be exchanged for money. This good woman had evidently no faith in new fashions; she dressed as she did thirty years ago, and every dish that she cooked for me was kept warm by a pewter brazier filled with embers from the hearth. One of these dishes was a goose's liver half roasted, half stewed, and sprinkled with capers.

While at Martel I was arrested as a spy by an old *garde champêtre*, who, seeing me taking notes of the church, wished to know who gave me permission to 'make a plan of the town.' I did not reply to him with the politeness that he evidently considered himself entitled to. It is probable that I should have chosen my words with more circumspection had I guessed what an important person he was; but as he wore a blouse, and was squatting upon a heap of stones which he had been pulling about, I underestimated his dignity. That he united the functions of *cantonnier* and *garde* did not occur to me. He sprang to his feet, put on his official badge, and, seizing me by the arm, shouted: 'I arrest you!' Then, when I took the liberty of removing his hand, he called out: '*Au secours!*'

But those to whom he appealed were women, who preferred to let him manage his own business, and who, moreover, were too much amused to interfere. When he had calmed down a little I walked with him to the deputy-mayor, whose office was over a little shop. After hearing me and examining my papers, this gentleman was satisfied that I was not a very dangerous person, and he told me that I had better forget the incident.

The fierce old man could not understand why I was released. He even protested: '*Il dit qu'il est un anglais; mais il le dit!*'

The deputy-mayor tried to calm him by observing that I had a right to be an Englishman. The *garde* then walked out, looking very hot and puzzled. From his childhood he had heard of the English as the worst tyrants that the region had known. Was not the country strewn with the ruins of the fortresses they had built? To his mind they were more dangerous enemies than the Germans, who never came near Martel. I bear no grudge against the old man. He believed that he was doing his duty in arresting me, and if I had made more allowance for his age and prejudices the unpleasantness might have been avoided. To him the old struggle with the English was almost as fresh as if it had taken place in his father's time.

People who remain in the same place all their days, and who never read, live much more in the past than others, and remember injuries done to their remote ancestors as if they, the latest descendants, were still suffering from them. I remember asking a woman in an inn not far from Martel how an old gateway and other mediæval buildings close by had been brought to such a sad state of ruin.

'It was you,' she exclaimed, 'who did that—*vous autres anglais!*'

And she looked so resentful for a few moments that I wished I had let the sleeping dog lie.

IN UPPER PÉRIGORD.

LEAVING Martel, I crossed the valley of the Dordogne, and passed on to other valleys southward and eastward, as recounted in the story of my wanderings by 'Southern Waters.' Many months went by, and then one summer day found me wayfaring again by the Dordogne towards the sea. A little below the point where I had crossed in search of the Ouysse I came to the small town of Souillac. This place, although fortified in the Middle Ages, played a much less important part in the wars of the Quercy than the neighbouring burgs of Martel and Gourdon. Its interest lies mainly in its twelfth-century church, and here chiefly in a very remarkable bas-relief of the Last Judgment. This astonishing work of art is to be found not where one would expect it to be, namely, in the tympanum of the portal, but in the interior, against a wall at the west end, over a Gothic arch, whose transition from the preceding style is marked by a billet-moulding. The sculpture is in a high degree typical of the uncouth vigour of the period. The two pillars supporting the arch are so carved as to represent figures of the damned going down into hell. The artist might have been inspired by Dante had he not lived before the poet who collected and fixed upon the sombre canvas of his verse all the woeful visions of eternal punishment that haunted the mediæval mind. A man and woman are descending to the abyss, he holding her by the hair, and she clasping him by the waist, the faces of both terribly expressive of horror that is new, and utter despair. The meaning is plain enough: each was the cause of the other's doom, and the sentence of the Judge in the panel above has united them in hell for all eternity. On the opposite pillar are another couple, also clasping one another; but their faces express the blank and passionless misery of a doom foreknown. Monk or layman, he who designed the composition felt the necessity of giving this tragic warning to his fellow-beings. Centuries later an English poet expressed the same idea in verse:

'The woman's cause is man's! they rise or sink
Together, dwarfed or god-like, bond or free.'

One of the less conspicuous figures is going down head foremost in the company of an animal that looks very like a pig. This beast having been damned by ecclesiastical sculptors in France as early as the twelfth century, and probably earlier, it is not surprising that a polite peasant, when he mentions it by name, often excuses himself for his supposed breach of good manners by adding: '*Sauf votre respect.*'

Nearing a village not far from Souillac, and wondering the while what had become of the picturesque, I saw, as if by enchantment, a few yards away, a little old church covered with ivy, and surrounded by tombstones that were stained with the dead colours of last winter's lichen; one leaning this way, another that, but all going down into the grassy graves. A few chairs and a single bench told that the people who came here to pray were not many nor rich. Most of the flagstones were broken, and the altar was almost simple enough to please a Calvinist. It was the simplicity, not of intention, but of poverty. Are such churches—lost amidst the pensive trees, or bathed by the tender evening light upon the vine-clad hillside—doubly hallowed, or is it the poetry of old memories and ideal pictures stored away behind a multitude of newer impressions that moves us like the wind-blown strains of half-forgotten melodies as we pass them in our wanderings?

Evening found me by the Dordogne, that flowed calmly in a salmon-coloured light, thrown down by a wasteful stony hill, itself lit up by a reflected glow of the sinking sun. The meadows through which the little path ran were dotted all over with golden spots of lotus, and near the water the pale, pure yellow of the evening primrose shone against the darkening willows. The voices of unseen peasants, labouring somewhere in the fields so long as the daylight lasted, were carried up the valley by the breeze, just loosened from its leash; but the sound was only a little louder than the whispering of the poplars.

The gloaming lingered until I reached the village of Cazoulès. At the inn where I decided to pass the night I fell among bicyclists—quite a crowd of them—all young, frantic with the excitement of some break-neck run, and noisy enough to shock the dog's sense of decorum, for he slunk off with his tail between his legs. Having slaked their thirst, the jovial band of enthusiasts sprang upon their steel horses and dashed off into the darkness, where their voices were quickly lost.

While waiting for dinner, I found nothing so amusing as listening to a high dispute between the hostess and a travelling butcher, with whom she had long had dealings, but whom she had lately deserted because she had found another who sold cheaper. The butcher called his rival a 'dirty sparrow,' but at length proposed to yield the sou on each pound of meat by means of which the 'sparrow' had scored his victory. In future all his meat was to be sold at eleven sous, and on these terms he was restored to favour. Thus, by playing one man off against the other, the artful woman was able to save quite a pile of sous every week on her general expenses. The Frenchwoman of ordinary intelligence, whether she belongs to the north or the south, the east or the west, may be safely trusted to beat any man of her own race at bargaining.

For a rural inn this one at Cazoulès was good and

substantial, but it provided a little too much irritation at night to be consistent with peaceful slumber and happy dreams. This was not, perhaps, the fault of the inn, but of the Dordogne Valley. As soon as the day broke another enemy entered the field. The flies then awoke, refreshed but hungry, and determined to make the most of a good opportunity. The house-flies of the North, when compared to those of the South, seem to have been well brought up, and trained to live with human beings on terms of civility, if not of friendship. The flies of Southern France must be descended from those that were sent to worry Pharaoh, and when one has lived with them during the months of August and September, one can quite believe that their ancestors exasperated the Egyptian king to the point of promising anything so that they might be taken from him.

It was not until I had walked away from Cazoulès that I realized where I was. I had left the Quercy while wandering through those meadows as the sun was sinking, and had entered Périgord—once famous for troubadours, and now for truffles. Nobody can live there to-day by making verses, and the representative of the jongleur, who once sang from castle to castle to the accompaniment of the mediæval fiddle, and who was so heartily welcomed at all the baronial feasts and merrymakings, is now a wandering beggar, who gathers crusts from the peasants by his rude minstrelsy, that changes from the pious to the obscene, or from the obscene to the pious, as the character and taste of the audience may decide. Many persons, however, contrive to prosper by hunting for truffles in the exhilarating company of pigs. It is not in this fertile valley that they find them, but on the hillsides and stony tablelands, where the oak flourishes, but never grows tall.

I passed almost at the foot of one of those darkly-wooded, precipitous hills or cliffs which now approach the water's edge and now recede for a mile or more in this part of the valley; widening or diminishing the cultivated land accordingly as the rocky sides of the fissure resisted the washing and mining of the ancient waters.

On the top of the cliff stood a high round tower —the keep of a small feudal stronghold. It is called the Tour de Mareuil. Its position leaves little doubt that in old times its owners, like so many other nobles whose ruined castles crown the heights on both sides of the Dordogne, levied toll upon the boats that came up or went down the river. Navigation must have been always difficult on account of the strong current and the numerous rapids and shallows; but the stream was a means of communication between Bordeaux, Périgord, and the Haut-Quercy that was not to be despised, and probably some care was taken to keep the channel open. According to tradition, the English made frequent use of it. The tolls were an important source of income to the nobles whose fortresses overlooked the river. A sharp look-out was always kept from the towers for approaching boats.

I was on my way to the castle where Fénelon first saw the light, and in order to reach it I had to cross the river. An old flat-bottomed boat, built for conveying men, asses, and other animals from one side to the other, lay off the bank, and two girls, who were in charge of a flock of geese as well as of the ferry, were willing to take me across. While the elder ferried, the younger examined me carefully at close quarters, and apparently with much interest. Presently she asked me if I sold writing-paper. After landing, I soon reached the village of St. Mondane. Here I halted at an inn in the shadow of old walnut-trees. A few yards off, under one of the great trees, was a high wooden crucifix, around which some twenty or thirty geese were standing or lying down, all in a digestive or contemplative mood, and through the openings between the boles and the branches were seen the sunlit meadows sloping to the low willows and the flashing river.

From St. Mondane a charming road or lane between very high banks that are almost cliffs leads upward to the Château de la Motte-Fénelon, where, in 1651, was born François de Salignac de la Motte, known to the world as Fénelon. Having reached the top of the hill, I soon came in view of a picturesque mass of masonry with round towers capped with pointed roofs, and with Gothic gables hanging lightly in the air over dormer windows; the whole rising out of a dense grove of trees in the midst of a quiet sunny landscape. When quite near I found that the grove was a sombre little wood of evergreen oaks. The same wood, if not the actual oaks, may have been there in Fénelon's time, for the ilex is one of the commonest trees in Périgord on the hills about the Dordogne. As a boy, while climbing here, he may have torn his hose into tatters, notwithstanding his precocious knowledge of Greek. The future churchman may even have robbed a jay's nest on this very spot. What quietude and what deep shadow! Not a leaf stirred; only a fiery shaft of sunshine forced its way here and there through the dark roof of unchanging green to the brown soil and the rampart's mossy wall.

Although the present castle was raised when feudalism was nothing more than a tradition and a sentiment, the outworks, consisting of two walls, the inner one standing on ground considerably higher than the other, were of exceptional strength, and as they were originally, so they remain at the present day. I passed through the outer and then the inner gateway, and, in my search for a human being, accident led me to the kitchen, which was very large and entirely paved with pebbles. Here I found the cook, who, I had been told, was the only person in authority at that time. Surrounded by four great walls, on which hung utensils that were rarely handled except for the periodical scouring, she looked as solemn as a cloistered nun. She consented, however, to show me the interior of the castle, with a pathetic readiness which said that the

CHÂTEAU DE FÉNELON.

appearance of an occasional visitor kept her from sinking into hopeless melancholy.

The most interesting room is the one in which Fénelon slept. Here is to be seen his four-post bedstead, each of the posts a slender twisted column, the silk hangings and fringe looking very worn and faded after being exposed to the light of over two hundred years. Adjoining this room is the *salle à manger*, the immense hearth, with seats at the ingle corners, being covered by an elliptical arch. Most of the furniture here and elsewhere is of massive oak, carved in the style of the seventeenth and eighteenth centuries. The family into whose possession this castle has passed, although distinct from that of Salignac de la Motte, which has now no representative, reverently preserves all that associates the spot with the memory of the illustrious author of 'Télémaque.'

From the top of one of the machicolated towers I saw a vast expanse of country, singularly grand, but very solemn. From each side of the Dordogne Valley rose and stretched away into the distance a seemingly endless succession of hills, broken up by narrow gorges and glens. Over all, or nearly all these hills lay a dark and scarcely varying mantle of forest. This tract of country is well named Périgord Noir. It is one of the few districts of France which still draw a sum from the Government yearly in the form of prize money for the wolves that are killed there.

I returned to St. Mondane and continued my journey westward by the valley, which brought me every day a little nearer to the sea—still so far away. As I had no need to hurry, I sat awhile in the late afternoon upon a low mossy wall, in the deep shade of a dripping, whispering rock, from which hung delicate green tresses of the maiden's-hair fern. Above, the rock was lost in a steep wilderness of trees and dense undergrowth, which met the radiant sky somewhere where the eye could not follow. The bell-like tinkle of water out of sight was the only sound until I heard a patter-patter of webbed feet coming along the road. A flock of geese were moving homeward, followed by a woman, whose feet were as bare as theirs, and whose eyes were fixed upon her distaff and spindle. She would not have noticed me had not the birds, true to their ancient reputation, given the alarm.

A little later I had left the shadow of the wooded rocks and was on the margin of the river, which spread out broadly here between its shelving banks of pebbly shingle. Then, to reach by the shortest way the village where I intended to pass the night, I had to turn once more from the water and cross some wooded hills. Here the jays mocked at the solemnity of the evergreen oaks, and the dark forest echoed as with the laughter of fiends.

Groléjac was the curious name of the village I was seeking, and which I at length found partly on a hill and partly in the valley of the Dordogne. Chance taking me to a house that bore the sign of an inn, although it was at the back of a farm-yard,

I thought I might as well stop there as anywhere else.

I am waiting for dinner—seldom a cheerful way of killing time. I do not, however, expose myself to the risk of being irritated by the sight of my willing but mechanical hostess scraping the white ashes from the embers, parcelling out these into little heaps of fire upon the hearth, throwing salt into the swinging pot with a hand the colour of which may be distressing to the imagination, then tasting the soup: all this, and much more, I leave her to accomplish in the gathering darkness of the kitchen, and, sparing her the pain of lighting lamp or candle while there is still a gleam of day, I wander out beyond the houses of the village to a quiet woodside, there to watch the coming of night, which, whether it be accompanied by wailing winds and storm-rack brimming with tears, or by that grand serenity which grows in beauty as the light fails, is always like the coming of death.

In the clear-obscure, the brown and yellow rocks of bare limestone, at the foot of which is the small inn, seem to be drawing nearer. All their details become luminously distinct as the air grows darker, while the caverns gape like the black mouths of some stealthily approaching, monstrous, many-headed form. Two men are still working in a field of tobacco, and they go on until lights flash forth from all the houses in the valley. Then they slowly move off into the dusk with their ox and waggon.

All about the fields, where the night crickets are now chirruping and the flying beetles are droning, there is a general movement of life towards the village— of men carrying their mattocks on their shoulder or walking in front of the ox that has done his long day's ploughing, of women and children, geese, turkeys, and sheep.

I wonder if the wooden cross beside the tobacco-field was put there to mark the spot where somebody

RETURNING FROM THE FIELDS.

died, in accordance with an old and beautiful custom still much practised in these rural districts of France; but the thought of the laid table at the auberge changes the train of ideas, so, following in the wake of the last goose, I, too, take refuge from the night in the now animated village.

Sitting alone at a great table in a room large enough for a marriage feast, ill-lighted by an oil-lamp, whose flame appears to be afflicted with St. Vitus's dance—a room quite free from ornament, with furniture responding exclusively to the purposes of resting, eating, and drinking, with curtainless windows looking out upon the moonless night that is beginning to sigh and moan at the approach of a storm—my dinner is not a very cheerful one. Not that I am necessarily unhappy when I take a solitary meal. In this matter all depends upon the mood, and the mood frequently depends upon influences too subtle to be analyzed. The dinner was as good as I had a right to expect it to be. A dish on which the hostess had evidently striven to use her best art was of orange mushrooms in a sauce of verjuice; but the substantial one was a roast fowl—an unfortunate bird that was just going to roost with an easy mind, when my coming upset the arrangements of the inn and the poultry house. One fowl, at all events, had had good reason to think it was an ill wind that blew me into the village.

It is a bad custom in rural France to kill fowls just when they are wanted for the spit. Not only is it unpleasant to think that a creature is not allowed time to cool before it begins to turn in front of the fire, but the art of cooking is placed at a disadvantage by the practice. It is of no use, however, trying to convince the people of their error, even when they kill poultry for themselves and can choose their time: they will never do things otherwise than in the way to which they have been accustomed. The French are stubbornly conservative in everything except politics.

As I felt the need of talking to-night, I fetched the farming innkeeper from his kitchen and persuaded him to drink some of his own cognac. This he did without wincing, but he soon returned the compliment by bringing out of a cupboard a bottle of clear greenish liquor, which he said was *eau de vie de figues*. It was something new to me. I had tasted alcohol distilled from a considerable variety of the earth's fruits, but never from figs before. It retained a strong flavour of its origin, and might have been correctly described as fire-water, for it was almost pure spirit.

I drew this man into conversation upon the peasant's life. All that he said was only confirmation of the opinion I had already formed from other testimony respecting the occupation of Adam when he had to struggle with nature outside of the terrestrial paradise. Let a man own as much soil as he can till with his hands, let him have an ox, too, to help him: he can only live at the price of almost incessant labour and rigorous frugality. This is the normal condition of the peasant-proprietor's existence.

'The peasant who works seriously,' said the farmer, 'does not sleep more than four hours a night during the summer months. He goes to bed at ten, and gets up at two. This would not hurt him if he were better fed, but he eats little besides his soup, and drinks bad *piquette*.'

The man went back to his kitchen, and then

to his bed close by; the flame of the lamp became sick unto death, for it now wanted oil, and the house grew so quiet that the squeaking of the rats and the pattering of their feet could be heard from places that seemed far away. But for the rumbling of the thunder, the only sound from the mysterious world outside would have been the scream, now like the cry of a cat, now like a puppy's bark, of an owl flying with muffled wings up and down the valley. Very different, however, was this little owl's cry from the madman's shout of the great eagle owl, which I had often heard in the rocky vale of the Alzon. I threw open the window of my bedroom and looked out upon the night. It was illumined, not by moon nor by stars, but by lightning flashes, which followed one another with such rapidity that there was no darkness. The quivering flame threw an awful brightness into the great woods upon the tops of the hills.

A few hours later I was wandering through these woods, which were now filled with another light that dried the dripping leaves.

Some miles of forest, then cultivated slopes, and at length the Dordogne again. I was growing rather weary of searching for the mediæval town of Domme, when I recognised it by its old ramparts upon the summit of a high bare hill, which looked very forbidding indeed where it changed to rock, whose naked escarpments seemed to float as inaccessible as a cloud in the blue air far above the valley. As I climbed the shadeless stony hill in the mid-day sun-glare, I thought that if the soldiers of five or six centuries ago used strong language as they toiled up here in their heavy armour, it was excusable. I was wellnigh repenting of my resolution to reach Domme, when, by a turn of the road, I found myself not many yards in front of a fortified gateway of the fourteenth century, with a drum-tower on each side connected by a curtain with the ramparts. At first glance nothing seemed to be wanting. The towers, however, were ruinous in the upper part, and the battlements had disappeared.

With the help of a local pork-butcher, who kept the key, I was able to enter the towers of this gateway. In each was a guard-room of considerable size, and the men-at-arms while on duty there evidently found that in time of peace the hours lagged, for some of them had carved upon the wall with their knives or daggers crucifixes and representations of the Virgin and Child, all closely imitated from church sculpture, painting or window decoration of the Gothic period. Many names are cut in Gothic character on the same walls; a further proof that the vanity of man has ever sprouted in much the same way as now. The antiquary, because he has his own prejudices, perceives an abyss between the act of the Cockney tourist of to-day who carves his name upon an old tower or a menhir, and that of a man who five centuries ago, for no better reason than the other, left upon a guard-room wall a similar record of his passage. The man of the present is a vulgar defacer of interesting monuments, whereas he of the past added to their interest, and prepared a pleasant little surprise for the archæologist who might walk that way a few centuries later.

Enough of the fortifications of Domme remains to show what a very strong place it was in the Middle Ages. Much of the wall where the town was not naturally defended by the high naked rock, forming a frightful precipice that no besiegers would have attempted to scale, has been well preserved. Standing upon some bastion of this rampart, with the deep valley far below him and the sky above him, the wanderer may allow his fancy almost to convince him that he is really standing upon some 'castle in the air.' Of the many rock-perched towns of the South, this is one of the most remarkable; although, with the exception of the fortifications, little remains of archæological interest.

According to the chronicles of Jean Tarde, a canon of the neighbouring town of Sarlat, who wrote at the end of the sixteenth and beginning of the seventeenth century, Domme was first taken by the English in 1346, but not without the help of '*quelques traistres.*' From this stronghold they harassed the surrounding country, 'while the armies of one and the other party were in Normandy and Picardy, and that battle of Cressi (Crecy) was fought to the disadvantage of the party of France. Towards the end of the year a truce was accorded, but it was in no way observed in Périgord by the English.'

The correct date of the capture of Domme appears to have been 1347. The men who treasonably delivered up the place were afterwards hanged by the French party when they regained possession of the stronghold. In 1369 the English again invested the rock, this time under the command of Robert Knolles. (Tarde, who spelt all English names as he had heard them pronounced in the country, writes Robert Canole.) The place was then so well defended, and success appeared so far off to the partisans of Edward III., that the siege was raised in despair at the end of a month; and the annalist goes on to say that the English then marched into the Quercy and took Roc-Amadour. Domme, however, fell into the English power again; but in 1415 it was once more in the hands of the French. Then we read that the seneschal sent the crier into the public place to proclaim '*de par le Roy*' that every inhabitant of Domme was forbidden to leave the town with the intention of living elsewhere, under the penalty of having any property that he might possess in the town confiscated. The motive of this ordinance is explained as follows: 'The wars had already rendered the country so desolate, that at Domme, where the ordinary number of inhabitants who were heads of families was a thousand, there were now no more than a hundred and twenty. The people who had left had abandoned everything, and gone to Spain or elsewhere.'

From the bare and windy hill I went down again into the quiet valley, where, when a few more miles were left behind, I came to La Roque-Gageac, a village at the foot of high-reaching rocks of fantastic outline, not far from the Dordogne. Many houses long ago seem to have climbed far up the warm limestone under the shelter of cornice and canopy, fashioned by the sculptor Time, braving all the storms of centuries, and the danger of being hurled in fragments towards the valley by some falling crag.

In an open space, forming a little square, a man and a woman were holding down a pig, one at each end of a board, where the animal had been stretched out against its inclination, while a third person had the knife ready for action. And the spot chosen for the execution was immediately in front of a very old and interesting shrine, with gabled roof, surmounted by a rude Gothic crucifix. I caught a glimpse of the pale statue and the flowers before it; but only a glimpse, for the struggles of the doomed pig, and the momentary expectation of seeing the red stream gush forth, made me turn away. One sees much that is anything but poetical in the romantic land of the troubadours.

Near this strikingly-picturesque village is a cave such as one might read of in a story of fanciful adventure. It is in a rock beside the Dordogne, where the river rests in a deep pool. The entrance is under water, and it can only be reached with safety by a good diver when, the sun shining at a certain hour, and the light striking in a particular way, the passage into the cavern is lit up. A boy had made the dive successfully not long before my visit to this place, but he found so much to interest him in the cave while it was lighted a little by the borrowed gleam from the water, that he lingered there until, the sun moving on his course, the angle of refraction suddenly changed. The child had not the courage to take a plunge into the dark gulf, where there was no beacon to guide him, and where he might have struck against the rock. He therefore remained the rest of the day and all night in the cavern. When the sun again lit up the passage leading from his prison, the boy plunged, and a few seconds afterwards he was sitting on the riverbank drying himself in the sun.

* * * * *

I have entered upon the tenancy of a small house beside the Dordogne at Beynac, a village a few miles below La Roque, partly crouching beneath a very high rock, and partly built upon its terraces or ledges up to the inner wall of a feudal castle that was much modified and refashioned in later ages under the pressure of two forces—time, that ruins, and the eternal striving of each generation to attain its own ideal of comfort and elegance. But the grand old keep still rears its rectangular mass behind and far above the later masonry, and when the evening sun shines upon it, the stones, no longer gray, wear again their bright colour of six or seven centuries ago. Presently, as the glow moves higher, the battlements and machicolations take a golden clearness that marks every detail against the blue depth of sky whose fire is fading and preparing to change into the calm splendour that mingles with

BEYNAC.

the dusk. Between the base of the rock and the river is just space enough for a road, which is dazzlingly white now, and well powdered with dust; but in winter it not infrequently disappears under water.

On the opposite shore, above a shelving beach of yellow pebbles and a broken line of osiers, stretch meadows that are intensely green in spring, and would be quickly so again if rain were to fall; but now they are very brown, and the long-tailed sheep that wander over them, tinkling their bells, like to keep near the Dordogne, where they can moisten their mouths from time to time, and thus help themselves to imagine that they are eating grass. Beyond the reach of meadow, almost at the foot of high wooded hills which mark the boundary of the valley on that side, is a modern château; but the architect found his model for it in the past, when castles were more picturesque than comfortable. When the amber-tinted towers are seen through the haze of a summer morning against the background of wooded hill, one thinks that in just such a castle as this Tasso or Spenser would have put an enchantress, whose wiles, combined with the indolent influence of the valley, few pilgrim knights taking the eastward way to Roc-Amadour would have been able to resist.

I found the valley so hot in the steady blaze of summer that, having reached Beynac, I felt no inclination to go any farther. I thought I would stop there until cooler weather came, and live meanwhile principally in the Dordogne. Several families from different parts of Périgord had already come here to spend a mildly exciting and not too costly river season; and there they were, fathers, mothers, sons and daughters, splashing in the blue tepid water, with their clothes laid carefully in little heaps upon the pebbly beach or upon the brown grass by the osiers. Despising the shelter which in more fashionable watering-places is thought indispensable, they lazily undressed and dressed in the open air with an appreciation of sunshine and regardlessness of apparel that was almost lizard-like in its freedom from conventional restraint.

I was charmed by the spectacle as I meditated upon the opposite bank. The more I meditated the better I liked the idea of tarrying in a spot where Arcadian simplicity of life was so unaffectedly cultivated. I resolved that I, too, would take a house at Beynac if there was one to be had, and that I would have what I figuratively termed my 'caravan' brought up here. At the auberge—the only one in the place—I learnt that there was but a single house still vacant, and that it was not a very beautiful one. A young fisherman started off barefoot to fetch the owner from his village, four miles away. The country had to be scoured for him, so that it was long before he showed himself.

While waiting, I went out and amused the fish in the Dordogne by pointing a borrowed rod at them, and tempting them with the fattest house-flies I could find; but as soon as they saw the bait they all turned their tails to it. My angling was a complete failure. And yet there were multitudes of fish swimming on the surface; the water seemed alive with them. I concluded that they were observing a solemn fast.

At length the fisherman returned, looking very hot and dusty, and of course thirsty. He was accompanied by a hard-baked man of about sixty— a peasant, apparently, but one who had put on his best clothes in view of an important bargain that was to be made. He had cunning little eyes, and a mouth that seemed to have acquired from many ancestors, and from the habits of a lifetime, a concentrated expression of rustic chicanery which told me that no business was to be done with him without a fight.

He led the way to his house, which was on the road just above the river. I came to terms with him for a month, after the expected fight; but it was not until he had gone away that I began to realize that I had not distinguished myself by my wisdom in this transaction. Even the villagers, who are not dainty in the matter of lodging, described the house as a *baraque*. It gave me the same impression when I saw the inside of it; but I closed my eyes to its drawbacks, because I had taken a fancy to Beynac, and this was the only furnished dwelling to be obtained there. I thought all the little drawbacks belonging to it, such as the rustic hearth to cook upon, pots with holes in them, rusty frying-pans, deficiency of crockery, and more than a sufficiency of fleas, would be overcome somehow, as they had been elsewhere during my peregrinations in out-of-the-way districts, where the traveller who nurses his dignity, and has a proper regard for the comforts of life, never thinks of stopping. But things did not settle down this time quite so quickly as I had expected.

After the arrival of the 'caravan' I took to fishing —always with the same rod borrowed of the blacksmith-innkeeper—with a zeal that I had not known since I was a boy. I found that things settled down better when I was out of the way. But there was something that settled down only too rapidly. This was the kitchen floor. There was a bare rock forming the back wall of the house, and adown it a runnel of water gently trickled. In the wet season it lost all modesty, made a lake that rose above the boards, and tried to find an exit by the back of the chimney. This explained why the fire needed two days' coaxing and blowing before it would burn, notwithstanding that our servant had been reared in the knowledge of such chimney-places and their humours. It also explained why somebody's foot went through the floor in a fresh place two or three times a day. At the end of the first week one had to stride or jump over half a dozen chasms to get from one side to another. About the same time four or five of the lower stairs gave way from rottenness, so that it needed no little agility to reach the bedrooms. The old man had to come and mend his house, and because he had a guilty conscience he brought a basket of figs with him; but, instead of owning that the wood was rotten, he insinuated that it had been maliciously danced upon.

8

But the heat was the worst tribulation. The house, with all its windows without *persiennes*—a detail I had quite overlooked—faced the south, so that during the hottest hours of the day the sun was full upon it, and the heat was over one hundred degrees Fahrenheit in the shade. It was the most scorching August that had been known even in the South of France for years. The recollection of those burning hours in that shanty will be ever green.

Nevertheless, the time spent at Beynac left some pleasant memories. The days were fiery, and, when the south wind blew, almost suffocating; but when the sun went down into the west there usually came a beneficent change. During the few minutes that the golden circle lay seemingly upon the edge of the world, a boat crossing the river appeared to glide over unfathomable depths of splendour; then gradually over the fields of maize and tobacco, and where the yellow stubble of the corn long since reaped had been left, there spread the deep-toned lustre of evening. As the brown dusk filled the valley, and under the sombre walnut-trees the wayside cross became like the spectre of one, shrill voices of old women were heard calling the geese and turkeys that still lingered in the fields.

The geese were often left to come home by themselves, after spending the day along the banks of the river. They belonged to various people, but, being eminently sociable birds, they started off together in flocks of fifty or more. Although there must have been causes of jealousy and rivalry among them, they never seemed to quarrel. They knew when it was time to go home by the failing light, and in the dusk I often met them marching along the road like a regiment of soldiers. As they reached houses to which some of them belonged, detachments would fall out and the others would go on. Every bird would return to the place which had for it the sweet associations of its gosling innocence.

It is now night—the calm summer night without a moon, but spangled with stars. Among those which the Dordogne reflects and holds as if they were its own, is the planet Mars, which gleams redly in the midst of a swarm of lesser yellow lights. The river here is broad and still; there is not ripple enough to make a beam tremble. If the stars in the water flash, it is because the rays are flashed from above. Just below the village there are rapids, and a faint murmur comes up from them, but it is borne under by the shrilling of the crickets that have climbed into the osiers and poplars all along by the water's edge. Now and again there is a great splash in the middle of the stream, which makes one think that a fish large enough to swallow some unsuspecting Jonah of Périgord must be there in a playful mood; but this is merely the effect upon the imagination of a sudden noise breaking in upon the monotonous sounds of the night which are so much like silence.

Lured by the freshness of the air and the serene glory of the starlit sky, I wander off down the valley to a spot where the river, all in turmoil, washes and wears away the flanks of rocks rising sheer from its bed like a wall. Looking back, I can see very distinctly the dark mass of the castle and the church by its side high above me against the sky, and every minute or so the lightning-flash from a storm far away in the west brightens the sombre masonry and the rock beneath.

Centuries ago in this light, the rock, the fortress, and its church must have looked much the same as now. An Englishman, who had campaigned with the Black Prince, standing where I am—the road was probably a mule track then—would have seen against the sky the picture that sets me dreaming of the past. But the quietude of the summer night might have been disturbed by sounds that are not heard now. It is unlikely that so large a castle, containing so many men-at-arms and officials as must have been deemed necessary to its safety and dignity, would at this early hour have been wrapped in silence more complete than that of the valley. There would surely have been some people breathing the cool air on the platform of the keep besides the watchman, some soldiers pacing the *chemin de ronde*, although peaceful days may have returned to the unlucky land of Guyenne; and the clamour of strong voices would have come down to the river. But now the castle is quiet as its rock which was beaten by the waves of a vanished sea, and those who still live in it are like the keepers of a cemetery. That *donjon*, whose dark form seems to stand amidst the stars, only serves to mark one of the many tombs of feudalism which rise above the smiling but capricious Dordogne like menhirs—monuments of older illusions—along the ocean-scalloped coast of Brittany.

Animated as Beynac became late in the afternoon, when the little society, composed of extraneous particles, met in costumes that were airy, fantastic, elementary, anything but ceremonious, to exchange civilities in the water, life on the whole was so mildly exciting that when one day a small caravan, drawn by a donkey and preceded by a young man half hidden by a great straw hat and wildly beating a drum, entered the place, there was a great and tumultuous movement of the population. Everybody wanted to know what the donkey and the young man proposed to do at Beynac. On the caravan had been painted '*Théâtre de la Gaîté*,' which threw light upon the object of the intruders. The donkey drew up in front of the inn, and the excited crowd waited with ill-contained impatience to see the company of players descend from the battered travelling trunk on wheels. At length a pretty little girl of about twelve, with large and lustrous brown eyes, came out of the box. She was the company. She was in the charge of her mother, who superintended the artistic arrangements, as well as the culinary and financial, but did not venture upon the stage. The young man looked after the donkey and the drum, and filled up his time by catching fish for the company and her mother. The stable of the auberge was hired for evening use as a *salle de spectacle*, and at one end a very diminutive stage was set up by means of rough planks and old pieces of carpet.

Everybody who could afford to spend a penny or twopence upon vanity and worldliness went to see the performance. It was quite a fashionable gathering. The best society were by common consent allowed to take the best seats—very hard benches—the less ambitious crowded behind, with minds fully made up not to allow themselves to be carried by enthusiasm beyond the expenditure of two sous when the plate went round; while favoured children, who were not expected to pay anything, because they had nothing, climbed into the mangers, and packed themselves as close together as aphides on a rose-stalk. The stable had been carefully cleansed, but the horsey odour that belonged to it could not be swept out. This, with the bad ventilation, and a temperature almost equal to the hatching of eggs without hens, was a drawback; but the audience was in no humour to be critical. A small handbell was rung, two pieces of old carpet were drawn back, and the little girl made her bow to the audience in a costume as near to that of Mignon as she and her mother could make it. She sang:

'Connais-tu le pays où fleurit l'oranger?'

and other airs from the opera in a small, bird-like voice, unaccompanied by any music. For three hours the child sang, acted, and danced in the suffocating stable, lighted by two petroleum lamps. The next day I saw Mignon sitting on one of the shafts of the caravan and gnawing the 'drumstick' of a fowl. The child-actress was the prop of her mother and the donkey; her talent also kept the youth, who began to agitate the nerves of Beynac with his diabolical *rataplan* hours before each performance.

One morning, soon after sunrise, the donkey, which had begun to think that this time it had really been pensioned off, was put into the shafts, and the caravan gradually disappeared upon the white road. Then the village became quite dull again; but it was roused from its torpor by the annual fête. This was the chief event of the year. The peasants came in from the scattered villages and from the isolated farms lying in the midst of the chestnut woods. All the women coifed themselves with their best kerchiefs, the heads of most of the young girls being resplendent with brilliant-coloured silk. This coiffure resembles that of the Bordelaise, but it is not so small, nor is it folded so coquettishly. There was much love-making—sometimes exquisitely comic by its rustic naïveté—and there was a good deal of dancing to the maddening music of two screaming hurdy-gurdies.

At Beynac I made the acquaintance of a Frenchman who, after angling for riches—a sport at which he lost much bait and caught nothing—turned all his attention to the fish in the Dordogne. He resolved that he would run no more risk by casting his bread upon the wider waters, but that he would make the most of what remained to him by withdrawing to some riverside nook, where his love of the unconventional, and his taste for a free life in the open air, could expand, emancipated from all servitude to society, including the necessity of keeping up what is called 'an appearance.'

What, to my mind, helps greatly to make France such a pleasant country to live in is the large amount of social liberty that one enjoys there. Except in great towns, and in those places which are thronged at certain seasons by cosmopolitan crowds, people can live as simply as they please, and they can wear anything, however cheap or even shabby, without risk of being diminished on this account in the opinion of others. They are liked or disliked, respected or despised, as their conduct and dealings become known and judged.

The Otter—this nickname had been given to my new acquaintance by those who were jealous of his fishing skill—when he was out in his boat never wore anything finer than corduroy trousers, a short blue jacket of the cotton material from which blouses are made, a straw-hat, and *espadrilles*, into which he put his bare feet. No heavier clothing is consistent with happiness in such a climate as that of the Dordogne Valley during the summer months. When, by gliding over the transparent water, which revealed the pebbles at the bottom almost in the deepest places, and the shoals of fish as they passed up and down the stream, the temptation to plunge became irresistible, the blue jacket and the other garments were thrown off in a few seconds, and the fish were startled by the descent of a black head and beard, followed by the rest of that human form which Carlyle has compared to a forked radish.

Sometimes the Otter made nocturnal expeditions far up the channels of the little streams that fall into the Dordogne. Then he was after crayfish. The ordinary method of catching these crustacea, namely, with a piece of netting covering a small wire hoop, and baited with meat, had little charm for him. There was another much more in keeping with his passion for movement. He would walk up the beds of the streams quite heedless of the water, holding in one hand a lantern, and having the other free to make a grab at every crayfish he might see scuttling out of harm's way over the stones or sand. As he went slowly up the narrow valleys, the gleam of his lantern through the osiers, the tall loose-strife and hemp-agrimony startled the owls, the hedgehogs and the weasles; but not the sound of water wailing in the darkness, nor the cries of disturbed animals, nor the weird blackness of overhanging trees that hid the stars, troubled his nerves. On he went, through water-meadows, at the bottom of gloomy little gorges, and by the fringe of the forest, until he had wandered miles away from Beynac. We very nearly met one night, both being out with the same object in view. I, however, had very little of his zeal for the sport, and was less interested by the crayfish than by the fantastic indistinctness of trees and shrubs and flowers, which, in the light of the stars and the lantern, seemed to belong to a world with which I was but vaguely familiar, although I had travelled all over it in dreams.

Sometimes I used to go out fishing with the Otter on the Dordogne. When the casting-net was left at home (it was of little use when the water was clear) chub-fishing with the flying-line was generally the chosen form of sport. Here I may say that my companion, who could turn his hand to anything, made his own rods from hazel-sticks. Where the water was sufficiently deep, the boat was rowed and steered with a single-bladed paddle, but where it was shallow much better progress could be made by polling. These are the two methods invariably used by the fishermen and ferrymen of the Dordogne, and it is astonishing with what success they can get a boat up the rapids without having recourse to the towing-line.

When we went chub-fishing, we took the boat a mile or so up-stream, and then let it drift down with the current near a bank that was fringed with willows and acacias. Although we needed only six inches of water, the depth was sometimes miscalculated, and we went aground on a bank of pebbles. Then the Otter, whose bare feet were always ready for such emergencies, stepped out into the sparkling current, and hauled or pushed the boat over the obstacle. What with rapids and banks of pebbles, the excitement of boating on the Dordogne above Lalinde never flags. It looked very easy to throw a line with a worm on it towards the shore, and then draw it back, but the chub showed such little eagerness to be caught by me that I generally preferred to steer and watch my companion pulling them out as he stood in the prow, his face nearly hidden under the thatch of his straw hat. When the fish were in a biting humour, he had one on his hook every time he threw the line.

There are few trout in this part of the Dordogne, but in tributary streams, like the charming little Céou, they are plentiful. Carp are abundant, but they are very difficult to take with the line, and even with the net, except in time of flood, when they get washed out of their holes, and the water being no longer clear, their very sharp eyes are of little use to them. Then a lucky throw will sometimes bring out two or three carp weighing several pounds each. The fish commonly caught are mullet, perch, barbel, gudgeon, bream, and chub. As a food-supplying river, the Dordogne is one of the most valuable in France, and, owing to the rapid current and the purity of the water, the fish is of excellent quality.

The fixed belief of all the riverside people in this and other valleys is that fish should be cooked alive. You enter an inn and ask for a *friture* of gudgeon. In a few minutes you see the victims, which have been pulled out of a tank with a small net on the end of a stick, jumping on the kitchen table, and they are still jumping when they go into the boiling grease. I am not among those who have grown callous to such sights, common as they are in France. To see fish scraped, opened, and cooked while still alive gives me disgust for it when it afterwards appears on the table. I can imagine somebody saying: 'Why look at what goes on in the kitchen?' That somebody does not quite understand what rural France is. In a country inn we invariably pass through the kitchen to reach the room set apart for guests, and it has often fallen to my lot to seek rest, shelter, and food in a poor auberge, where the kitchen is also the common room of the family and outsiders.

A Beynac character that left on my memory a lasting impression was old Suzette. Suzette might have been any age between fifty and seventy. She had no beauty, but she must have had a little vanity left, for when I showed her a photograph I had taken of her, she put her hard old hands together, swayed her head from shoulder to shoulder, and actually wept. She could not speak much French, but she said as well as she could that she did not know that she had grown so ugly. I have noticed, however, that my photographs have a tendency to draw tears or angry expressions from most of those on whom I operate, which I can only account for by the reason that these people have not the pleasure of paying for their portraits. What is done for nothing is seldom appreciated. Suzette, not wishing to hurt my feelings, soon wiped out her eyes with her largest knuckle, and, having composed her countenance, thanked me for having photographed her. She had had a rough life, but as she had known little else but hardship and privation, she was contented with what Providence considered enough for her. This was now a two-roomed cottage to live in, and for food a bunch of grapes, a peach or a pear to eat with her bread in the fruit season, a few walnuts to go with it in autumn or winter, chestnuts to boil or roast, and a piece of fat bacon hanging to a beam, from which she cut only just enough at a time to disguise the water which, when thickened with bread, a handful of haricots, and some scraps of other vegetables, made her daily soup. She was a widow now, but although whenever she spoke of her dead husband her head began to wag and the tears to start from her eyes, she had less care and worry and pain as a lonely woman than when she was bearing children and working harder than any pack-mule to bring them up. Her husband was a fisherman of the Dordogne, and she sold his fish in the Sarlat market, some eight miles distant from where they lived by the river. In order to be early in the market, she had to start at about two in the morning, and the road, which was uphill all the way, ran between woods where the wolves, descending from the vaster forests of Black Périgord, often howled in winter. She told me it frequently happened when she reached the market that her arms and hands were so benumbed with the cold that she could not take the basket of fish from her head. As a widow, she had lived for a while with a married son, but the young woman soon turned the old one out. Poor Suzette told the story without bitterness; she recognised the law of nature in this expulsion of the mother when she was of no further use to her children, and accepted thankfully the ten francs a month which her son allowed her. She managed to live by fetching and carrying for anyone who would give her two or three sous for an hour's trudging. She used to take my letters to post at the nearest railway-station, and no one who merely noted how nimbly her bare feet moved along the hot, dusty road would have supposed that she had left her youth so far behind her. Battered and pinched and harassed as she had been by destiny, she still believed in the working out of eternal justice, and one day before sunrise she started off on a pilgrimage to a distant sanctuary, and did not return until after many hours. With all this she was gay, and could tell a lively story with plenty of Southern salt. She was a good bit of human nature, worth studying.

Sarlat, where old Suzette went to sell her husband's fish, was a very important stronghold of Black Périgord in the Middle Ages, and the chief place in that Sarladais which the English kings of Norman and Angévin descent found such a tough bone to pick. The way to it from Beynac leads up steep valleys and gorges, covered with dense forest. Here wolves are to be seen occasionally in winter, but the wolf country begins a little to the north of Sarlat, and stretches towards the Limousin. The town appears to be composed of one long street, and to be dismally uninteresting. There is, however, an old Sarlat that lies a little off the main artery, and which a lazy visitor who does not like the trouble of asking questions might easily miss. There are few scenes more original and picturesque in France than that presented by the ruinous old church, half open to the weather, and the ancient houses that form a framework round it. Under the lofty Gothic vaulting are wooden shops and shanties, and, looking up, you see the smoke from bakers' ovens hanging about the ribs of the great arches, which it has blackened.

Of the old houses, one of the most remarkable is that which was the residence of the philosophical writer, Etienne de la Boëtie, the friend of Montaigne. It is an interesting example of the French Renaissance, the exterior being richly ornamented with carvings.

A very rough, bad time had the men of Sarlat during the long years that they were fighting intermittently for their lives and property with the lawless bands of so-called English, who had turned so many rocks into fastnesses, and who issued from their fortified caverns, that they made almost impregnable, to prey upon the unfortunate people who strove to live by husbandry. These hardened ruffians and freebooters had no respect for treaties, and inasmuch as peace never lasted long, and the English kings of that epoch always liked to feel that they were ready for anything that might happen in France, the companies of brigand soldiers who preferred to serve under the leopards rather than under the golden lilies were left to do pretty much what they pleased in the wilder parts of Guyenne.

After the treaty that followed the battle of Poitiers they continued their depredations, heedless of the orders communicated to them by the English commissioners. They carried their raids up to the walls of Sarlat, even at the time of vintage, although this season was much respected in the Middle Ages by violent men, from a motive that was perhaps not disinterested. They seized the bullocks that were harnessed to the waggons, and bore them off to their strongholds. It is but fair to add, however, that the Sarladais did not formally submit to English authority until 1361—five years after the battle of Poitiers. Then Chandos went to Sarlat and received the submission of the burghers. Soon afterwards Edward III. confirmed all the privileges they had been enjoying under the kings of France. But

they did not remain quiet long. Persuaded by
Talleyrand and other nobles, they rebelled in 1369,
and the town became again French. Speaking of
this event, Tarde observes :

'And behold how and when the salamander*
was again placed under the three fleurs-de-lys,
having carried the leopards in chief only eight years
two months and a half.'

The people of Sarlat often boast that their town
never submitted to the English. In this matter,
however, they are in error.

September came, and I was still at Beynac,
although I had found another house. The fruit
season was then at its height. Peaches were sold
at three sous the dozen, a good melon cost about the
same sum, and figs were to be had almost for
nothing. On these terms quite a mountain of fruit
could be placed upon the table for half a franc.
There was often no necessity to run into this ex-
travagance, for the people at Beynac are good-
natured, and they would frequently send a basket of
their earliest grapes or other fruit. Although the
present might have been made by a woman with
bare feet, her feelings would have been hurt had
money been offered in return.

One day rather late in the month, having grown
ashamed of inactivity, I carried my knapsack down
to the river and put it into the Otter's smallest boat,

* This reptile was borne in the arms of Sarlat.

which he called the *périssoire*, although it was not really a canoe. He was the chief builder of it, and as a contrivance for bringing home to man the solemn truth that life hangs to a thread or floats upon a plank — perhaps the worst state of the two — it certainly did him infinite credit. It was a flat-bottomed outrigged deal boat, very long, and so narrow that to look over one's shoulder in it was a manœuvre of extreme delicacy, especially where the rapids caused the water to be in wild commotion. I was told that it would go down stream like an arrow, and so it did. There was no need to row hard, for the current took the fragile skiff along with it so fast that the trees on the banks sped by as if they were running races, and every few minutes brought a change of landscape. It was very delightful; only one sensation of movement could have been better—that of flying.

The water was as blue as the sky above, and over the valley, the wooded hills, and naked rocks lay the sunshine of early autumn, tender in its strength, mingling a balm with its burning. I seemed to be floating swiftly but gently down some lovely but treacherous river of enchanted land. And where is the river that lends itself better to this illusion than the Dordogne—ever charming, changing, and luring like a capricious, fascinating, and rather wicked woman? Now it flows without a sound by the forest, where the imagination places the fairy people and the sylvan deities; now it roars in the shadow of the castle-crowned and savage rock, over which the solitary hawk circles and repeats its melancholy cry; now it seems to sleep like a blue lake in the midst of a broad, fair valley, where in the sunny fields the flocks feed drowsily.

The depth of the water was as variable as the strength of the current. Sometimes I saw the stony bed seven or ten feet below, and then quite suddenly the boat would get into rushing water that sparkled with crystal clearness over a bank of pebbles, and I expected momentarily to hear a grating noise and to feel myself aground; but the little boat went over the shallows like a leaf. I passed a bank large enough to be called an island. The water had not covered it for months, and it was all thickly overgrown with persicaria, which the late summer had stained a carmine red, so that the island was all aflame. The swallows that dipped their wings in the water, the kingfishers that flew along the banks or perched on the willow stumps, and the graceful wagtails, were for some miles my only river companions — excepting, of course, the fish, with which a treacherous current or a sunken rock might have placed me at any moment on terms of still closer intimacy.

But time flew like the boat, and I soon came in sight of a charming little village whose houses with peaked roofs seemed to have been piled one upon another. Here upon stones in the water I recognised the human form supported by two bare legs, and in the posture as of a person about to take a dive, which is not perhaps very graceful, but is one that certainly lends character to the riverside scenery of France. Two or three women were rinsing their linen.

On nearing St. Cyprien the current became swifter and the turmoil of the rapids so great that I prepared my mind here to being swamped by the waves. The question whether I would abandon or try to rescue my knapsack after the wreck was distressing. The risk being over, it was with a sigh of relief that I beached the boat, now half full of water, at the nearest spot to the small town. Having moored it and given the sculls in charge of a man whose house was close by, I was soon walking in the warm glow of the September afternoon by cottage gardens where the last flowers of summer were blooming.

The small burg of less than three thousand inhabitants which bears the name of the African saint was probably, like many others, much more important in the Middle Ages than it is now. In accordance with the building spirit of the past, so strongly pronounced throughout Aquitaine, and obviously inspired by a defensive motive, the houses are closely packed together on a steep hillside. A few ancient dwellings, notably one with a long exterior gallery, show themselves very picturesquely here and there. The town grew up at the foot of an abbey, of which the church still existing exhibits a massive tower that might easily be mistaken at a little distance for an early feudal keep. The lower part of this tower is Romanesque. The interior of the church is in the very simple pointed style of the twelfth century, but the interest has suffered much from restoration. What is chiefly remarkable here is the carved oak of the reredoses and pulpit.

The English in 1422 took the town of St. Cyprien and besieged the abbey, which was a veritable citadel where the inhabitants in the last resort found shelter. A French force coming, however, to the relief of the people, the English, who were probably not very numerous, deemed it prudent to retire.

There being still an hour or more of daylight, I continued the ascent of the hill above the houses and the solemn old church to find a certain Château de Fâges, which I knew to be somewhere in the locality. A woman working her distaff and spindle with that meditative air which the rustic spinners so often have, her bare feet slowly and noiselessly moving over the rough stones, pointed out to me a little lane that wound up the deserted hill between briars bedecked with scarlet hips and bits of ancient wall to which ferns and moss and ivy clung, tinged by the waning golden light. I passed through vineyards from which the grapes had been gathered, then rose by broom and blackthorn to the level land.

I looked in vain for the castle. I might have searched for it until darkness came, but for the help of a boy who was taking home a goat. At length I found it lying in a hollow, a sufficient sign that it was never a stronghold. In feudal times it was probably a small castellated manor belonging perhaps to a knight who could not afford to build himself a *donjon* on some eminence and to fortify it with walls; but centuries later what remained of the original structure was patched up and considerably enlarged. Now, as I saw it in the dusk, it seemed a very ghost-haunted place. The building had not fallen into ruin; it was still roofed, and might easily have been made habitable; but there was no glass in the windows; all the rooms were silent with that silence so deep and sad of the long-deserted house which is not sufficiently wrecked by time and decay to have lost the pathos of human associations. The breath of the dying twilight stirred the ivy leaves upon the wall of the detached chapel where never a person had prayed for many a year, and the goblin bats came out from the shadowy places to flutter against the pale sky. Then I felt that I had lingered long enough on this desolate spot, and the thought of the awaking hearths brightening the little town with the blaze of wood made me hasten through the heather and gorse that had grown up on the grave of many a vine.

The next morning saw me afloat again. As I was getting away from the shore a man called out to me:

'Your boat is worth nothing! If you try to pass the third bridge you will go to the bottom!'

He spoke very seriously, and I wished to take further counsel of him; but having once got into the current, it carried me off at such a rate that while I was thinking of putting a question I was taken out of speaking distance. I shot through one of the arches of the first bridge, and soon found myself in water that was a little rough for my poor skiff. Here were the rapids again. I had been warned against these before I left the inn. There was no turning back now, and if the commotion of water had been ever so great I should have had to take my chance in it. The Otter's advice when I came to rapids was to pull as hard as I could in the middle of the current. I followed it, and my shallow boat, which had just been described as worthless, darted into the midst of the turmoil, and went through it all as swift as a swallow on the wing. The river, however, had risen considerably during the night, and the strength of the current having much increased in consequence, my belief in the *périssoire's* worthiness was not sufficient to make me run the risk of being swamped at the third bridge. I therefore landed at the next one, which was close to the village of Siorac. It seemed that I had only just started from St. Cyprien, and yet I had travelled about six miles. With the help of a willing man the boat was carried to the railway-station, which was not far off, and its journey home having been paid, I ceased for awhile to be a waterfarer, and became again a wayfarer.

Although there was not much to interest me at Siorac, I stayed there to lunch in a small inn, where an old woman grilled me a chop over the embers, and then set before me a pile of grapes, another of pears, and a third of fresh walnuts. The fruit was to me the best part of the meal, for the long hot summer had caused me to look upon meat very much as a necessary evil in the routine of life. While I was seated at the table, the old woman, who now dozed over her distaff in the chimney-corner, would start up every five minutes or so, as if from the beginning of a nightmare, and rush at the flies, which were ravenously busy upon the grapes and pears that I had set aside for them. She hated them with a hatred so fierce and bitter that I thought it rather unbecoming at her time of life.

'*On ne peut rien manger,*' she said, '*sans que ces diables y touchent.*'

This was quite true; but it was not the flies' fault that their parents were prolific, and that they had been hatched in a climate eminently conducive to their vigour and happiness. Their numbers and their voracity showed that they, too, were compelled by the struggle for life to be active and enterprising. Unlike some beings of a higher order, they did not take this trouble sadly; but, then, they were Southern flies.

Having driven them from the table, the aged woman nodded her head with vindictive satisfaction, and murmured, '*C'est égal; elles vont bientôt crever*'—unmindful of the fact that she, too, had reached the season of life when the frost comes suddenly and catches people unawares.

I returned to the river and crossed the bridge. On one side of it was a high statue of the Madonna and Child, with these words on the pedestal: '*Protectrice du pont, priez pour nous.*' The inscription further stated that the statue was raised in remembrance of the flood of 1866. That was in the time of the Empire; nowadays the Government despises all heavenly assistance in the department of roads and bridges, and religious statues are no longer erected in such places. Just before reaching a village called Coux, I was confronted by a very large army of geese, and while the foremost row advanced to the attack with outstretched necks and bills laid near the ground, the others cheered them on. For a minute or so matters looked very serious; then goose and gander courage failed completely, until the army worked round to my rear, when the screams of defiance arose again.

Poor wretches! their high spirits were not going to last long. They would soon have to undergo the cramming process, which a goose detests, for, unlike a pig, it will never of its own will eat more than it needs. In a few weeks the livers of most of them would be made into those excellent truffled *pâtés de foie gras*, which it is the pride and profit of Périgord to send far and wide.

A grand old elm, such as one does not often see in France, stood in front of the village church—a Transition building with a Romanesque portal. Beyond this place the land became marshy, and considerable tracts of it had been planted with Jerusalem artichokes, each of which had now its yellow head that tells its relationship to the sunflower. These artichokes are much grown by damp woodsides, and on other land of little value, in the valleys of Périgord. They are rarely used as food for man, for the French, notwithstanding the wide range of their gastronomy, including as it does squirrels and tomtits, and even snakes in certain localities, as well as various herbs and vegetables seldom or never eaten in England, have not been able to acquire a liking for the tubers of the artichoke. The plant is cultivated for feeding cattle, the whole of it doing good service in a region where there is but little grass. The multitude of golden flowers floating, as it were, on sombre green waves light up the autumnal landscape with a new flame when the skies turn gray.

A solitary man whom I found working a loom in a cottage by the side of the river kept a ferry-boat, and with his help I crossed again to the other bank. Wandering on with a somewhat vague purpose, I soon found myself—now under a gray sky—on a marshy flat, which a backwater of the Dordogne had almost made an island. Here there were many low shrubs of dwarf elder covered with berries; pools, and wide ditches, where the dark water scarcely moved, all fringed with tall reeds; while here and there was the gleam of a white flower upon the erect stem of a marsh-mallow. But what gave to this spot a strange and almost weird character was the number of great hoary willows, thirty or forty feet high, with gnarled and twisted boles, scattered over the dark green grass. It was a melancholy grove of fantastic dream-haunted willows, such as belongs to the South and the Virgilian muse:

'Umbrarum hic locus est, somni noctisque soporæ.'

And the sad solitude, in which there was not a sound of moving leaf or singing bird, seemed to be peopled by the ghosts of men who were waiting and weeping out their hundred years on the Stygian shore.

Hoary willows, dark alders, and then the road. This led me to Le Buisson—a place possessed of the blue devils, and which exists merely out of compliment to the railway-junction here. Having made arrangements for returning to the inn, I wandered out again to look at the river in the gray evening, and at the bridge where it was predicted that I should go to the bottom if I remained in the little boat. I crossed fields from which tobacco and maize had lately been carried, and reached the bridge of evil prophecy. The river certainly seemed to be doing its best to sweep away the piers, and when it escaped from the arches it raised its voice to a roar; but it seemed to me that on one side the *périssoire* would have gone through gaily without being swamped. The cry of troubled water in the dusk fascinated me. I lingered, and yet felt the strong impulse to hurry back to the society of men, out of the sound of the angry river, whose slaty waves flashed out strange gleams. What is it in the gloom and horror of nature that so draws us and yet warns us to flee? The day was ending stormily. The poplars wailed, and bent under the lash of the rising wind; dark masses of cloud stood still in the sky, whilst others, torn and scattered below them, rushed hither and thither madly. Every few minutes the faint gleam of lightning, still far off, brought to the black woods along the hills a momentary return of radiance, as though it were the fitful flashing of the day's dying lamp.

The roaring and wailing of the turbid flood now seemed to be repeating in cruel mockery the despairing cries of all the drowning people who were ever the prey of the water-fiends that draw downward in whirlpools to depths where twilight passes into darkness, and take the form of the long waving weeds that look so innocent, but whose grasp is deadly, or guide the current that utters never a sound as it seizes its victim and bears him into an unfathomed gulf under the pitiless rock. A voice within me cried 'Home!' but home had I none anywhere of the staple sort: mine was like a home on wheels.

As I returned to the inn across the fields, I saw some scattered peasant figures moving slowly the same way under the wild sky; men with the ox that was weary like themselves, women with bundles of forage on their heads—melancholy forms or phantoms in the dusky air, at one with nature in unconscious sympathy. Then across the dim and dreary plain, where the narrow path was lost to sight after the first few yards, a railway lamp flashed like the large red eye of some unimaginable monster of the primordial marsh.

In the morning I was on the road to Cadouin. The air was keen and a little frosty, for the hour was early. Men were mowing the last crop of grass, which was powdered with rime. After the meadows came the woods, for the road went south, and was therefore carried over the hills which rise above the valley of the Dordogne. The woods were mainly of chestnut, and, under the action of the storm, followed by the first frost, many a nut lay shining on the road within its gaping prickly shell. After two or three miles of ascent the road sloped downward, and it was not long before I entered a very neat and trim little town, which, however, was altogether village-like. This was Cadouin, and in the centre stood its venerable

Romanesque church. I entered the building, which was silent and very dim ; not a soul was there but myself. Presently there was a moan in the tower, which seemed so far away : the clock was striking one of the quarters. Now the dim light brightened suddenly, for the sun had risen high enough to dart its rays through a window, and to flash upon a column the brilliant colours of the glass. With the exception of the apse, which is purely Romanesque, the interior of this church is Gothic of the Transition ; but most of the capitals of the pier-columns have a plain Romanesque outline. There is no clerestory, the light being admitted from small round-headed windows in the aisle walls. Much of the building dates from the foundation of the abbey of Cadouin, in the early part of the twelfth century ; but the existing cloisters, which are what is most remarkable here, date from the fifteenth century, and owe much of their interest to the partial transformation of their style which they afterwards underwent when the spirit of the Renaissance set in. The Gothic tracery of the arches that face the quadrangle unites the strength of stone with the delicacy of pencil drawing. In the late Gothic and Renaissance part, the ceilings are richly and floridly groined, angelic and other figures forming the termination of the low-reaching bosses, the groins converging in fan-like order towards elaborately-carved canopies against the wall. At one end of this wing is a doorway, the jambs and lintels of which are heavily over-worked with carvings very typical of the exuberant fancy of the early French Renaissance.

For centuries Cadouin was a famous place of pilgrimage, in consequence of the claim laid by the abbey to the possession of the Holy Shroud. The

CLOISTERS OF THE ABBEY OF CADOUIN.

following is the history of the celebrated relic, according to Jean Tarde :

'In the year 1100 Hugh, surnamed the Great, brother of the King of France, and Bishop of Le Puy, in Auvergne, having gone on a voyage beyond the seas with Godefrey de Bouillon, found means, after the taking of Jerusalem, to recover this holy relic, and, dying in Palestine, he left it in charge of a priest, his chaplain. The priest falling ill on board ship, and perceiving that his end was drawing near, gave the shroud into the hands of a clerk, a native of Périgord. He, after the death of his master, took a small barrel, in the middle of which he placed a partition. In one half he put the sacred sheet, and his drink in the other. In this manner he carried the relic back to his native land, and placed it in a church near Cadouin, of which he had charge. Fearing that someone might steal his treasure, he left it in the barrel, which he put away in a chest near the altar, showing it only to a few of the monks of Cadouin. But one day, while he was absent, fire broke out and gained the whole village. All that was in the church was consumed, excepting the chest that contained the barrel. The monks of Cadouin, informed of the fire, hastened to the spot, and, having broken open the chest, took away the barrel, and carried it to their own church. The clerk, on his return, asked for what had been taken from him; but the monks said that, inasmuch as they had risked their lives in saving it from the flames, it belonged to them. The difference was arranged in this wise: the clerk was received as a religious, and the keeping of the relic was entrusted to him during his lifetime. He himself thought it safer there than in a rural church.'

In 1392, when the country was distracted by the dynastic wars between the crowns of France and England, the Holy Shroud was taken for safety to

Toulouse. Subsequently, the people of Périgord wished to have it replaced at Cadouin, and the Abbot and Chapter of St. Etienne at Toulouse resisting, much litigation ensued. In 1455 some monks of Cadouin took it away by stealth, and brought it back to their abbey. Tarde mentions, among other circumstances which tended to increase the importance of the abbey of Cadouin, '*les bienfaictz d'une reyne d'Angleterre.*'

Had it not been for other plans, I should have continued my journey southward from Cadouin as far as the Château de Biron, one of the most instructive relics of the past in Périgord, and have taken on my way Modières, one of the English *bastides* which Edward I. farmed for ten years; but I made my way back to the Dordogne, with the intention of ascending the valley of its tributary the Vézère. I did not, however, return to Buisson, but took the road to Ales, which lies a little lower down the stream.

While I was recrossing the hills the sun warmed the world again, and led back the trembling summer which had been scared by the early morning's frost. The half-benumbed butterflies opened and shut their wings many times upon the bramble leaves before they could bring themselves to believe that that pinch of winter was only a joke. It seemed a cruel jest while the bloom of honeysuckle was upon the hedges.

At Ales—a mere group of houses round a little

old church with a broad squat tower—I lunched in a very wretched inn. If a pig had not been killed at an early hour that morning I should have been obliged to be satisfied with vegetable and egg diet; and the knowledge that the pig had met with such

CHÂTEAU DE BIRON: THE LODGE.

bad luck only a few hours before did not dispose me in favour of the various dishes prepared from the external and internal parts of him. The *aubergiste* was an old boatman of the Dordogne, who had steered many a cargo of wine floating with him down-stream in time of partial flood; but that was before the phylloxera had played havoc with the vines. Now he had to get along as well as he could by combining husbandry, pig-rearing, and innkeeping.

On reaching the river again, I perceived that the annual descent of the Auvergnats had commenced. All the people who live by the higher waters of the Dordogne, whether they belong to the Puy de Dôme, the Cantal, or the Corrèze, are called Auvergnats in Périgord, or, rather, such of them as come down the stream with their small barges laden with wood, when the autumnal rains have commenced, and there is sufficient water in the river for their purpose. Sometimes, in their anxiety to turn their wood into money, they start a little too early, and being misled by an increase of the current which is not maintained, they go aground after a few days' navigation. I have seen one of these boats stuck fast on a bank almost in mid-stream, with the rapids nearly breaking over it with a roar that could be heard a mile away. The wood is cut in the forests, which stretch almost without a break for many a league on both sides of the Upper Dordogne, and is seasoned, dressed, and shaped for barrel-making before it is put afloat. The boats, which are some thirty or forty feet long, are necessarily flat-bottomed, and are so roughly built that there are usually gaping spaces between the planks, which are calked with moss. They are good enough for the voyage, which is their first and last. The men return, but never the boats. These are sold as firewood at Libourne, when they have discharged their cargoes. Where the water is deep and comparatively quiet the speed is increased by rowing with very long oars ; but where the current is strong the boat has only to be steered. This, however, is work that needs thorough knowledge of the river.

The autumn is a merry time for these Auvergnats. They look forward to it during the long months that they are working in the woods. The annual voyage to the Bordelais gives them an opportunity of again seeing the old friends whom they have been meeting for years at the waterside inns where they frequently put up at night, because the descent of the Dordogne in the dark is rather too exciting. They always say that they will start again in the morning at sunrise, but it often happens that the sun is very high indeed before they are afloat. After all, an Auvergnat is a man no less than another, and because he lives on next to nothing eleven months in the year is perhaps a reason why he should feel that he has earned the right to let his sentiments expand, and to light the lamp of conviviality in his breast during the remaining two or three weeks that he may be away from home.

There is this, however, to be said: whatever money he may possess, he trusts himself with very little when he goes off on his annual river-voyage, and when he has sold his wood he is anxious to get out of danger as quickly as possible.

I had to return some distance up-stream before I was able to cross to Limeuil. This is one of the most picturesque villages on the banks of the Dordogne. It is built on the side of an isolated rock, close to the point where the Vézère falls into the broader river. Before crossing the bridge I lingered awhile gazing at all those high-gabled roofs with red and lichen-stained tiles rising from the blue water towards the blue sky; vine trellises mingling their sunny green with the red of the roofs. Where no houses clung, the yellow rock was splashed with the now crimson sumach.

Then I climbed the long street over the rock and cobble stones between walls half green with pellitory, houses with high gables and rough wooden balconies where geraniums shone in the shadow, and from which the trailing plants hung low in that supreme luxuriance which is the beginning of their death. A few old women sat at their doors spinning, and geese, in small companies of three or four, waddled out of the way; but there was no sound of any kind— Limeuil was as silent as a cemetery. And yet there were cafés, which gave the place a false air of liveliness. Some tourists, attracted by the caverns in the valley of the Vézère, had possibly wandered as far as Limeuil; but where were the inhabitants now? Had there been an epidemic, and were the old women, whose heads were bent towards their knees while they clutched their distaffs, the few survivors?

Taking the road to Bugues, I passed a small church with an open belfry with a tiled roof supported by wooden pillars. It stood in a grove of tall cypresses and weeping willows, and the gravestones lay scattered round about. The waning sunshine seemed to fall more tenderly here than upon the open fields where the ruddy pumpkins flamed. It was nearly dark when I reached the little town of Bugues.

TRUFFLE-HUNTERS.

IN THE VALLEY OF THE VÉZÈRE.

THE spring has come again, and I am now at Les Eyzies, in the valley of the Vézère : a paradise of exceptional richness to the scientific bone and flint grubber on account of the very marked predilection shown for it by the men of the Stone Age, polished and unpolished. It is about five in the morning, and the woods along the cliffs are just beginning to catch the pale fire of the rising sun. Just outside my open window are about twenty chickens in the charge of two mother hens, and as they have not been long awake, they do their utmost to make a noise in the world like other creatures that are empty. As soon as the neighbour's door is open they enter in a body, and march towards the kitchen. A female voice is heard to address something sharply to them in patois; there is a scuffle in the passage, and all the chickens scream together as they rush before the broom into the road. This is how the village day opens.

I am waiting for a man who has undertaken to show me some caverns in the neighbouring rocks. Meanwhile, another comes along, and makes mysterious signs to me from the road. He is barefoot and ragged, and does not look as if he had a taste for regular work, but rather as if he belonged to the somewhat numerous class who live by expedients, and have representatives in all ranks of society. He has a small sack in his hand, to which he points while he addresses me in patois. I tell him to come in. The sack contains crayfish, and now I know the reason of his mysterious air, for all fishing is prohibited at this time, and he is running the gauntlet of the *garde-pêche*, who lives close by. The poor ragamuffin has been out all night, wading in the streams, and his wife, who looks, if possible, more eager and hungry than himself, is waiting near, keeping watch. He offers his crayfish for three sous the dozen, and I buy them of him without feeling that respect for the law and the spawning season which I know I ought to have. But I have suffered a good deal from bad example. There was a *Procureur de la République* not far from here the other day, and the first thing he asked for at the hotel was fish.

Presently the other man—the one I am waiting for—shows himself. He is a lean old soldier of the Empire, with a white moustache, kept short and stiff like a nailbrush. He is still active, and if he has any disease he is in happy ignorance of it; nevertheless, he confides to me that it is in the legs that he begins to feel his seventy-two years. His face has a very startling appearance. It is so scratched and torn that it makes me think of the man of the nursery-rhyme who jumped into the quickset-hedge; and, as it turns out, this one was just such another, only his movement was involuntary. He tells me how he came to be so disfigured. He was coming home with some cronies, at a late hour, from one of those Friendly Society meetings which in France, as in England, move the bottle as well as the soul, when, owing to an irregularity of the road, for which he was in no way to blame, he took an unintentional dive down a very steep bank, at the bottom of which was a dense forest of brambles. As he was quite unable to extricate himself, his companions, after a consultation, decided to haul him up by the legs; and it was to this manner of being rescued that he attributed most of the damage done to his ears.

We passed under the ruined castle of Les Eyzies, which was never very large, because the shelf of rock on which it was built would not have admitted of this; but when defended it must have been almost inaccessible. The ruin is very picturesque, with the overleaning rock above, and the clustered roofs below. The village is continued up the marshy valley of the Beüne, which here joins that of the Vézère. In the face of the overleaning

CHÂTEAU DES EYZIES.

rocks are orifices that strike the attention at once by their shape, which distinguishes them from natural caverns. They have been all fashioned like common doors or windows on the rectangular principle, which proves that they are the artificial openings of human dwellings. The men who made their homes in the side of the precipice, and who cut the rock to suit their needs, must have let themselves down from the top by means of a rope. To what age these Troglodytes belonged nobody knows, but it is not doubted that they came after the flint-working savages, whose implements are found in the natural caverns and shelters near the ground.

We continued up the valley of the Beüne. The banks under the rocks were starred with primroses, and from the rocks themselves there hung with cotoneaster the large and graceful white blossoms of that limestone-loving shrub, the amelanchier. In the centre of the valley stretched the marsh, flaming gold with flags and caltha, and dotted with white valerian. The green frogs leapt into the pools and runnels, burying themselves in the mud at the shock of a footstep; but the tadpoles sported recklessly in the sunny water, for as yet their legs as well as their troubles were to come. I confess that this long morass by the sparkling Beüne, frequented by the heron, the snipe, the water-hen, and other creatures that seek the solitude, interested me more than the caverns which I had set out to see. I nevertheless followed the old man into them, and tried to admire all that he showed me; but there was not a stalactite six inches long the end of which had not been knocked off with a stick or stone. The anger that one feels at such mutilation of the water's beautiful work destroys the pleasure that one would otherwise derive from these caves in the limestone.

A visit, however, to the now celebrated cavern known as the Grotte de Miremont repaid me for the trouble of reaching it. It lies a few miles to the north of Les Eyzies, in the midst of very wild and barren country. From any one of the heights the landscape on every side is seen to be composed of hills covered with dark forest and separated by narrow valleys. Here and there the white rock stands out from the enveloping woods of oak, ilex, and chestnut, or the arid slope shows its waste of stones, whose nakedness the dry lavender vainly tries to cover with a light mantle of blue-gray tufts. It is these sterile places which yield the best truffles of Périgord. Sometimes trained dogs are used to hunt for the cryptogams, but, as in the Quercy, the pig is much more frequently employed for the purpose. A comical and ungainly-looking beast this often is : bony and haggard, with a long limp tail and exaggerated ears. A collar round the neck adds to its grotesqueness.

One has to climb or descend a steep wooded hill to reach the cavern, for the entrance is on the side of it. The *métayer* acts as guide, and his services are indispensable, for there are few subterranean labyrinths so extensive and so puzzling as this.

Although the principal gallery is barely a mile in length, there are so many ramifications that one may walk for hours without making a complete exploration of the dædalian corridors, even with the help of the guide. With sufficient string to lay down and candles to light him, a stranger might enter these depths alone and come to no harm; but if he despised the string and trusted to his memory he would soon have reason to wish that he had remained on the surface of the earth, where, if he lost himself, there would be fellow-creatures to help him. Now with the sticky and tenacious clay trying to pull off his boots at every step, now walking like a monkey on hands and feet to keep his head from contact with the rock, he would grow weary after an hour or so, and begin to wish to go home, or, at any rate, to the hotel; but the more his desire to see daylight again took shape and clearness, the more bewildered he would become, and farther and farther he would probably wander from the small opening in the side of the hill. Thus he might at length hear the moan of water, and if it did not scare him, he would see by the glimmer of his solitary candle the gleam of a stream rushing madly along, then plunging deeper into the earth, to reappear nobody knows where. This cavern offers little of the beauty of stalactite and stalagmite; but the roof in many places has a very curious and fantastic appearance, derived from layers of flints embedded in the solid limestone, and exposed to view by the disintegration of the rock or the washing action of water. They can be best likened to the gnarled and brown roots of old trees, but they take all manner of fanciful forms.

The little house in which I am living stands almost on the spot where some particularly precious skeletons, attributed to prehistoric men and women, were dug up about twenty years ago, when the late Mr. Christy was here busily disturbing the soil that had been allowed to remain unmoved for ages. The overleaning rock, which is separated from my temporary home only by a few yards, probably afforded shelter to generations of those degraded human beings from whom the anthropologist who puts no bridle on his hobby-horse is pleased to claim descent. Near the base is one of those symmetrically scooped-out hollows which are such a striking peculiarity of the formation here, and which suggest to the irreverent that a cheese-taster of prehistoric dimensions must have been brought to bear upon the rocks when their consistency was about the same as that of fresh gruyère. According to one theory, they were washed out by the sea, that retired from the interior of Aquitaine long before the interesting savages who made arrow-heads and skin-scrapers out of flints, and needles out of bone, came to this valley and worked for M. Lartet and Mr. Christy. Others say that the sea had nothing to do with the fashioning of these hollows, but that they were made by the breaking and crumbling away of the more friable parts of the limestone under the action of air, frost, and water. While members of learned societies discuss such questions with upturned noses, a rock above them will sometimes be unable to keep its own countenance, but, simulating without flattery one of the human visages below, will wear an expression of humour fiendish enough to startle the least superstitious of men.

Upon the lower part of my rock is hanging the wild rose in flower, and above it is a patch of grass that is already brown, although we are in the first week of May; then upon a higher grass-grown steep is a solitary ilex, looking more worthy of a classic reputation than many others of its race. Its trunk appears to rise above the uppermost ridge of bare rock, and the outspread branches, with the sombre yet glittering foliage, are marked against the sky that is blue like the bluebell, as motionless as if they had been fixed there by heat, like a painted tree on porcelain.

On the other side of the house is a small balcony that looks upon the road, the peaceful valley, and the darkly-wooded cliffs just beyond the Vézère. During the brief twilight—the twilight of the South, that lays suddenly and almost without warning a rosy kiss upon the river and the reedy pool—I sometimes watch from the balcony the barefooted children of the neighbours playing upon the white road. Poor village children! As soon as a wanderer gets to know them, he leaves them never to see them again. Living in a great city is apt to dull the sensibility, and to close men up in themselves. In a village you become forcibly interested in surrounding humanity, and enter into the lives and feelings of others. A young woman died yesterday in child-birth, and was buried to-day. Everybody felt as if the awful shadow that descended upon the lonely house across the river had passed close to him and her, and left a chill in the heart. When the uncovered waggon bearing the deal coffin wrapped in a sheet, and having at the head an upright cross of flowers and leaves that shook and swayed with the jolting of this rustic hearse, moved towards the church, nearly the whole of the population followed. Only the day before another woman was carried along the same white road towards the little cemetery, but the coffin then was borne upon the shoulders of four persons of her own sex. Now and again fatigue brought the bearers to a standstill: then they would change shoulders by changing places. And the white coffin, moving up and down as a waif on the swell of the sea, passed on towards the glowing west, where presently the purple-tinted wings of evening covered it.

But the peasants are not sentimentalists—far from it. Always practical, they are very quick to perceive the futility of nursing grief, and especially the unreasonableness of wishing people back in the world who were no longer able to do their share of its work. A young man came into the village with a donkey and cart to fetch a coffin for his father who had just died.

'*Apé!* I dare say he was old,' was the reflection

of our servant—a Quercynoise. If it had been the old father who had come to fetch a coffin for the young man, she would have found something more sympathetic to say than that.

Sometimes at sunset I climb the rugged hill behind the house. Then the stony soil no longer dazzles by its white glitter, but takes a soft tint of orange, or rose, or lilac, according to the stain of the sky, and there is no light in the rocky South that so tenderly touches the soul as this. Here the spurge drinks of the wine of heaven with golden lips wide open; but the hellebore, which has already lost all its vernal greenness, and is parched by the drought, ripens its drooping seeds sullenly on the shadowy side of the jutting crag, and seems to hate the sun. Higher and yet far below the plateau is a little field where the lately cut grass has been thrown into mounds. Here the light seems to gain a deeper feeling, and the small vineyard by the side holds it too. It is one of the very few old vineyards which, after being stricken nearly unto death by the phylloxera, have revived, and by some unknown virtue have recovered the sap and spirit of life. The ancient stocks gnarled and knotted, and as thick as a man's arm, together with the fresh green leaves and the hanging bunches of buds that promise wine, wear a colour that cannot be rightly named—a transparent, subtle, vaporous tint of golden pink or purple, which is the gift of this warm and wonderful light. A cricket that has climbed up one of the tender shoots strikes a low note, which is like the drowsy chirrup of a roosting bird. It is the first touch of a fiddler in the night's orchestra, and will soon be taken up by thousands of other crickets, bell-tinkling toads, croaking frogs in the valley, and the solitary owl that hoots from the hills. Below, how the river seems to sleep under the dusky wings of gathering dreams where the white bridge spans it! Beyond, where the blue-green sky is cut by a broken line of hill and tree, the rocks become animated in the clear-obscure, and the apparently dead matter, rousing from its apathy, takes awful forms and expressions of life.

My small boat had been lying on the Vézère several days doing nothing, when I decided upon a little water-faring up the stream. This canoe had been knocked together with a few deal boards. It had, as a matter of course, a flat bottom, for a boat with a keel would be quite unsuitable for travelling long distances on rivers where, if you cannot float in four inches of water, you must hold yourself in constant readiness to get out and drag or push your craft over the stones. This exercise is very amusing at the age of twenty, but the fun grows feeble as time goes on. My boat was not made to be rowed, but to be paddled, either with the short single-bladed paddle which is used by the fishermen of the Dordogne, and which they call a 'shovel,' or by the one that is dipped on both sides of the canoe alternately. There being rapids about every half-mile on the Vézère, and the current in places being very strong, I realized that no paddler would be able to get up the stream without help, and so I induced my landlord to accompany me and to bring a pole. He was a good-tempered man, somewhat adventurous, with plenty of information, and a full-flavoured local accent which often gave to what he said a point of humour that was not intended. The voyage, therefore, commenced under circumstances that promised nothing but pleasantness. It was a perfectly beautiful May afternoon, with a fresh north breeze blowing that tempered the ardour of the sun.

The water changed like the moods of a child who has only to choose the form and manner of his pleasure. Now it pictured in its large eye, whose depth seemed to meet eternity, the lights and forms and colours of the sky, the rocks, and the trees; now it leapt from the shaded quietude, and, splitting into two or more currents, separated by willowy islets or banks of pebbles, rushed with an eager and joyous cry a hundred yards or so; then it stopped to take breath, and moved dreamily on again. Where the water was shallow was many a broad patch of blooming ranunculus; so that it seemed as if the fairies had been holding a great battle of white flowers upon the river. We glided by the side of meadows where all the waving grass was full of sunshine. On the bank stood purple torches of dame's violet, and the dog-rose climbing upon the guelder rose was pictured with it in the water. On the opposite bank stood the great rocks which have caused this part of the river to be called the Gorge of Hell. Here human beings in perpetual terror of their own kind cut themselves holes in the face of the precipice, and lived where now the jackdaw, the hawk, the owl, and the bat are the only inhabitants. In the Middle Ages the English companies turned the side of the rock into a stronghold which was the terror of the surrounding district.

This fastness was called La Roque de Tayac, because the village of Tayac faces it on the other side of the river. Although only a few fragments of the masonry that was formerly attached to the rock remain, the chambers cut in the solid limestone are strange testimony of the habits and contrivances of England's lawless partisans in these remote valleys. The lower excavations evidently served for stables, as the mangers roughly cut in the rock testify. The horses or mules were led up and down a steep narrow ledge. A perpendicular boring, shaped like a well, connects the lowest chamber with those above, and there can be no doubt that the nethermost part served the purpose of a well or cistern. By means of a hanging rope a man could easily pull himself up to the higher stages and let himself down in the same manner. In the event of a surprise the rope would, of course, be pulled up. Woe to those who exposed their heads in this cylindrical passage to the stones which the defenders above had in readiness to hurl down! But the river flowing deeply at the base of the rock, no part of the fortress could have been easy of access. Such was the stronghold which obtained so evil a reputation throughout a wide district as an almost impregnable den of bandits and cut-throats.

We read that the English, who had fortified themselves at the Roque de Tayac, having ravaged the country of Sarlat in 1408, the men of Sarlat laid an ambush for them, and, taking them by surprise, cut them in pieces. But the next year, their numbers being again largely increased, they resumed their forays with the result that the Sarladais marched to the valley of the Vézère and regularly besieged the Roque de Tayac. The struggle was marked with great ferocity on both sides. The fortress was eventually captured, but the defenders sold their lives dearly, and many of the Sarladais, instead of returning to their homes, remained under the pavement of the church across the water.

Having passed the first rapids easily, we talked, and the conversation turned upon—cockchafers! My companion had been much impressed by the strange doings of a party of gipsy children whom he had lately passed on the highroad. One of them had climbed up a tree, the foliage of which had attracted a multitude of cockchafers, and he was shaking down the insects for the others to collect.

But it was not this that made the teller of the story stop and gaze with astonishment; it was the use to which the cockchafers were put. As they were picked up they were crammed into the children's mouths and devoured, legs, wings, and all. At first he thought the small gipsies were feasting on cherries. He declared that the sight disgusted him, and spoilt his appetite for the rest of the day. In this I thought his stomach somewhat inconsistent, for I knew of a little weakness that he had for raw snails, which, to my mind, are scarcely less revolting as food than live cockchafers. He would take advantage of a rainy day or a shower to catch his favourite prey upon his fruit-trees and cabbages. Having relieved them of their shells, and given them a rinse in some water, he would swallow them as people eat oysters. He had a firm belief in their invaluable medicinal action upon the throat and lungs. His brother, he said, would have died at twenty-three instead of at fifty-three had it not been for snails. He told me, too, of a man who, from bravado, tried to swallow in his presence, and at a single gulp, one of the big pale-shelled snails—known in Paris, where they are eaten, after being cooked with butter and garlic, as *escargots de Bourgogne*—but it stuck in his throat, and a catastrophe would have happened but for the sturdy blow which his companion gave him on the 'chine.' That a snail-eater should criticise gipsies for eating cockchafers shows what creatures of prejudice we all are.

After passing the Nine Brothers—a name given to nine rocks of rounded outline standing by the water like towers of a fortress built by demi-gods—we had our worst fight with the rapids, and were nearly beaten. It was the last push of the pole from the man behind me, when he had no more breath in his body, that saved us from being whirled round and carried back. Before one gets used to it, the sensation of struggling up a river where it descends a rocky channel at a rather steep gradient is a little bewildering. The flash of the water dazzles, and its rapid movement makes one giddy. There is no excitement, however, so exhilarating as that which comes of a hard battle with one of the forces of nature, especially when nature does not get the best of it. This tug-of-war over, we were going along smoothly upon rather deep water, when I heard a splash behind me, and on looking round saw my companion in a position that did not afford him much opportunity for gesticulation. He was up to his middle in the water, but hitched on to the side of the boat with his heels and hands. He had given a vigorous push with his pole upon a stone that rolled, and he rolled too. Now, the boat being very light and narrow, an effort on his part to return to his former position would have filled it with water; so he remained still while I, bringing my weight to bear on the other side, managed to haul him up by the arms. After this experience, he was restless and apparently uncomfortable, and we had not gone much farther before he expressed a wish to land on the edge of a field. Here he took off the garments which he now felt were superfluous, vigorously wrung the water out of them, and spread them in the sun to dry. I left him there fighting with the flies, whose curiosity and enterprise were naturally excited by such rare good luck, and went to dream awhile in the shadow of the rock, on the very edge of which are the ramparts of the ruined castle of La Madeleine. This is the most picturesque bit of the valley of the Vézère ; but to feel all the romance of it, and all the poetry of a perfect union of rocks and ruin, trees and water, one must glide upon the river, that here is deep and calm, and is full of that mystery of infinitely-intermingled shadow and reflection which is the hope and the despair of the landscape-painter. Now, in this month of May, the shrubs that clung to the furrowed face of the white rock were freshly green, and the low plaint of the nightingale, and the jocund cry of the more distant cuckoo, broke the sameness of the great chorus of grasshoppers in the sunny meadows.

When I returned to my companion, I found that he was clothed again, but not in a contented frame of mind. He accompanied me as far as Tursac, and then started off home on foot. He had had enough of the river. There was still sufficient daylight for me to continue the voyage to Le Moustier, but, apart from the fact that I could not get up the rapids alone, I was quite willing to pass the night at Tursac.

Having chained the boat to a willow, I walked through the meadows towards a group of houses, in the midst of which stood a church, easily distinguished by its walls and tower. When I had arranged matters for the night, I passed through the doorway of this little church, under whose vault the same human story that begins with the christening, receives a new impetus from marriage, and is brought to an end by the funeral, had been repeated by so many sons after their fathers. The air was heavy with the fragrance of roses from the Lady Chapel, where a little lamp gleamed on the ground beside the altar. As the sun went down, the roses and leaves began to brighten with the shine of the lamp, like a garden corner in the early moonlight.

At the inn I met one of those commercial travellers who work about in the rural districts of France, driving from village to village with their samples, fiercely competing for the favours of the rustic shopkeeper, doing their utmost to get before one another, and be the first bee that sucks the flower, taking advantage of one another's errors and accidents, but always good friends and excellent table companions when they meet. I learnt that my new acquaintance was 'in the drapery.' We were comparing notes of our experience in the rough country of the Corrèze, when he, as he rolled up another cigarette, said:

'I had learnt to put up with a good deal in the Corrèze, but one day I had a surprise which was too much for me. I had dined at one of those auberges that you have been speaking of, and then asked for some coffee. It was an old man who made it, and he strained it through—guess what he strained it through!'

I guessed it was something not very appropriate, but was too discreet to give it a name.

'*Eh bien!* It was the heel of an old woollen stocking!'

'And did you drink the coffee?'

'No. I said that I had changed my mind.'

We did not take any coffee that evening. We had something less likely to set the fancy exploring the secrets of the kitchen, where, through the open doorway, we could see our old peasant hostess seated on her little bench in the ingle and nodding her head over the dying embers of her hearth. Her husband was induced by the traveller to bring up from the cherished corner of his cellar a bottle of the old wine of Tursac, made from the patriarchal vines before the pestilential insect drew the life out of them. The hillsides above the Vézère are growing green again with vineyards, and again the juice of the grape is beginning to flow abundantly; but years must pass before it will be worthy of being put into the same cellar with the few bottles of the old wine which have been treasured up here and there by the grower, but which he thinks it a sacrilege to drink on occasions less solemn than marriages or christenings in the family.

'You can often coax the old wine from them,' said my knowing companion, 'if you go the right way to work.'

'And what is the secret?'

'Flattery: there is nothing like it. Flatter the peasant and you will be almost sure to move him. Say, "Ah, what a time that was when you had the old wine in your cellars!" He will say, "*N'est-ce pas, monsieur?*" and brighten up at the thought of it. Then you will continue: "Yes, indeed, that was a wine worth drinking. There was nothing like it to be found within fifty kilomètres. What a bouquet! What a fine *goût du terroir!*" He will not be able to bear much more of this if he has any of the wine. Unless you are pretty sure that he has some, it is not worth while talking about it. Expect him to disappear, and to come back presently with a dirty-looking bottle, which he will handle as tenderly as if it were a new baby.'

Those whose travelling in France is carried out according to the directions given in guide-books—the writers of which nurse the reader's respectability with the fondest care—will of course conclude that the best hotels in the wine districts are those in which the best wine of the country is to be had. This is an error. The wine in the larger hotels is almost invariably the 'wine of commerce'; that is to say, a mixture of different sorts more or less 'doctored' with sulphate of lime, to overcome a natural aversion to travelling. The hotel-keeper, in order to keep on good terms with the representatives of the wine-merchants—all mixers—who stop at his house, distributes his custom among them. Those who set value on a pure *vin du pays* with a specific flavour belonging to the soil, should look for it in the little out-of-the-way auberge lying amongst the vineyards. There it is probable that some of the old stock is still left, and if the vigneron-innkeeper says it is the old wine, the traveller may confidently believe him. I have never known in such cases any attempt at deception.

The next morning I reached Le Moustier. Here the valley is broad, but the rocks, which are like the footstools of the hills, shut in the landscape all around. These naked perpendicular masses of limestone, yellow like ochre or as white as chalk, and reflecting the brilliance of the sun, must have afforded shelter to quite a dense population in the days when man made his weapons and implements from flints, and is supposed to have lived contemporaneously with the reindeer. Notwithstanding all the digging and searching that has gone on of late years on this spot, the soil in the neighbourhood of the once inhabited caverns and shelters is still full of the traces of prehistoric man.

Shortly before my coming, a *savant*—everybody is called a *savant* here who goes about with his nose towards the ground—gave a man two francs to be allowed to dig for a few hours in a corner of his garden. The man was willing enough to have his ground cleared of stones on these terms. The *savant* therefore went to work, and when he left in the evening he took with him half a sackful of flints and bones.

In a side valley close to Le Moustier is a line of high vertical or overleaning rocks. A ledge accessible from the ground runs along the face, and nearly in the centre, and at the back of it, are numerous hollows in the calcareous stone, some natural, others partly scooped out with the aid of metal implements, whose marks can still be seen. Each of these shelters was inhabited. Holes and recesses have been cut in the walls to serve for various domestic purposes, and on the ground are traces of fireplaces, reservoirs for water, etc. The original inhabitants of these hollows may have been savages no more advanced in the arts than those who worked flints, but it is certain that the latest occupiers were much more civilized. Rows of holes roughly cut in the limestone show where the ends of beams once rested, and the use of these timbers was evidently to support a roof that covered much of the ledge. It is quite certain that people lived here in the Middle Ages, and they might do so now but for the difficulty of bringing up water. The security which the position afforded could hardly have been lost sight of in the days when the inhabitants of Guyenne were in constant dread of being attacked. One must therefore be guarded against wild talk about prehistoric man in connection with these rock dwellings, which in many cases were used as fortresses during the three hundred years' struggle between the English and French in Aquitaine.

My waterfaring back to Les Eyzies was far easier than the voyage up-stream. Nevertheless, there was some excitement in it, for when the rapids were reached, the current snatched the boat, as it were, from me, but carried me with it, by little reefs each marked out as an islet as white as snow, by the floating flowers of the water ranunculus; but when its strength failed, it left me to drift where, in the dark shadow of rock and tree, the water rested from its race. Presently the rapids were seen again dancing in the sun, and the boat, gliding on to just where the smooth surface curved and the current took its leap without a ripple, darted forward like a startled water-bird. Once a back current whirled my fragile boat completely round. Then I remembered the good advice of the friendly Otter at Beynac with reference to going down these streams, where the water has to be watched with some attention if one does not wish to get capsized: '*Tenez-vous toujours dans le plus fort du courant.*'

Again in calm water, I recognised, beyond the still grass and the scattered flame of the poppies, the high walls of the fortress-like church of Tayac, with the light of the sinking sun upon them. Then a little lower down at the ford, which was my stopping-place, a pair of bullocks were crossing the river with a waggon-load of hay; so that the picturesque, the idyllic, and the sentiment of peace were all blended so perfectly as to make me feel that the pen was powerless, and that the painter's brush alone could save the scene from passing away for ever.

Tayac and Les Eyzies form one very straggling commune, and the church where the slain men of Sarlat lie serves for the entire population. This edifice of the eleventh and twelfth centuries deserves a brief description. There is much grandeur in its vast, deeply-recessed Romanesque portal, with marble columns in the jambs and numerous archivolts. Then its high, narrow windows, and the low, square towers, pierced with loopholes, give to it that air of the fortress which immediately impresses the beholder. Without doubt it was built like so many other churches of the same stormy and uncertain period, to be used as a place of refuge in case of danger. The entrance to the principal tower is artfully concealed at the back of a chapel at the east end, and can only be reached with a ladder. The very narrow passage makes two or more right angles before it leads to the foot of the spiral staircase—a disposition of great value in defence.

Having heard of a cavern in the garden of the presbytery which, in the memory of living people, was the refuge of a murderer whom the gendarmes were afraid to follow underground, because it was believed that he would knock them on the head one after the other while they were wriggling through the passage, and then quietly walk out by a back way unknown to anyone but himself, I felt a strong desire to explore this cave of evil repute. The idea was all the more enticing because I was assured that nobody had entered it but the murderer. I called upon the curé, and asked him how he felt at the prospect of a little trip underground in his own garden. He did not seem to feel very eager for the adventure; but when I proposed to go alone, he was too polite to let me depart with his best wishes. He decided to accompany me. When he had put on his oldest *soutane*, we started with a packet of candles and a ball of string.

Priests' gardens are often very interesting, and the one through which we now passed pleased me greatly. It was a long strip, in two or three terraces, upon the rocky hillside. Many fruit-trees, but chiefly almond, cherry, and peach, were scattered over it. There was also a straggling vine-trellis, from which there now spread in the June air that sweet fragrance of the freshly-opened flower-buds of which the poet-king Solomon sung. In the highest part was the cavern. We had to crawl in upon our hands and knees, and in some places to lie out almost flat. As my friend the curé insisted upon going first, I could not help thinking that the back view of him, as he wormed his way along the low gallery, was not exactly sacerdotal. Sometimes we passed over smooth sand—evidently left by a stream that once issued here; at other times over small stones, which were bad for the knees. We kept a keen look-out for the remains of prehistoric men and beasts, but only found the shells of eggs which a fox had probably stolen from the curé's fowl-house. There were also rabbits' bones, whose presence there was to be explained in the same way. My companion, however, having once entered his cave, was resolved upon returning another day and digging conscientiously in the sand, which appeared to be very deep in places. He may since have unearthed some prehistoric treasures there. The cavern was interesting as showing the honeycombing effects of water on limestone rock, but it did not lead very far into the hill. The belief that the murderer escaped by another opening than the one by which he entered was founded on fiction.

After the cave exploration, the curé was so good as to accompany me to a mysterious ruin in the neighbourhood, which he believed to be of English origin, because it was always spoken of by the people of the locality as William's Chapel. The English pronunciation of the name William had been preserved in the patois. After this, I did not doubt that his supposition was correct. Some Englishman was connected with the history of the building; but was it really a chapel? The hill that we had to climb to it was very high, and, although covered with herbage, almost precipitous. The building was not on the summit, but on a ledge of rock some distance down the cliff. The ruin consisted of only a few fragments of wall, built very strongly of well-shaped stones laid together without mortar. Holes cut in the rock showed where the ends of beams had rested. The position was rather one for a fortress than for a chapel; but no doubt Englishmen of an eccentrically religious turn appeared as early as the thirteenth or fourteenth century, if not earlier. If the people of the valley climbed up to William's Chapel to say their prayers, they must have been very pious indeed.

The strength of the current in the Vézère had turned me from my first plan, which was to ascend the river as far as Montignac, and take the road thence to Hautefort, the birthplace of Bertrand de Born, who was put into hell by Dante for having encouraged Henry Plantagenet's sons to rebel against their father. The sombre Florentine treated the troubadour baron with excessive harshness, for it is recorded of Bertrand that his repentance for the sins of his restless and agitated life was so sincere that he ended his days as a monk in the monastery of Citeaux.*

Bertrand de Born was an evil counsellor to Henry Court-Mantel, but a singularly attractive figure of the twelfth century was this troubadour noble, whose life in the world was divided between the soothing charm of the '*gai sçavoir*' and the excitement of war, and who was equally at his ease

---

* ' Mobile, agité, comme son aventureuse existence qui commença au donjon d'Hautefort et s'éteint dans le silence du cloître de Citeaux.—' *Discours sur les célébrités du Périgord*,' par L. Sauveroche.

whether he was holding the lance or the pen. He had the tenderest friendship for the young Prince, and mourned his death in the best elegy that appeared at the dawn of modern literature.

CHATEAU DE HAUTEFORT.

Of the ancient fortress of Bertrand de Born, Viscount of Hautefort, a few vestiges are left, which may be easily distinguished from the later masonry of the castle with which they are combined.

A HOUSE AT PÉRIGUEUX.

IN THE VALLEY OF THE ISLE.

It was in the full flame of noon on a hot June day that we arrived at the headquarters which I had chosen for my second summer in Périgord. It was a little château, of which I was to occupy a small wing, and also a low building that was quite detached—all very plain and rustic, as, indeed, most of the really old châteaux that are still inhabited are. At this burning hour the place seemed as quiet as the ideal retreat of a literary hermit could be. In the large old-fashioned garden, where magnolias and firs mingled with all kinds of fruit-trees, and lettuce-beds were fringed with balsams, golden apricots hung upon the branches that were breaking with their weight, and seemed to say: 'There is nobody here to eat us. We are quite tired of waiting to be gathered.'

Suddenly there was a great noise of barking, and three or four dogs that had smelt or heard strangers rushed through the archway that led to the court, which was so much like a farm-yard that no one would know the difference from the description.

'Mees! Mees! Black! Black!' cried a voice from within.

There was nothing in the sound of these words to cause astonishment, for most French dogs that move in good society have English names. If you were to call out at any respectable gathering of these animals, whether in the North or the South, 'Fox,' 'Stop,' 'Black,' 'Mees' (not Miss), the chances are that they would all try to reply at once.

After the dogs came bare-footed domestics of both sexes, who stared at us wonderingly, while saluting politely, and evidently not wishing to show their curiosity. Then, when we entered the court, we were met by a great many fowls, ducks, and turkeys of various ages. Not a few had apparently just jumped out of their shells. Lastly came the master and mistress of the house, advancing in the slow and stately style of the times when the drawbridge would have had to be lowered, but moving in the midst of the poultry. They were gracious and hospitable, and very soon we settled down, altogether well pleased with our new quarters.

Here we were surrounded by trees just as Robinson Crusoe was by his grove when it had grown tall and thick. Now, the traveller in Southern France who lingers as I am wont to linger in my wanderings, will probably have cause to pine, as I have pined, for trees about his house to shelter him from the fury of the summer sun. There are few houses that are not hovels or ruins to be found, except where the land is fertile, and wherever it repays labour the owner loathes a tree that produces nothing but its wood. Thus we get those wide, burning plains, where so few trees are to be seen save poplars along the watercourses and walnuts bordering the roads. Even these become rare, as in journeying farther south the last low buttresses of the rocky highlands are left behind.

Here, close to this retreat that I had chosen on the banks of the Isle, some twenty miles below Périgueux, rose, on the opposite side of the river, high cliffs of white limestone with wooded brows. The château was on a small island formed by a curve of the river under the cliffs, and a short canal drawn across the loop to facilitate the navigation of the Isle.

A very lazy kind of navigation it was. Two or three barges would pass in a day on their way to Périgueux or Bordeaux. They were of considerable size, and were capable of some sea-faring, but their masts were now laid flat, and they were towed along at the rate of two or three yards a minute by a lean and melancholy horse that had ceased to care for cursing, and was almost indifferent to beating. As the navigation had been nearly killed by the railway, the canal was allowed to fill itself with water-plants, which were interesting to me, but exceedingly hurtful to the temper of the bargees. They vented their fury upon the engineer, who was absent, and the horse that was present—unfortunately for the poor brute, for somehow he seemed to be looked upon as a representative of the negligent functionary.

'You appear to be having a bad time,' said I one day to a great dark bargee who was streaming from every pore, as much from bad temper as from the exertion of cracking his whip, and whose haggard horse looked as if he would soon break off in the middle from the strain of trying to move the barge, which was stuck in the weeds.

'A bad time of it! I believe you. *Sacr-r-r-re!* If I could only send that pig of an engineer to Nouméa I should be a happy man!'

If wishes could have wafted him, he would have gone farther than New Caledonia long before.

One day, far on in the summer, this engineer actually appeared upon the canal in his steam yacht, and there was great excitement in the country. The peasants left their work in the fields and ran to the banks to gaze at him. He did not go very far before he got stuck in the weeds himself. Then he reversed his engine, made back as fast as he could, and was seen no more.

But I am going on too fast. I have not yet described the château. The picture of it is clearly engraved upon the memory, and a very pretty picture I still think it; more so now, perhaps, than when the reality was before me, for such is the way of the mind. I can see the extinguisher roofs of the small towers through openings in the foliage rising from a sunny space enclosed by trees. I can see the garden, with its old dove-cot like a low round tower, its scattered aviaries, its rambling vines that climb the laden fruit-trees, its firs, magnolias, great laurels, its glowing tomatoes and melons, its lettuces and capsicums and scattered flowers, all mingled with that carelessness which is art unconscious of its own grace; its dædalian paths, its statues so quaintly placed in unsuspected corners, its—well, the picture is finished, for now begins the effort to recall its details. The eye's memory is a judicious painter that never overcrowds the canvas. I can see on that side of the building, which looks upon a much wilder garden, where peach and plum trees stride over grassy ground adjoining the filbert-grove that dwindles away into the wooded warren, a broad line of tall nettles in the shade against the wall. Hard by, on the line—so it was said—of the filled-up moat, is a row of ancient quinces, with long crooked arms, green, gray, or black with moss and lichen, stretching down to the tall grass, where in the dewy hours of early darkness the glow-worms gleam.

This little château was never a stronghold to inspire an enemy with much respect; it was rather a castellated manor-house, dating from the times when even the residences of the small nobility were fortified. Marred as it had been by alterations made in the present century without any respect for the past, it was still very interesting. In one of the towers, said to be of the fourteenth, and certainly not later than the fifteenth, century, was a chapel on the ground-floor with Gothic vaulting, and which still served its original purpose. A contemporaneous tower flanking the entrance contained the old spiral staircase leading to the upper rooms. I often lingered upon it in astonishment at the mathematical science shown in its design, and the mechanical perfection of its workmanship. What seemed to be a slender column round which the spiral vaulting turned was not really one, for each of the stone steps was so cut as to include a section of the column as a part of its own block. The contrivances by which this staircase *en colimaçon* was made to hold together, and to hold so well as to have lasted several hundred years, with a promise to continue in the same way another century or two, were deftly hidden from the eye of those unversed in such technicalities. In the hollow at the foot of the stairs was what I took to be a very old and rough christening font, such as I had seen in village churches. But it was not that; it was called a *pierre à l'huile*. Its purpose a long time ago was to receive the oil taken from the first pressing of walnuts after the annual gathering. Then the priests came and fetched what they wanted of it to serve for the rites of the Church during the year.

All this summer we lived out of doors, except at night. Even Rosalie, our servant, did most of her cooking in the open air with the aid of a portable charcoal stove, which she placed in the shade of some noble plane-trees that were planted by accident on the day of Prince Louis Napoléon's *coup d'état*. They were already tall and strong when his Will-o'-the-wisp, which he had mistaken for a star, sank in the bloody swamp of Sedan. When the rising wind announced a storm, the swaying branches shed their dry bark, which was piled upon the hearth indoors, where a cheerful blaze shot up if by chance the rain fell and the air grew chilly. But very seldom did even a shower come to moisten the parched land and cool the heated air. Thus the plane-trees came to look upon the stove beneath them as a fixture.

These open-air kitchens are by no means uncommon in Southern France during the hot months. I have a pleasant recollection of dining one scented evening in May with my friend the Otter at Beynac in his garden terraced upon rocks above the Dordogne. The table was under a spreading chestnut-tree in full bloom. Not many yards away the swarthy Clodine had her kitchen beneath an acacia. Strange as it may seem, the hissing of her frying-pan as she dropped into it the shining fish did not mingle unpoetically with the murmur of lagging bees overhead and the soothing plaint of the river running over its shallows below. Nor, when the purple flush faded on the water's face, and little points of fire began to show between branches laden with the snow of flowers, did the fragrant steam that arose from Clodine's coffee-pot make a bad marriage with the amorous breath of all the seen and unseen blossoms. What is there better in life than hours such as those?

But now I am by the Isle. The plane-trees are on the edge of a little dell, in the centre of which is a smooth space encircled by many trees, forming a dense grove. A rough table has been set up here with the aid of planks and tressels. It is our dining-table, and the centre of the grove is our *salle à manger*. Wrens and blackcaps hop about the branches of the filbert-bushes, and when the *métayer's* lean cat comes sneaking along, followed by a hungry kitten that is only too willing to take lessons in craft and slaughter, the little birds follow them about from branch to branch, scolding the marauders at a safe distance, and giving the alarm to all the other feathered people in the grove. Here the nightingales warble day and night until they get their young, when, finding that hunting for worms and grubs to put into other beaks than their own is very prosaic business, they only sing when they have time to fly to some topmost twig and forget that they are married.

When the sun is near setting, a sound very different from the warble of a bird is heard close by. It is some leader of a frog orchestra in the sedges of the canal giving the first note. It is like a quirk of gluttony just rousing from the torpor of satisfaction. The note is almost immediately taken up by other frogs, and the croaking travels along the canal-banks as fire would if there were a gale to help it. But the music only lasts a few minutes, for the hour is yet too early for the great performance. The frogs are only beginning to feel a little lively. It is when the sun has gone quite down, and the stars begin to twinkle upon the water, that the ball really opens. Then the gay tumult seems to extinguish every other sound, and to fill the firmament. Oh! they must have a high time of it, these little green-backed frogs that make so much noise throughout the warm nights of June. Sometimes I creep into my canoe and paddle by the light of moon or stars as noiselessly as I can along the fringe of sedges and flags and bullrushes, hoping to watch them at their gambols. But the frog is a very sly reptile, and you must stay up very late indeed in order to be a match for him in craft, unless you dazzle his eyes with the light of a torch or lantern. Then he is a fool in the presence of that which is out of the order of his surroundings, and his amazement or curiosity paralyzes his muscles. It is in this way that those who want the jolly frog just to eat his hind-legs *à la poulette* or otherwise catch him with the hand, unless they have the patience and the cruelty to fish for him with a hook baited with a bit of red flannel.

Now I will speak of my own hermitage, my ideal nook for writing, reading, and doing nothing, which, after much wandering and vain searching, I found at length here. Yes, I found it at last; and I much fear that I shall never find another like it. It lay at the back of the château, beyond the shaded nettles and the ancient quinces. My ordinary way to it was through a piece of waste, which, with unintentional sarcasm, was called the 'Little Park.' It was overgrown by burdocks, to which it had been abandoned for years—who could tell how many?—and was rambled over by turkeys, guinea-hens, and other poultry. Then I passed through a little gate, crossed another bit of waste that was neither lawn nor field, skirted a patch of buckwheat, and entered a small wood or shrubbery, where plum and filbert trees grew with oaks and beeches, until I came to water. This was the *vivier* of the château—a fish-pond, long drawn out like a canal, and fed by a spring, but which had been left to itself until it was nearly shaded over by alders and other trees. At the end farthest from all habitations was a little structure built of stones, open on one side, and with small orifices in the three remaining walls. These could be closed, and yet they were not windows. Their purpose was much more like that of loopholes in a mediæval barbican. They were to enable the man inside to watch the movements of migratory birds, and to send his shot into the thick of them when, unsuspecting danger, they chanced to come within range. The little building was an *affût*. Near to it was a sort of fixed cage, intended for decoy birds, but it had long been without tenants when I took possession of this refuge from all the human noises of the world. The other sounds did not worry me, although they often drew me from my work. The splash of a fish would take me to the water's edge, where I would watch the small pikes lying like straight roots that jut from the banks under water. The cooing of the little brown turtles in the trees overhead, the movements of a pair of kingfishers that would often settle close by upon an old stump, the magpies and jays, and especially the oriels, would make my thoughts wander amongst the leaves while the ink was drying in the pen. The oriels tantalized me, because I could always hear them in the crests of the trees, until, about the middle of August, they went away on their long journey to the South, but could very rarely catch sight of their gold and black plumage. Although they will draw near to gardens to steal fruit when they have eaten the wild cherries, they are among the most suspicious and wary of birds.

The oriel is a strange singer. It generally begins by screeching harshly; then follow three or four flute-like notes, which seem to indicate that the bird could be a musician if it would only persevere. But it will not take the trouble. It goes on repeating its 'Lor-ē-oh!' just as its tree-top companions, the cicadas, keep up their monotonous creaking.

From my cabin I could see all the lights, colours, and shadows of the day change and pass, but the sweetest music of the summer hours was heard when the soft sunshine of evening fell in patches on the darkening water, and on the green grass on each side of the brown path strewn with last year's trodden leaves.

Sometimes a hedgehog would creep across the narrow path, shaded with nut-bushes, oaks, and alders towards the water, and at night—I was often there at night—the glow-worms gleamed all about upon the ground, and there were mysterious whisperings whose cause I could not trace. Yes, it was an ideal literary hermitage, but as perfection is not to be found anywhere on land or water, even this spot had its drawback. There were too many mosquitoes. My friend the owner of the château often said to me, '*La moustique de l'Isle n'est pas méchante;*' but on this point I could not agree with him. I bore upon me visible signs of its wickedness; but in course of time I and the '*mostique de l'Isle*' lived quite harmoniously together in the little shanty under the trees.

Where the weedy and shady avenue leading to the château made an angle with the highroad, there was often a caravan or tilt-cart stationed for days together. Sometimes it was the travelling house of a tinker and his family; in which case the man was generally to be seen working outside upon his pots and pans in the shade of a tree. Sometimes it belonged to a party of basket and rustic-chair makers, who gathered the reeds and hazel-sticks that they needed as they passed through the country. Some were gipsies, and some were not; but all were baked by the sun almost to the colour of Moors. Having a taste for nomadic life myself, I used to stay and talk to these people from time to time; but none of them interested me so much as the wandering cobbler and his dog, whose acquaintance I had made higher up the country amongst the rocks.

I can still see them both in the shade of the old gateway; the man seated in the entrance of the little tower, where, at the top of the spiral staircase, is the village prison: the dog lying with his nose upon his paws just within the line drawn by the gateway's shadow across the dazzling road. They both came one evening and took up their position here with as much assurance as if it had been theirs by right of inheritance. They soon set to work, the man mending boots and shoes, and the dog making himself disagreeable to all the male members of the canine population for a couple of miles or so around. Until the cobbler's companion settled down comfortably, he had several exhilarating fights with local dogs that looked upon him as an intruder and an impostor. He really was both. He had no great courage, but he had grown impudent and daring from the day that he had first worn a collar armed with spikes. When his enemies had taken a few bites at this, they came to the conclusion that there was something very wrong in his anatomy. After the first encounter they were not only willing to leave him alone, but were exceedingly anxious to 'cut' him when they met him unexpectedly. They approached the gateway as little as possible; but when they were obliged to pass it, they drew their tails under them, showed the whites of their eyes, and having crept very stealthily to within ten yards or so of the archway where the interloper appeared to be dozing, they made a valiant rush towards the opening. Notwithstanding these precautions, the cobbler's dog, which had been watching them all the while out of the corner of one eye, was often too quick for them.

Man and dog were ludicrously alike both in appearance and character. The beast was one of the ugliest of mongrels, and the man might well have been the final expression of the admixture of all races, whose types had been taken by destiny from the lowest grades of society. They were both grizzly, thick-set, and surly. They both seemed to have reached the decline of life with the same unconquerable loathing of water, except as a means of quenching thirst. The dog, although some remote bull-dog ancestor had bequeathed him short hair, had bristles all over his face just like his master. They were a couple of cynics, but they believed in one another, and loved one another with an affection that was quite edifying. The dog wished for nothing better than to lie hour after hour near his master, hoping always, however, for an occasional fight to keep him in health and spirits. The cobbler did nothing to make himself liked by the inhabitants, but he could afford to work more cheaply than others who were 'established,' and who had a wife and children to keep; consequently the pile of old boots and shoes that looked quite unmendable rose in front of him, and for three or four weeks he remained in the same place stitching and tapping. Having locked up his things at night in the tower—he had obtained permission to make this use of it—he disappeared with his dog, and what became of them until next day was a mystery.

I admired the blunt independence and practical philosophy of this homeless man. Although he was disagreeable to others, he was on good terms with himself, and seemed quite satisfied with his lot. If, when he had named his price for mending a pair of shoes, anybody tried to beat him down, he would say, 'Take them and mend them yourself!' His incivility obtained for him a reputation for honesty, and his prices were soon accepted without a murmur. He talked to nobody unless he was obliged to do

so, and by his moroseness he came to be respected.
I managed to draw him into conversation once by
feigning to be much impressed by the comeliness
and amiable nature of his dog, and he then told me
that he had been wandering ever since he was a boy
in Languedoc and Guyenne, stopping in a village as
long as there was work to do and then moving on
to another. Wherever people wore boots or shoes—
if it were only on Sundays—there was always something to be done by working cheaply.

The silent cobbler might have kept his open-air
shop longer than he did in the shadow of the
mediæval gateway, if his dog had not quarrelled
with the sole representative of police authority for
having put on his gala uniform, which included a
cocked-hat and a sword. For this want of respect
the animal was imprisoned in the room of the tower,
to the great joy of all the other dogs, but to the
intense grief of his master, who found it impossible
to turn a deaf ear to the plaintive moans that
reached him from above. And thus it came to pass
that they went away together rather suddenly in
search of a gateway somewhere else, the dog
earnestly praying, after his fashion, that it might
not be one with a tower.

One June morning, soon after sunrise, twenty-seven mowers came to the château to cut the grass
in the great meadow lying between the river under
the cliffs and my moat—I called it mine because
it was almost made over to me for the time being,

together with the bit of wood and the cabin. Each mower brought with him his scythe, an implement of husbandry which in France is in no danger of being classed with agricultural curiosities of the past. Here the reaping and the mowing machine make very little progress in the competition between manual and mechanical labour. In the southern provinces, few owners of the soil have ever seen such contrivances. People who cling to the poetic associations of the scythe and the sickle—and who does not that has been awakened by their music in his childhood?—must not cry out against the laws which have caused the land of France to be divided up into such a multitude of small properties, for it is just this that preserves the old simplicity of agriculture as effectually as if some idyllic poet with a fierce hatred of all machines were the autocratic ruler of the country. Whether the nation gains or loses by such a state of things is a question for political economists to wrangle over; but that the artist, the seeker of the picturesque, the romantic roamer, and the sentimental lover of old custom gain by it can hardly be denied.

Some of the mowers were men of sixty, others were youths of seventeen or eighteen: all were contented at the prospect of earning nothing, but of being treated with high good cheer. Now, victuals and drink are a great deal in this life, but not everything, and these men would not have come on such terms had they not been moved by a neighbourly spirit. They were themselves all landowners, or sons of landowners. Had wages been given, two francs for the day would have been considered high pay, and the food would have been very rough. No turkeys would have had their throats cut; no coffee and rum would have been served round. In short, this haymaking day was treated as an annual festival.

A goodly sight was the long line of mowers as their scythes swept round and the flowery swathes fell on the broad mead in the tender sunshine, while the edges of the belt of trees were still softened by the morning mist. After the mowers, all the workers employed on the home-farm, men, women, and boys, entered the field to turn the swathes, which in a few hours were dried by the burning sun. On the morrow a couple of oxen drew a creaking waggon into the field, and when the angelus sounded from the church-tower in the evening the haymaking was over. But I have not yet described the mowers' feast.

At about ten o'clock the big bell that hangs outside the château is rung, and the mowers, dropping their scythes, leave the field and troop into the great kitchen, which has changed so little for centuries. The pots and pans hanging against the walls, and the pieces of bacon from the beams, have been renewed, but not much else. There is the same floor paved with stones, now much cracked and worn into hollows, the same hearth and broad chimney with hanging chain; and the long table and benches stretching from end to end, although their age is uncertain, were certainly fashioned upon the exact model of others that preceded them. Richard Cœur-de-Lion, when campaigning in Guyenne, may have sat down many a time to such a table as this, and to just such a meal as the one that is about to be served to the mowers, with the exception of the coffee and rum.

Let us take a look into the great caldrons, which appear to have come out of Gargantua's kitchen. One contains two full-sized turkeys and several fowls, another a leg of pork, and a third a considerable portion of a calf. Then there is a caldron of soup, made very 'thick and slab.' Home-baked loaves, round like trenchers, and weighing 10 lb. each, are on the side table, together with an immense bowl of salad and a regiment of bottles filled with wine newly drawn from the cask.

In the evening, when all the grass has been cut, there is another and a greater feast. The work being done, the men linger long at the table. Then all the household is assembled in the great kitchen, including the *châtelain* and *châtelaine*, and the young men who are known to have voices are called upon to sing. They do not need much pressing, for what with the heat of the sun during the day, then the wine, the coffee and rum, their blood is rushing rather hotly through the veins. One after another they stand up on the benches and give out their voices from their sturdy chests, which are burnt to the colour of terra-cotta. They make so much noise that the old warming-pan trembles against the wall. Although they all speak patois among themselves, they are reluctant to sing the songs of Périgord in the presence of strangers. The young men are proud of their French, bad as it is, and a song in the café-concert style of music and poetry fires their ambition to excel on a festive occasion like this, whilst their patois ditties seem then only fit to be sung at home or in the fields. At length, however, they allow themselves to be persuaded, and they sing in chorus a 'Reapers' Song,' composed long ago by some unknown Périgourdin poet, who was perhaps a jongleur or a troubadour. The notes are so arranged as to imitate the rhythmic movements of the reaper; first the drawing back of the right arm, then the stroke of the sickle, and lastly, the laying down of the cut corn. There is something of sadness as well as of joy in the repeated cadences of the simple song, and it moves the heart, for now the old men join in, and the sound gathers such strength that the little martins under the eaves must be pressing troubled breasts against their young.

This château had remained in the same family for centuries, and the actual owner, although by no means indifferent to the noble exploits of his ancestors, had long ago settled down to the life of an agricultural gentleman, and devoted what energy may have come down to him from the Crusaders to the cultivation of tobacco, the improvement of stock, the rearing of pigeons and poultry, the planting of trees, and a great deal more belonging to the same order of interest. He was a strongly marked type of the *gentilhomme campagnard*, in whom blue blood combines perfectly with rustic tastes and simplicity of manners. Like most men who live greatly to themselves, he had his hobbies, and they were all of a very respectable kind. One was to surround himself with trees; another was to have all kinds of captive birds about him. I was never able to know exactly how many aviaries he possessed, for I was always finding a fresh one curiously hidden in some neglected corner. He liked to mix up all sorts of birds together, such as pigeons, doves—tame and wild—blackbirds, linnets, canaries, chaffinches, sparrows, tomtits—no, the tomtits had been turned out. I asked why.

'Because,' said M. de V., 'there is no bird so wicked for its size as the titmouse. It pecks other birds with which it is shut up so often in the same part of the head that at length it makes a hole and picks out the brains.'

He used to catch his birds by means of a long net, and his favourite place for spreading it was along the side of the patch of buckwheat which was sown to feed the captives. He was a true lover of birds, and by observing them had stored up in his mind a fund of curious knowledge respecting their characters and habits. He only worked a portion of his land with the aid of the servants of the château; the rest was farmed on the system of *métayage*, for which he had a very strong liking. He said it was far preferable from the landlord's point of view to leasing, because the owner of the soil remained absolute master of his property. He could take care that nothing was done which did not please him, for the *métayer* or *colon* was on no firmer footing than that of an upper servant. If the landlord was not satisfied with the manner in which his land was treated, or if he suspected his *métayer* of trying to take an unfair advantage of him in the division of proceeds, all he had to do was to change him for another. But it was the interest of both to work well together, and it was the duty of the landlord to assist the *métayer* as much as possible, especially when times were hard.

On this estate the *colons* were housed free, but they paid one-third of the taxes. At the time of sowing, the seed was found by the landlord, but the *colon* returned half of the amount when the crop was gathered.

Métayage, or the system of sharing results between the landowner and the labouring peasant, still flourishes in France, notwithstanding the severe denunciations passed upon it by various writers. If it were a very bad system, it would have fallen into disuse long before now, for although the French have a tendency to keep their wheels in old ruts, they are as keen as any other people in protecting their own interests. It is a system that would soon become impossible without trustfulness and honesty. On both sides there must be fair dealing. The *colon* must feel that the landlord will help him in time of trial and need, and the landlord must feel that the *colon* is not trying to cheat him. In the great majority of cases, the man who does the ploughing, the sowing and the harvesting quite realizes that honesty with him is the best policy, and the owner of the soil knows that it is to his interest to support his *métayer*, and encourage him with judicious aid when the times are bad. The *métayer*, who has hope of making a little money over and above what is barely sufficient to support himself and his family, and knows that results will depend largely upon his own sagacity and industry, works with a steady zeal that it would be unreasonable to expect of the hired labourer, who, having his measured wage always in his mind's eye, has no incentive to do more than what is rigorously expected of him.

It may happen that the *métayer*, with all his labour—carried sometimes to an extreme that degrades the man physically and mentally—and all his frugality, which so often entails constitutional enfeeblement and degeneration, because the nutrition is not sufficient to correct the exhaustion of toil, obtains really less value for his work than an English farm labourer, and is not so well housed;

but, on the other hand, he enjoys a large amount of liberty and independence, and has the hope, if he is young, of being able to save money, buy some land, and become his own master. A *métairie* is seldom so large as to be beyond the working capabilities of a man and his family. In Guyenne an estate of a few hundred acres, if the land is productive, is often divided up into several *métairies*.

Farm labourers are not an overfed or overpaid class in Périgord. Food that is almost bread and vegetables, and a wage of one franc a day, are the ordinary conditions on which men work from sunrise to darkness. Lodging is not always included. I have known men in the full vigour of life earning only the equivalent of ninepence halfpenny a day, paying rent out of it, and presumably supporting a wife and children.

The daily life at the château was quite old-fashioned in its simplicity. Everybody rose with the sun, or very soon afterwards. At nine o'clock the bell in the court rang for the principal meal, which was called dinner. Kings dined at about the same hour in the times of the Crusaders. Early in the afternoon the bell rang again. This was for *collation*, a very light repast, which was often nothing more than salad or fruit and a *frotte*—a piece of crusty bread rubbed with garlic. At about seven o'clock the bell rang for supper.

The small châteaux with which the whole country hereabouts is strewn, notwithstanding that most of them have been partially rebuilt or grossly and wantonly mangled without a purpose such as the rational desire of increasing homely comfort may excuse, even when combined with no respect for the past, nevertheless contain numerous details that call up in the mind pictures of the life of old France. In the rat-haunted lofts and lumber-rooms may still be seen, worm-eaten and covered with dust, the *cacolet*—a wooden structure shaped like the gable roof of a house, and which, when set upon a horse's back, afforded sitting accommodation for two or three persons on each side. There are people who can still remember, on the roads of Périgord, the *cacolets* carrying merry parties to marriage feasts and other gatherings. In a few of the great dining-rooms the visitor will still notice the *alcôve volante*—a bedstead, that is a little house in itself, put into a cosy quiet nook where a person can get into bed without being observed by others in the room. A pretty sentiment caused it to be especially reserved for the grandmothers, who, stretched upon the warm feathers on the winter evenings, could rest their weary limbs while listening to the talk of their descendants and friends, until drowsiness began to make confusion of the present and the past, and then they would pull the cords which closed the curtains and go to sleep. Poor old ladies, now in their graves under the paving-stones of little churches or beneath the grass of rural cemeteries, how happy for them that they did not dream of the future in their snug alcoves near the fire—of a revolution that would kill or scatter their descendants, and of the strangers to their blood who would lie in their beds!

The detached dovecot is seen in almost every old manorial garden. Although pigeons are seldom kept in it, the structure has been preserved because of its usefulness for various purposes and the solidity of its masonry. In some of them is to be seen the old spiral ladder or staircase winding like a serpent round the interior wall from the ground to the domed or pointed roof. By means of this ladder the pigeons could be easily taken from their nests as they were wanted. These great dovecots are an interesting remnant of feudalism. Down to the Revolution the right of keeping pigeons was still a *droit seigneurial*. To those who enjoyed the privilege, the business was therefore a profitable one, for the birds fed largely at other people's expense.

It is rare to find the ancient walls and towers which stud the hills that rise above these valleys in the hands of families who owned them even in the last century. Terror of the Revolutionists caused most of the small nobility of the country to forsake their homes and lands, which were consequently sold by the State *révolutionnairement*, and they who acquired them were thrifty, sagacious people of the agricultural, mercantile, or official class, whose political principles bent easily before the wind that was blowing, and whose savings enabled them to profit by the misfortunes of those who had so long enjoyed the advantages of a privileged position. The descendants of the men who seized their opportunity, and who purchased the estates of the refugees —often at the price 'of an old song'—generally cultivate anti-Republican politics, for they have the best of reasons to be suspicious of the 'great and glorious principles' by virtue of which property was made to change hands so unceremoniously at the close of the last century.

The present owners of most of the country houses in Périgord, whether they belong to the old families or the new families, whether they put the noble particle before their names or not, have very much the same habits and manners. Not a few of them have never been to Paris, and in speech they often use old French forms, which sound strange in the ears of the modernized society of the North. Although the accent is often drawling or sing-song, their language is more grammatically correct than that now ordinarily used in conversation. They observe the true distinction of the tenses with an exactitude that sounds stiff and pedantic to those French people who move about, and who consider that they live in the 'world.' To the unprejudiced foreigner, however, it is not unpleasant to hear this old-fashioned literary French spoken in an easy, simple manner that removes all suspicion of affectation.

In the relations of master and servant, something

of the old régime still survives. The master still says *tu* and *toi* to his servant; but if the latter were to take the liberty of replying with the same pronoun, his insolence would be considered quite unpardonable. And yet no people appear to be troubled less with false pride than the class of whom I am speaking. Relatively large landowners, whose names count for a good deal in the district, think there is nothing derogatory in sending a maid-servant to market to sell the surplus fruit and eggs. Those who buy are equally practical. They haggle over sous with their friends' servant just as if she were a peasant driving a bargain on her own account. It is the exception, however, when to this keen appreciation of money warm-hearted hospitality and disinterested kindness are not joined.

There was a château combining the country house, the farm, and the ruin on the summit of the steep hill that rose above our little island just beyond the river. It often tempted me to climb to it, and one day at the end of summer I wended my way up the stony path. I met with that courteous reception which so rarely fails in France to place the visitor completely at his ease. I was surprised to find how extensive the ramparts were, and how easily the castle behind the modern house could have been rendered habitable. But all the windows were open to the weather. A Gothic chapel with groined vaulting at the base of one of the towers had been turned into a coach-house. Following an old servant who carried a lantern along a dark passage leading to an *oubliette*, I saw what looked like a large cattle trough, and inquired the use of it in such a place. It was put to no purpose now, was the reply, but it was intended for keeping a whole bullock in salt. In the tumultuous ages it was always necessary to be prepared to take immediate measures in view of a siege, and at no period more than during the wars of religion, when the owners of these castles, whether they were Huguenots or Catholics, had to be continually on the alert. When there was fighting to be done, a salted bullock gave less trouble than a live one.

The old man, having tied a string to the top of the lantern, let it down through the round hole of the *oubliette* until it touched the ground many feet below. Then he told me that, when the dungeon was discovered years ago, immediately beneath the opening an old tree was found stuck about with rusty blades and spikes, with their points turned upwards. This story was confirmed by others.

In the garden on the edge of the cliff the myrtle flourished in a little Provence sheltered from the cold winds; the physalis—beautiful southern weed—now laid its large bladders of a vivid scarlet along the edges of the paths, and the walls flamed with the red fruit of the pomegranate.

The most important feudal ruin in this district is that of the Château de Grignols, the cradle of the Talleyrand family. It was raised by Hély Talleyrand, Seigneur de Grignols, at the close of the twelfth century. Much of the outer wall and a few fragments of the interior buildings remain.

I lived a good deal upon the water when I was not in my hermitage under the trees or wandering across country. I found in the water an ever-growing interest and charm. It often drew me from my work, for my canoe was on the canal only a few paces from my dwelling. On each side the high banks were glorious with their many-coloured clothing of summer flowers. There were patches of purple thyme, of blue stachys, and yellow gallium; there were countless spikes of yellow agrimony and heads of wild carrot, and white ox-eyes looked out from amidst the long grasses like snowflakes of summer. Near the water's edge, mingling with sedges, flags, marsh-mallows, bur-reed, and alisma, were the golden flowers of the shrubby lysimachia in dense multitudes, while from the canal itself rose many a spike of water-stachys, with here and there blossoming butomus, near the fringe of the banks. Then there were the pond-weeds, and other true water-plants, whose summer luxuriance nearly stopped the navigation of the canal, and whose pollen in July, collecting near the locks, lay there upon the water like a thick scum. As my little boat moved over them, I could note all the wondrous beauty and delicacy of the strange foliage that lives below the air, and preserves so much of the character of the earliest vegetation of the earth.

It is twilight, and I am paddling up to the river, gliding now along by one bank and now by another. A humming-bird moth, that seems to have been just created, for the eye cannot follow its movement in the dusky air, appears suddenly upon the topmost flower of a stachys, and in another moment it has vanished. Upon the broader and more open river the day appears to revive. There is a faint lustre upon the distant chalky hills and their corn-fields that rise against the quiet sky. But the pale moon just above them is brightening; already the rays are glinting upon the water. A little later the boat is moving up a long brilliant track, where small waves lap and quiver like liquid fire. It is now night, and the forms of the alders in the air and on the water have become weird and awful. I often come alone at this hour, or later, to be filled with the horror of them. There is a strong fascination in their terrible and fantastic shapes, which may be because the sublime and the horrible are so thinly separated. Rarely does the same tree wear the same ghostly appearance when seen a second time, and a shape that may seem to one person appallingly life-like may convey no meaning to another.

Had the gendarmes met me while water-wandering at night, they would certainly have concluded that I was a fish-poacher. All fishing by night in French rivers and streams is illegal, but it is much practised notwithstanding.

There are many carp in the Isle, weighing from

fifteen to twenty pounds, but they are very rarely caught. The river is full of very deep pools, caused by the washing away of the sand down to the solid rock, and the carp seldom get within reach of a net except when they are stirred up and washed out of their lairs in time of flood. Then, when an old fish gets entangled in a net, it is almost certain to break through it, so that it is not with a feeling of pure pleasure that the fisherman recognises by the weight and tug that he has thrown his meshes over one of these monsters. Nor does any better success attend the angler—at all events, the angler who is known in these parts. It is quite an extraordinary event when a carp weighing more than five pounds is taken with the line. The bait commonly used is boiled maize or a piece of boiled chestnut. There is another method of hooking these fish which I have seen practised on the quays at Périgueux. The fisher has a very strong rod, and also a strong line many yards long, at the end of which is fastened, not a bait, but a piece of lead two or three inches in length. To this large hooks are fixed, with barbs turned in all directions. The man, whose eyes have become very keen with practice, sees some carp coming up or going down the stream, and, throwing the plummet far out into the river, he draws it rapidly through the water, across the spot where he believes the fish then to be. It is not often that he feels a tug, but he does sometimes, and then follows a deadly struggle, which may result in his landing a splendid carp that is worth more than he might earn by any other industry in two days.

Among the peasants in this part of Périgord there is a deeply-engrained superstitious horror of what is called a *rencontre*. If a person falls suddenly ill, especially if his sickness be not a familiar ailment, he will begin to probe his memory, and to ask himself if he has lately sat upon a stone or the stump of a tree. If he remembers having done so, he murmurs, unless he should be free from the popular superstition, 'Ah! I thought so. This is a *rencontre!*'—by which he means that he has met one of the three unholy reptiles, the snake, the toad, or the lizard, although it was hidden under the stone or stump.

'Marie,' said I to an old farm woman who was hobbling about with a rheumatic leg, 'what is the matter?'

'Oh, mossieu,' said she, 'it's a *rencontre*. I sat down the other day upon a stone.'

This made me inquire what was meant by a *rencontre*.

I will only set down a few impressions of Périgueux, there being already quite enough written respecting the ancient capital of the Petrocorii. The upper part of the town commands a pleasant view of the valley of the curving Isle, with the wooded hills that lead away towards the upper and wilder country of Périgord; but it is in the lower town near the river, where the odours are strong, that the interest really lies. Here is the cathedral of St. Front, a church in the Byzantine style of the tenth century, and closely imitated from St. Mark's at Venice. It is impossible to see it now, however, without regret and disappointment. In many it stirs both sorrow and anger. It is no longer one of the most precious monuments of old France. What we see now on the site of St. Front is a new church, scrupulously rebuilt, it is true, according to the original plan, and with a great deal of the original material, but its interest is that which belongs to a model: its venerable character, with all the associations of the past, is gone. Whether those responsible for the complete demolition of the ancient structure when it threatened to fall and become a heap of ruins were right or wrong in their decision is a technical question on which very few persons are now competent to give an opinion. The plan of the church is a Greek cross, and, like St. Mark's and St. Sophia's, it has five domes; but the building has, nevertheless, a feature of its own which makes it one of the most original of churches. It possesses a Byzantine tower.

In common with many towns of Southern France, Périgueux shows remarkable vestiges of different races and dominations. Remnants of Roman or Gallo-Roman architecture stand with others that belong to the dawn of mediæval art, and others, again, that are marked by the florid and graceful fancy of the Renaissance. The ruins of the amphi-

theatre are insignificant compared to those at Nimes
and Arles, and there is no beautiful example of
Roman art like the Maison Carrée at Nimes ; but
there is an exceedingly curious monument of antiquity, which was long a puzzle to archæologists, but

THE TOUR DE VÉSONE.

which is now generally believed to be the *cella* of
a Gallo-Roman temple dedicated to the city's tute-
lary divinities. It is called the Tour de Vésone,
and, indeed, it was supposed for centuries to have
been originally a tower. Its cylindrical shape and
its height (ninety feet) give it all the appearance of

one. It is built of rubble, faced inside and out with small well-shaped stones, and has chains of brick in the upper part. The circle of the tower is no longer complete, for about a fourth of the wall has been broken down from top to bottom. The ground is strewn with fragments of immense columns and entire capitals, some Corinthian, others Tuscan. These, doubtless, were parts of the peristyle, which, with the exception of such scattered fragments, has quite disappeared. There is something decidedly barbaric in the fantastic structure that has come down to us, and it is difficult to understand the motive of its height. Such a cylinder rising far above the peristyle could not have had a classic effect. This ruin stands in an open field, and the foulness of the spot, although quite in accordance with the Southern manner of showing respect for antiquities, is nevertheless a disgrace to the ædiles of modern Vesunna.

Another curiosity of the lower town is the ruin of a very early mediæval castle, said to have been built by Wulgrin, surnamed Taillefer, the first of the hereditary Counts of Périgord. Close to this picturesque ruin is one of the ancient gateways of the town. It goes by the name of La Porte Normande, but its slightly pointed arch disposes of the suggestion that the Normans were in some manner concerned in its construction.

What interested me most at Périgueux was something that very few strangers, or even townspeople, for that matter, ever see, because it is hidden from public view. This is a considerable fragment of one of the early walls of the town, which, tradition says, was thrown up in great haste at the approach

THE 'NORMAN GATE' AT PÉRIGUEUX.

of the Normans during one of the incursions of these adventurers up the valley of the Dordogne and, its tributary, the Isle, in the tenth century. It is a bit of wall that speaks to us in a language by no means common. It is not built of stones such as could be found anywhere in all ages, but is put together with the fragments of temples and palaces which even now tell of the power and splendour of Rome. The shafts of fluted columns, capitals wearing the acanthus, pieces of cornice and frieze, all mortared together with undistinguishable rubbish, bear testimony in the quiet garden of the Ursuline convent to the vanity of human works. Vesunna, splendid city of Southern Gaul, completely Latinized, with native poets, orators, and historians speaking and writing the language of Virgil and Cicero, raised temples, palaces, thermæ, and a vast amphitheatre to be used centuries later as material for building a wall to keep out the Northern barbarians!

THE DRONNE AT BOURDEILLES.

FROM PÉRIGUEUX TO RIBERAC (BY BRANTÔME).

FROM Périgueux I made my way to Brantôme in the neighbouring valley of the Dronne—a tributary of the Isle, which nobody who has not stifled the love of beauty in his soul can see without feeling the sweet and winning charm of its gracious influence. Between the two valleys are some fifteen miles of chalky hills almost bare of trees, a dreary track to cross at any time, but especially detestable when the dust lies thick upon the white road and the summer sun is blazing overhead. But how delightful is the contrast when, going down at length from these cretaceous uplands, where even the potato plants look as if they had been white-washed, you see below the verdant valley of the Dronne, that seems to be blessed with eternal spring, the gay flash of the winding stream, the grand rocks that appear to be standing in its bed, and the cool green woods that slope up to the sky beyond! The pleasure grows as you descend, and when at length you reach the little town you are quite enchanted with the grace and elegance, the poetic and romantic charm, of the scene. Although the church, with its tower half built upon a rock, dates from the eleventh and twelfth centuries, the influence of the sixteenth century is so strong that no other is felt. The eye follows the terraces with graceful balustrades in the shadow of old trees, dwells on the fanciful Renaissance bridge, that looks as if its first intention was to span the stream in the usual manner, but, having gone some distance across, changed its mind, and turned off at an abrupt angle; then the little pavilion in the style of Francis I., connected with a machicolated gateway, fixes the attention. There is something in the air of the place which calls up the spirit of Shakespeare, of Spenser, and of all the poets and romancers of the sixteenth century; you feel that everything here belongs to them, that you are in their world, and that the nineteenth century has nothing to do with it. Upon these balustraded terraces, beside the limpid river full of waving weeds, you can picture without effort ladies in farthingales and great ruffs, gentlemen in high hose and brilliant doublets; you can almost hear the lovers of three centuries ago kissing under the trees—lovers like Romeo and Juliet, who kissed with a will and meant it, and who were afraid of nothing. But Brantôme has clearer and more precise associations with letters than such as these, which belong purely to the imagination. Its name has been inextricably entangled with literature by Pierre de Bourdeilles, Seigneur de Brantôme, author of the famous and scandalous 'Mémoires'— terrible chronicles of sixteenth-century venality, intrigue, and corruption, written in a spirit of the gayest cynicism. Brantôme—he is known to the world by no other name now—was the spiritual as well as the temporal lord here, for he was abbot of the ancient abbey which was founded on this spot in the eleventh century or earlier. His ecclesiastical function, however, was confined to the enjoyment of the title and benefice, for if ever man was penetrated to the marrow by the spirit of worldliness, it was Pierre de Bourdeilles. What he has written about the women of his time is something more than the critical observations of a chronicler who was also a caustic analyst of the female character. Such was his cynicism that he, the Abbot of Brantôme, laughed in his sleeve at the horrible strife of Catholics and Huguenots in his own and neighbouring provinces. It is true that he fought at Jarnac against Coligny, but the admiral had met him in the court of the Valois before these wars, and knew him to be an *abbé joyeux*, without prejudices, if ever there was one. The astute chronicler played his cards so well as to keep on safe terms with both sides, and it was by this diplomacy of their lord and abbot that the inhabitants of Brantôme escaped the sword and the rope when Coligny and his terrible German mercenaries entered the weakly-defended place on two occasions in 1569. On the first of these Coligny was accompanied by the young Henry of Navarre and the Prince of Orange. They were all made very welcome by Brantôme, and treated by him with 'good cheer' in his abbey. He was rewarded for his diplomatic talent, for he tells us that no harm was done to his house, nor was a single image or window broken in the church. No doubt he had turned to good profit his distant relationship with Madame de Coligny. On the second occasion the admiral merely hurried through Brantôme with his *reîtres* in full flight after the bad defeat at Montcontour.

The abbey church of Brantôme is not without beauty, but it is the tower that is the truly remarkable feature. It was raised in the eleventh century, and although the architect—probably a monastic one—observed the prevailing principle of Romanesque taste, he showed so much originality in the design that it served as a model, which was much imitated in the Middle Ages. It is not only one of the oldest church towers in France, but its position is one of the most peculiar, it being built, not on the church, but behind it, and partly grafted upon the rock.

Of the old abbey little remains; but there is a cavern, formerly in communication with the conventual buildings, which contains sculptures cut upon the rock in relief, which are a great curiosity to ecclesiologists. They are the work of the monks, who used this old quarry as a chapel, and, it would appear, likewise as an ossuary in a limited sense, if the rows of square holes cut in the rock were to serve as

THE ABBEY OF BRANTÔME.

niches for skulls, as some have maintained. One of the compositions in relief has given rise to discussion among archæologists. The first impression that it conveys is that of an exceedingly uncouth representation of the Last Judgment, but the Marquis de Fayolle's explanation, namely, that the idea which the sculptor-monk endeavoured to work out here was the triumph of Death over Life, meets with fewer objections. There are three figures or heads symbolizing Death, of which the central one wears a diadem that bristles with dead men's bones. Immediately below is Death's scutcheon emblazoned with allegorical bearings. On each side of this is a row of heads rising from the tomb, in which a pope, an emperor, a bishop, and a peasant are to be recognised. In the middle part of the composition are two kneeling angels blowing trumpets, and above these is a vast and awful figure, apparently unfinished, and scarcely more human in its shape than some stalagmites I have met underground. Are we to see here the Eternal Father, or Christ sitting in final judgment? It depends upon the interpretation placed upon the work of the monk, who, with slow and painful effort, gave fantastic life to his solemn thoughts in the gloom of this old quarry, from which stone had been taken to build the church. He was a rude artist, such as might have belonged to the darkest age, but certain ornamental details of the bas-relief indicate that he was a man of the sixteenth century. The walls of the cavern have been blackened by the damp, and these awful shapes reveal themselves but slowly to the eye, so that they look like a vague and dreadful company of ghosts advancing from the darkness.

A visit to this sepulchral cavern gives an appetite for lunch at the good inn which is hard by, and at whose threshold sits or did sit a very fat, broad-faced landlord, seemingly fashioned upon the model of an ideal tapster of old time. Here a *friture* of the famous gudgeons of the Dronne is placed before the guest, whether the fishing be open or closed, and a magistrate would feel as much aggrieved as anybody if the law were not laughed at when its observance would lay a penalty upon his stomach. At the hospitable board of this inn I made the acquaintance of a somewhat eccentric gentleman who lived alone in a large old house, where he pursued the innocent occupation of hatching pheasants with the help of hens. In almost every room there was a hen sitting upon eggs or leading about a brood of little pheasants. This gentleman was more sad than joyous, for he could not take his handkerchief from his pocket without bringing out the corpse of a baby pheasant with it—one that had been trodden to death by a too fussy foster-mother. I owe him a debt for having led me a charming walk by moonlight to see a dolmen—the largest and best preserved of all those I had already seen in Southern France and elsewhere.

It was not without a little pang that I broke away from the spell of coquettish Brantôme and began my wanderings down the valley of the Dronne. A few miles below the little town the stream passes into the shadow of great rocks. I looked at these with something of the regret that one feels when awaking from a long dream of wonderland. I knew that they were almost the last vestiges towards the west, in the watershed of the Gironde, of the stern jurassic desert, gashed and seamed with lovely valleys, and deep gorges full of the poet's 'religious awe,' where I had spent the greater part of three long summers. And now, on the outskirts of the broad plain or gradual slope of undulating land that leads on from the darker and rockier Périgord, through the greenness of the lusty vine—led captive from the New World and rejoicing in the ancient soil of France—or the yellow splendour of the sunlit cornfields, towards the sea that rolls against the pine-clad dunes, I felt tempted to turn from my course and go back to my naked crags and stone-strewn wastes. But I did not go back. Life being so short in this world of endless variety, we cannot afford to return upon our path.

A little beyond where the double line of rocks ended, I saw a round tower of unusual height with machicolations and embattlements, in apparently perfect preservation, rising from the midst of what once must have been a fortress of great strength, which on the side of the river had no need of a moat, for it was there defended by the escarped rock, to the edge of which the outer ramparts were carried. This was the castle of Bourdeilles, the seat of the family of which the Abbé de

Brantôme was a younger son. I was soon able to get a closer view of it. It is one of the most instructive remnants of feudalism in Périgord, and one of the most picturesque, by the contrast of its great gloomy keep and frowning ramparts with the peaceful beauty of the valley below. The tall *donjon*, 130 feet high, and most of the outer wall, are of the fourteenth century. The inner wall encloses a sixteenth-

CHÂTEAU DE BOURDEILLES.

century mansion, marked with none of the picturesqueness of the Renaissance period, but heavy and graceless. In the interior, however, are sculptured chimney-pieces and other interesting details. This residence was built by the sister-in-law of Pierre de Bourdeilles. The burg itself, which lies close to the castle and is much embowered with trees, has something of the open, spacious, and decorative air of

Brantôme. It tells the stranger that it has known better days. The broad terrace, planted with trees so as to form a *quinconce*, where the people stroll and gossip in the summer evenings, is quite out of keeping with a little place that has scarcely more than a thousand inhabitants.

Near the castle gateway is the 'Logis des Sénéchaux,' a small building of the fifteenth century with turrets capped by extinguisher-like roofs, and within a stone's throw of this is a small church, dating from the twelfth century, the artistic interest of which has been lamentably deteriorated by renovation and scraping. The influence of the Byzantine cathedral that rose in the old Roman city by the Isle spread far, and numerous churches in Périgord bear witness to the imitative zeal which it inspired, especially in the application of domes to the vaulting of the nave. This arrangement is frequently to be found in connection with the pointed arch, and such is the case at Bourdeilles. The apse is beautiful, with its five tall windows and its columns with Corinthian capitals in the intervening wall spaces. Although the church is in no style that is recognised as pure, it is typical of one that has been developed in the district, and which is by no means without grace ; but the scraping that it has undergone has robbed it of the proper tint and tone of its age, and the ideal interest that belongs to this.

But here is something from which the gray mantle that the centuries have silently spun has not been lifted. I have gone down to the waterside to follow the stream onward, and am held by the quiet charm of a half Gothic bridge that was thrown across it five or six hundred years ago; the miller's house just below, with its bright little garden flaming with flowers a few inches above the water, and two great wheels turning slowly, slowly, as if time and change and the rush of life were the vain words of tiresome fools. On the side of the bridge looking up-stream, each pier is built out in the form of a sharp angle. This was intended to lessen the push of the current upon the masonry in time of flood. A great many old bridges in Guyenne show a similar design.

My road had now on one side the reedy Dronne, and on the other overleaning rocks topped with trees or shrubs, whose foliage reached downward as if it were ever troubled by the futile longing to touch the cool green water, and every little ridge or shelf was marked out by a line of ancient moss. Old alders had plunged their roots deep into the banks of the river, and wherever the sunshine struck upon the upper leaves was a cicada scratching out its monotonous note in joyous frenzy.

A long range of densely-wooded, rocky cliffs now stretched along the right bank; but I, keeping to the road on the other side, soon left the stream and rose upon a hill dotted with low juniper bushes. The scene in the widening valley below was full of summer light and gladness. Men were mowing, and women were turning the fallen swathes in the waterside meadows, and upon all the slopes above were patches of yellow corn ready for the sickle. In the green depth between the hills the river flowed vaguely on in the shadow of tall poplars, and was sometimes hidden by its reeds.

Here and there upon the higher ground, half concealed by walnut-trees, were small châteaux or farmhouses, with a castellated air derived from great dovecots and towers, which last once served for the defence of the manor-house or the little castle. When the fury of the religious wars followed upon that tidal wave of dilettantism and sensuality which swept over Europe from the south to the north, and which we call the Renaissance, and when Huguenots and Leaguers gave such frequent dressings of blood to the vineyards of Périgord, every house and church that was in any way fortified was used as a stronghold in the event of sudden attack.

From the broad landscape I turn to the wayside flowers: the agrimony, the little lotus, the candy-tuft—getting rare now that I have left the arid stony region—the blue scabious, and, pleasanter than all, the purple patches of dwarf thyme.

It was not yet evening when I came to Lisle, a rather large village near the Dronne. Here I fell in with a plasterer, and he being a good-tempered man, with some spare time on his hands, he offered to show me before dinner the picturesque ruin of an old bridge, known in the district as the Pont d'Ambon. On our way to the river he talked much, and especially about his village, in which he took a very lively interest. It had not changed its principles, he said, for a hundred years.

'And what are its principles?'

'Republican. We don't go to church here, although there is no ill-will towards the curé.'

'And is all the country about here Republican?'

'Oh no, not at all. There is a village close by that is full of religion. We are often called savages. When the curé asked the commune to give him 200 francs a year for saying an extra mass on Sundays, the majority of the inhabitants signed their names to a paper offering him 300 francs a year if he would say no mass at all.'

I said to myself that the curé of Lisle was not to be envied the piece of vineyard that he had been sent to look after. I had often heard stories such as this. Faction fighting provides the chief intellectual stimulus in many a village and small town of France. Where Republicanism is strong, the mayor's party is often at bitter feud with those who share the views and uphold the authority of *M. le curé*. The sign that the 'advanced' Republicans give of their political faith is never to set foot inside the church unless it be at a wedding or a funeral. But what is especially worth the attention of the philosophical observer is the extent to which prevailing ideas in politics and religion differ in the same district. Within a few miles of a commune where Republicans and Freethinkers have complete control of local affairs, may be another that is altogether Royalist or Bonapartist, and where the curé is both popular and powerful. There is, moreover, a very marked difference in the character of the inhabitants of neighbouring places. In one the prevailing characteristic may be mildness and affability of manners, whereas in another it may be truculence and incivility. Neither the influence of politics nor of religion sufficiently accounts for these differences in character. They seem to rest rather upon obscure and remote causes, such as racial and congenital tendencies. All this is especially observable in the South of France, where the present population has been formed from the blood of so many races, which is very unequally mixed even to this day.

When my talkative plasterer left the subject of local politics, he took up that of the moon. Like all country people, whether in France or in England, he had the strongest faith in the influence of the moon upon the weather. He, moreover, maintained that moonbeams had a very corrosive and destructive action upon zinc. This fact, he said, had come under his observation scores of times in his business, which was that of roofing as well as plastering.

Thus talking, we came to the bridge, or, rather, its sole remaining arch, now almost completely hidden by ivy, briars, and other vegetation, by which it has been gradually overgrown. The plasterer had a sense of the picturesque, and he had not over-rated the beauty of this spot. A little below the early Gothic arch, from which the briars reached down to the water, was an old mill, in the shadow of a high, overleaning rock, and great trees made a vaulting over the grassy lane, at the end of which the turning-wheel could be seen, with just a sparkle of evening sunshine upon the dropping water.

The inn where I put up that night was a substantial hostelry, containing all that was needful for the entertainment of man and beast. Had I been a *Procureur de la République* the law could not have been broken in a more solicitous manner than it was in my behoof. Not only did I have gudgeons, *en temps prohibé*, but also partridge. It was not until the bones were carried out that I felt that I had missed an excellent opportunity of setting a good example by declining to eat partridge in the month of June.

I must have been put into the best bedroom, for among other works of art which it contained was a bridal wreath of orange-blossoms under a glass. I surmised that when it decked the head of my hostess, her form would not have taken up so much room in the kitchen as when I saw it downstairs, passing with a slow and dignified movement in the midst of the saucepans and platters. I have often slept in rooms where there have been bridal orange-blossoms under glass. They always interest me, just as the faded family photographs do which so frequently deck the walls of the same room. They get me on the lines of thought or sentiment which make us enter when we are by ourselves into all that is human.

The next morning, after seeing the church—a Romanesque and Gothic structure of considerable beauty—I returned to the Dronne, and, after crossing it, continued upon the road eastward until I saw the picturesque ruins of the Château de Marouette upon a hill above me. Then I left the road, and climbed the hill by a rocky path. This castle, dating from the close of the sixteenth century, shows a blending of feudal architecture with the Renaissance style. In this respect it is like many others in the district, but it is truly remarkable in having preserved an outer wall, strengthened with round towers at intervals, and enclosing two or three acres of land. The fortress was raised by a Baron de Jarnac, and must have been one of the last built to combine the double character of family residence and stronghold. The outer and inner ramparts, and the high, frowning, machicolated keep, perched upon the rock and overlooking the valley, prove that it was truly a *château-fort*, and one that ought to have been able to give a very good account of itself. A fantastic effect has been produced by attaching a plain modern house without any character to the best-preserved parts of the ruin. Agriculture must possess the thoughts of those who are now living there. The wide space between the outer and inner walls, as I saw it in the early sunshine of the June morning, was a level floor of golden ears, nearly ready for the reaper.

A storm overnight had moistened the earth; the breath that came from the flowery banks and the glistening leaves of oak and chestnut was very fresh; all the birds that could sing were singing; the sound of the sweeping scythe and the voices of mowers rose from the valley, and the spirit of peace and gladness was over the land.

I took a road somewhat at random, and it led me by many windings away from the Dronne, up hills, where there were vines but no cornfields, and where the wayside trees were chiefly plums, laden with fruit fast purpling. And as I looked at the plums I thought of the time when, after being dried in the sun, they would become 'prunes,' and be scattered about the world, many of them, perchance, in England, where children would buy them with their pennies, as I had bought others myself, when I never supposed that I should walk by the trees that bore them under southern skies.

A road-mender whom I passed saluted me with the words, '*Bon soir!*' although the hour was eight in the morning. In these parts, however, *bon soir* is frequently said at all hours. It is a colloquial peculiarity. Another is to address or speak of a gentleman and a lady as '*Ces messieurs.*'

At length I reached a plateau, where I saw not far off, in a hollow surrounded by cornfields and ruit-trees, such a number of red roofs that I concluded I must have come to the little town of Montagrier. A young peasant soon undeceived me: I was near the village of Grand-Brassac. It was clear that I had gone much farther from the Dronne than I had intended, but, after all, it mattered little where I wandered. I now said that I would see Grand-Brassac, and that I might find something there worth the walk. I was rewarded beyond aught that I had expected or hoped for.

Here I found a very remarkable Byzantine-Gothic church of the thirteenth century, with a richly-decorated front in strong contrast to the defensive motive so clearly expressed by the solidity of the structure, the smallness of the windows, and especially by the height of the entrance—some ten feet above the level of the ground. It is reached by steps. Over the doorway, which has a pointed arch ornamented with a star moulding, is a semi-circular compartment containing several figures in high relief, the central one of which represents the Virgin enthroned. No satisfactory explanation of the others has yet been found. Beneath the compartment is a row of very fantastic bracket-heads, supposed to represent the Vices. Above it is a canopy with sculptured medallions on the under-surface, where the symbolical Lamb may be recognised amongst winged dragons and other monsters. Close to these is a monkey playing on the violin. Above this canopy is another, shaped like a low gable, and forming the upper frame of a further set of figures in relief, larger than those in the compartment below. The central and highest figure is that of Christ teaching. The Virgin is kneeling on the right, and St. John on the left. St. Paul is shown with the book of his Epistles, and St. Peter, wearing a bishop's mitre, is holding his keys. Among other details of this curious façade is the figure of a kneeling knight in a coat of mail. Upon the exterior side-walls are Roman arches *en saillie*, resting upon corbels and very wide pilaster-strips that are almost buttresses. In the interior, the Byzantine influence is very apparent in the three domes, which combine with the Gothic vaulting of the narrow, dimly-lighted nave. The main walls are carried so high as to hide the roof of the domes, and this goes far to give to the church that air of a mediæval fortress which at once impresses the beholder.

As the fortune of the road had cast me upon this village, I made up my mind to accept pot-luck here, for the morning was no longer young, and I knew not how far I might have to trudge before finding better quarters. So I resolved to take my chance at what looked like the best inn in the place, although it was a very rustic hostelry that would have repelled a wanderer less seasoned than myself to the vicissitudes of the highways and byways. I had, however, a cool little back-room with whitewashed walls to myself, and through the small square window near the table where I sat I could see something of the sunny world, with bits of tiled roof and green foliage, as well as the lemon-coloured butterflies that fluttered from garden to garden. There was no lack of food in the auberge, for a pig had been very recently killed. There were several dishes, but they were all made up from the same animal. When something fresh came, I thought, 'This, at all events, must be mutton or veal'; but although it may have been cunningly disguised with tomatoes or garlic, I perceived that it was pork again. It was long after this adventure that I could look at a pig with a lenient and unprejudiced mind.

When I left Grand-Brassac, I so shaped my course as to return to the valley of the Dronne, but at a point much lower than that where I had last crossed the river. The weather was now very sultry; not a breath of wind stirred, and thunder-clouds were gathering in the sky. As the sun glared between the layers of vapour, the cicadas screamed from the tops of the walnut-trees, while I upon the dazzling white road felt that there was no need of so much rejoicing.

A great dark cloud with fiery fringe now stretches far up the sky from the south, and there is a constant long-drawn-out groan of distant thunder. This storm is no loiterer; it is coming on at a rapid pace, and it will be a fierce one. Still, the haymakers keep in the meadow hard by the road, working for dear life to fill the waggon, to which a pair of oxen are harnessed, and to get it safely to the village on yonder hill before the floodgates of heaven are opened. I hasten on to this village, and reach it just before the rain begins to fall. It is almost deserted; everybody appears to be in the fields.

On the very top of the hill is a little old church surrounded by cypresses and acacias, and as the sun, about to vanish within the folds of the cloudy pall that is already drawn up to its flaming edge, darts burning rays upon the still motionless leaves, the cicadas again scratch out their note with the blind zeal of fiddlers who have made too merry at the marriage-feast.

According to my wont, I pay a visit to the dead, who lie scattered all around the old church. Scattered do I say? Why, the very ground on which I walk is made up of them. When another dead villager is buried, what occurs is merely a displacement of human remains. As one body goes down, the bones and dust of others come up to the surface. Wherever I walk I see bones, and if I were an anatomist I could tell the use and place of each in the human economy. One might well suppose that in these rural districts, where land is of so little value, there would be but slight disturbance of dead men's bones. Observation, however, tells a very different story. These country churchyards are very small, and nobody but the stranger seems to think that there is any reason why they should be larger. There is little or no buying of graves 'in perpetuity' here, and very little grave-marking, except by mounds and wooden crosses. Years pass quickly, while the briar and the thistle and the bindweed grow apace, like the new interests and affections that spring up in the minds and hearts of the mourners. Who are they who carry flowers to the graves of their grandfathers?

Think of the population of an entire village being swallowed up every fifty or seventy years by this patch of ground that would make but a small garden, and of this movement going on century after century! It is surely no matter for marvel that it has become as difficult to hide the bones as the pebbles whenever a bit of soil has been lately turned. They lie even about the sides of the rough path that goes round the church. Some fragments are so honeycombed that they are as light in the hand as touchwood; others have undergone little, if any, chemical change. Here people must often walk upon the bones of their not very remote ancestors; but they know, if they think about the matter at all, that their turn will come to be similarly treated by their own descendants. There is no better place for meditating upon all the vanities than one of these old rural cemeteries. Turn not away, you other wanderers who may chance to stray into these little fields consecrated to the dead, and excuse your unwillingness to reflect by muttering, 'Horrible!' There is nothing horrible, after all, in these poor bones. What matters it whether they are bleached by the sun or blackened by the clay? It is good for you and for me to see them here, and to realize how soon all men are forgotten, how quickly their bones, mingling with others, give no more clue to the individual life to which they once belonged than a particle of dust that dances in the sunbeam does to the matter from which it parted.

It is not good, however, to stay moralizing in a cemetery until a thunderstorm bursts over your head. I remained so long here that I had to run for refuge in a manner quite out of keeping with my solemn train of thoughts. I entered the first doorway that I saw open, and thus I found myself in a cobbler's shop. The cobbler was seated on a stool at a low table covered with tools and odds and ends in the middle of the room, sewing a boot, which he held to his knee with a strap passed under his foot. His apprentice was sitting near munching a piece of bread. Both looked up with an astonished, not to say startled, expression when I appeared simultaneously with a dazzling flash of lightning, followed immediately by a terrific thunder-clap. The thought expressed in the eyes of the cobbler as he looked up was, 'Are you a thunderbolt, or Robert the Devil?'

I spoke to him and calmed him; but although he was satisfied that I was human, he evidently could not make me out. Nor was this surprising, for the village—St. Victor by name—lies quite off the track of all but the inhabitants of a small district. The man, however, made me welcome, and offered me a chair. The sky was now the colour of dull lead, the lightning-flashes were almost momentary, and the thunder roared incessantly. Mingling with this sound and that of the splashing rain was another—the clang and scream of the bell in the church-tower. It was rung as the tocsin, with that quick and wild movement which had startled me elsewhere in the depth of night with the cry of 'Fire! Fire!' The bell, however, was not rung now to give the alarm of fire, and to summon everybody to lend a helping hand in extinguishing the flames, but to persuade the storm either to go somewhere else or to act with moderation. This old custom—now dying out—is no doubt founded on the religious belief that when the church bell is rung with faith a storm will do no harm; but the country people join to the religious idea the notion that the vibration of the atmosphere, caused by the ringing, dissipates the storm or turns it in another direction. Unfortunately for the ancient custom, churches have frequently been struck by lightning at the time when the bells were being rung, and science is positive in declaring that the electric fluid is attracted by an artificial commotion of the atmosphere. On the *causses* of the Quercy, the peasants place bottles of holy water on the tops of their chimneys as a protection against lightning. The idea is that the evil power will not strike the dwelling of those who put up a sign that their habitation is blessed. These bottles on the chimney-tops puzzled me greatly, until at length I inquired the reason why they were there.

There was to me something exceedingly grand and elevating in this storm that raged upon the hilltop, while the bell in the open tower, tossing like a cask on the sea, proclaimed over all the house-tops and the fields the fierceness of the struggle between the celestial guardians of the church and village, and the demons that thronged the air. I felt that I might never have such an opportunity as this again, and wished to make the most of it. The cobbler nearly lost his temper at seeing me so wickedly elated. Perhaps he thought that I might draw down a judgment upon myself, and that he ran some risk of being included in it for having harboured me. He not only looked frightened, but frankly owned that he was afraid. He was one of those men—of whom I have known several—who can never overcome their horror of a thunderstorm. At length the storm began to move off and the bell stopped ringing; then the cobbler became quite cheerful. He brought out a great jar of spirit distilled from plums, and insisted upon my drinking some with him. He also invited me to 'break a crust,' but this offer I declined. Before I took leave of the good-natured man, he seemed to have fairly shaken off the bad impression I had made upon him by watching a thunderstorm with interest and pleasure.

The sky having cleared, I continued my journey towards Riberac, and reached the Dronne when the stormy day was ending without a cloud. There was hardly a breath of wind to shake the drops from the still dripping leaves, and the last groan of distant thunder having died away, there would have been deep silence but for the warbling of blackbirds and nightingales.

THE DESERT OF THE DOUBLE.

I AM now at Riberac—the Ribeyrac of Dante's commentators, who generally prefer to abide by the old spelling. One might expect this ancient little town to offer much interest to the archæologist, but it does not. Its interest lies almost wholly in its literary associations of Arnaud Daniel, and of him mainly because Dante chanced to meet him in purgatory. Here was the castle—there is nothing of it now—where the thirteenth-century troubadour was born whom Petrarch described as '*Il grande maestro d'amore*,' and whom Dante made Guido speak of as a poet in these words of unqualified praise :

'Questi ch' io ti scerno
Fu miglior fabbro del parlar materno :
Versi d'amore e prose di romanzi
Soverchio tutti.'

Dante having asked for the name on earth of this gifted soul, the troubadour replied in the tongue that he had learned from his mother's lips at Riberac :

'Jeu sui Arnaulz che plor e vai cantan.'

Arnaud's modern critics admire him less than did Dante and Petrarch; but he had a gift of sweet song, and he owed it doubtless in no small measure to the influence of the lovely Dronne, on whose banks he must have often rambled in childhood—that season when impressions are unconsciously laid up which shape the future life of the intellect. No Englishman should pass through Arnaud's birthplace with indifference, for he was the first to put into literary form the story of Lancelot of the Lake.

Although Arnaud Daniel's castle has quite disappeared, much of the church, that was almost a new one in his time, still remains. It was originally Byzantine-Romanesque, but in the sixteenth century it underwent fantastic restoration, and was badly married to another style without a name. What struck me most on entering was the religious darkness through which one sees the suspended lamp of the sanctuary gleaming like a star, and behind it the dim outline of the altar. This crypt-like appearance is explained by the absence even of a single window in the apse, which is covered by a semi-dome. The Romanesque tower is very low and broad, with a broach spire roofed with stones.

What a contrast to the deep shadow of the church was the brilliant white light that I met outside, and to the grave-like silence the sawing sound of the cicadas, drunk with sunshine, in the neighbouring tree-tops!

I set out from Riberac to cross that tract of

country between the Dronne and the Isle which is known as the Double. It is still one of the most forlorn wildernesses in all France; but, like the Camargue, it has been much changed of late years by drainage and cultivation, and is destined to become productive and prosperous. For incalculable centuries it had remained a baneful solitude, overgrown with virgin forest, except in the hollows between the low hills, which succeed one another like the undulations of the sea; and here, almost hidden in summer by tall reeds and sedges, lay the pools and bogs that poisoned the air and rendered the climate abominable. In the midst of this marshy, cretaceous desert, stretching between the Isle and its tributary, the Dronne, and close to a wretched fever-stricken village called Échourgnac, a small community of Trappist monks established themselves in 1868. They did not go there merely as ascetics fleeing from the world, but also as philanthropists, prepared to sacrifice their lives for the good of humanity. Their mission was to drain and to cultivate this most unhealthy part of the Double, and to improve the condition of the peasants who eked out a miserable existence there. With what success the monks have applied themselves to their task of changing the climate by drainage, and assisting the peasants in their struggle, is proved by the sentiments of the people towards them. When, under the Third Republic, the unauthorized religious orders were expelled from France, the inhabitants of the

Double threatened to resist by force any official interference with the Trappists at Echourgnac, and the agitation was so great that the counsel given by the local authorities to the Government was to leave these monks alone. It was acted upon. The Trappists, like the Carthusians, were left undisturbed in this and in other parts of the country.

When I had turned south-westward, on the road to Montpont, I saw nothing for five or six miles that corresponded to what I had been told of the Double. Yellow corn-fields and green meadows covered the fertile plain. It was not until I had passed the village of St. Vauxains, and had reached the top of the line of hills beyond, that the character of the country changed decisively. Now, as I left the broad and favoured valley, and reached the brow of the hilly range that helps to keep the water stagnant and imprisoned in the Double, meadow and corn-field grew scarcer and scarcer, and then passed altogether into the wooded moorland. Cultivation returned at intervals, then vanished again. I was upon an undulating plateau with far-off higher hills closing the horizon all around. The reclaimed land was in the hollows or upon the surrounding slopes; but here, too, the scrubby forest might be seen stretching for miles without a break. The heat was intense, and the sky had become stormy.

When I left Riberac the blue above was without a spot, but now heavy masses of cloud were hovering in the sky. As yet there was not wind enough to rustle a leaf, and the dwarf oaks gave little shelter from the ardent sun. The air that rose from the heather and bracken was like the breath of a furnace. There were a few scattered cottages and farm-buildings, lying chiefly near the road, and the turkeys and geese that roamed around them were a sign that they were inhabited; but I rarely saw a human being.

I was resting awhile by a reedy pool fringed with gorse and heather, and was listening to the oriels answering one another upon their Pan-pipes, when I saw coming towards me a figure which might have disturbed me very much had I been living in those days when—if there is any truth in legendary lore—the devil only needed half a pretext for forcing his society upon lonely travellers. This man—for man it was—had a face so overgrown with coal-black hair that very little could be seen of it excepting the eyes and nose. Beard, whiskers, and moustache were inseparably mixed up. What skin was visible through the matted jungle of hair was little less swarthy than a Hindu's. All the upper part of this astonishing head was hidden by a large hat of black straw, shaped like an inverted washing-basin. The rest of the figure was clad in a frock of dark-brown serge, with hanging hood. Not expecting to see a Trappist where I was, I was startled for a moment by the apparition, but I quickly guessed that this was one of the brothers of the still distant monastery who had been sent out on some little expedition into the district. As he passed, he raised his hat just enough to show that the close-cropped black hair beneath it was turning gray.

The road led me through a little village where there was an old Romanesque church. There were numerous archivolts over the broad portal, and above these was a horizontal dog's-tooth moulding with grotesque heads at intervals; but time had effaced most of the carving. All about the church the long grass and gaudy mulleins stood over the bones of men and women who, like their parents before them, had clung to their old homes in the midst of the pestilential marshes, suffering continually from malaria, watching their children grow paler and paler, and yet never thinking of surrender. What a strange combination of heroism, obstinacy, and stupidity do we find in human nature! But now things had changed here. There was an air of prosperity in the village, and the people said that the fever had almost left them.

While crossing another bit of wild and deserted country, I saw the dark gleam of poisonous pools nearly hidden by sallows and reeds. The vibration of my footsteps disturbed the vipers that lay near the hot road; they slid down the banks and curved out of sight amongst the roots of the heather. These reptiles abound in the Double; conditions that are baneful to men are healthful to them. The sighing of the pines added to the sadness of the land, for these trees now appeared in clumps along the wayside, and the storm-wind had begun to blow. The sun was shining obliquely through a dun-coloured haze when I reached the village of Échourgnac in a cultivated valley. Here the cattle and the green fields were signs of the cheese-making industry carried on at the monastery. The conventual buildings were now visible on the top of the neighbouring hill, with the church spire higher against the sky than all the rest. I made my way towards this little fortress of asceticism hidden from the world amidst the woods and marshes.

I had made up my mind to spend the night with the Trappists, even if I was obliged to accept their charity and to allow myself to be classed with those tramps who have no literary pretext for their vagabond ways. Indeed, I had been given to understand by all to whom I had spoken on the subject in the district, that the reverend fathers gave money sometimes to the wayfarer, but accepted none in return for food and shelter. That part of me in which the conventional is concentrated said: 'Stop at the inn;' but the other part, which has the curiosity and the errantry of the man who has never been perfectly civilized, said: 'Go on, and whatever happens pass the night with the Trappists.'

Having reached the monastery gate, the next thing to do was to pull the bell. The porter opened first his wicket and then the door. The superior could not be approached for a quarter of an hour, so I was asked to wait in the lodge. Thus I had an opportunity of becoming acquainted with the porter. Although he was very much in religion, having been a brother at Échourgnac since the foundation, he might be termed without disrespect 'a jolly old soul.' He was, as he said, a man who had no pretensions whatever to be learned. His lack of book knowledge made him all the more natural. His age appeared to be about sixty-five, but he had a body that was still robust and vigorous under his dirty brown frock, although he had been living so many years on bread and cheese and vegetables, and short commons withal. The post of porter must have helped him not a little to bear up against the discipline, for it allowed him the use of his tongue, and the rule of silence would have been a more severe trial to him than to many another. He poured out some beer for me from a great stone jar that he kept near at hand. I had heard that the Trappists of Échourgnac added to their other accomplishments the arts of beer-brewing and wine-making, and was therefore not surprised by the porter's kindly offer; but when I noticed the yellow colour and soup-like consistency of the fluid that he poured out for me, I was sorry that I had accepted it.

'It is a little thick,' said the Trappist, whose keen eyes had noticed that there was a lack of warmth in the manner in which I took the glass from his hand, 'but the beer is good. It is rather new.'

'It must be very nourishing,' I replied, after heroically draining the cup of tribulation.

'Have some more?' said this good-natured Trappist as he raised the jar again. I saved myself from a second dose by an energetic '*Merci !*' and changed his thoughts by asking him if he had been a long time at the monastery.

'I was one of the first lot who came here in July, 1868. There were twenty-two of us in all, *pères et frères*, and two or three weeks afterwards seventeen were down with fever. You can have no idea of what it was here five-and-twenty years ago. The country was unfit for human beings. The people went shivering about in the heat of summer wrapped up as they would be in the depth of winter. It was pitiful to see them.'

He then entered into details respecting the clearing of the land, the draining of the pools, etc. Suddenly remembering the flight of time, he disappeared with my card, and left me in charge of the lodge. Presently he came back, and told me that the reverend father was unwell, and could not see anybody, but that I could pass the night in the monastery if I wished to do so. The porter led me through a great farmyard, then through a doorway into a room, in the centre of which was a large table, and in the corners were four very small and low wooden bedsteads with meagre mattresses, a couple of sheets, and a coloured quilt.

When we entered, two men were seated at the table eating bread and cheese and drinking home-brewed beer. One was quite young, perhaps five-and-twenty, and it was to him that the brother who parleyed with the outer world at the gate introduced me, with the recommendation that he should do all in his power for me, adding, with an emphasis by which he gained my friendship for ever: '*Je réponds sur vous.*' The young man said that as soon as he had finished his own meal he would see to my supper. I begged him to take his time, as I was in no hurry.

The good porter, still solicitous, asked where I was going to sleep, and the young man, who I afterwards learnt was a postulant, pointed to a bed in one of the corners. I was then left with my two new acquaintances. The postulant had very soon finished, and having brushed the crumbs off his part of the bare board with his hand, he disappeared, to see what he could find for me in the kitchen. The man who remained also brought his meal to a close, but he did not whisk the crumbs away; he brushed them into little heaps, and, wetting his forefinger, raised them by this means to his mouth. He was about fifty; his chin was shaved, but he wore whiskers, and a long rusty overcoat hung nearly down to his heels. He was very quiet, and I thought he looked like a repentant cabman. There was something about the man that excited my curiosity, but I felt that, considering where I was, it would be very bad taste to put any leading questions to him respecting his history. I nevertheless found a way of getting into conversation with him, and he did not need much persuasion to talk. He was rather incoherent, but I gathered from what he said that he had wandered a good deal from monastery to monastery, now in the world and now almost 'in religion,' without finding anchorage anywhere.

'The world,' he said, 'is like a rotten plank, and we are like smoke that comes and goes. If we do not think of eternity, we are shipwrecked.'

Feeling, perhaps, that something in the world was a little more solid after the bread and cheese and beer than it was before, he was working himself up to a communicative humour, and I was beginning to hope that I should soon know what sort of a character he really was, when the return of the postulant changed his ideas as effectually as if a bucket of water had been thrown in his face. When he ventured to speak again, the younger man told him that it was six o'clock, and that the whole community was now expected to observe the rule of silence.

'Do not be angry,' he added, as he heard the other mutter something that escaped me.

'I am not angry,' replied the owner of the long coat as he glided softly out of the room.

I was now alone with the postulant, who made matters pleasanter for me by giving a generous interpretation to the rule of silence in so far as it applied to himself. He told me that, as I had come after the hour of the second meal, the *frère cuisinier* was not in the kitchen, but at *salve;* consequently there was no possibility of getting even an omelet made for me. After looking, however, into all the corners of the kitchen, my providential man had discovered some cold macaroni, which he presented to me in a small tin plate. I do not know how it had been cooked, but its very dark colour made me suspicious of it. Although I knew it was quite wholesome, I thought it safer to leave it untouched, and to be satisfied with bread and cheese. Now, this cheese, made by the Trappists of the Double upon the Port-Salut recipe, which is a secret of the Order, is of excellent quality, and deserves its reputation. The monastery bread, made from the wheat grown by the monks, was of the substantial and honest kind which in England would probably be called 'farmhouse bread,' although the great wheel or trencher-shaped loaves of the French provinces might cause some surprise there. My meal, therefore, might have been worse than it was, and as it was given to me for nothing, it would have been very bad manners not to appear pleased. The truth is, the novelty of my position—that of a tramp taken in and fed on charity—amused me so much that I found everything perfect. I had an idea 'at the back of the head' that I should find a way of squaring matters financially with the holy men, but I did not wish to tell it even to myself then. I must confess that when a black bottle was placed beside the bread and cheese on the bare table, I was weak enough to hope that it contained some of the excellent white wine which I was told the Trappists made; but when the liquor came out the colour of pea soup, I recognised the religious beer which had already disappointed me. As I could get nothing better, and the water being distinctly bad, the most sensible thing to do was to be reconciled to the beer, and in this I succeeded very fairly. Necessity is not the mother of invention only. The wine, I afterwards learnt, is only drunk at the convent in winter. Much of it is sold to priests for sacramental use.

When I had taken the keen edge off my hunger, I began to feel a fresh interest in the postulant. Somehow, he did not appear to me to be of the stuff out of which monks, especially Trappists, are made, although I know that in all that relates to the interior workings of a man there are no outward signs to be relied upon. There is puzzle enough in our own contradictions to discourage us from trying to find consistency in others; but we try all the same. We have a fine sense of proportion and harmony when we analyze our fellow-beings, but none whatever when we turn the faculty introspectively. The sanctimonious undertone in which this young man spoke struck me as being false, for there was nothing in him that I could discover which linked him to the ascetic ideal of life. But then the question arose, Why was he there? He was strong and healthy; he had a deep colour on his cheeks, and a humorous twinkle in his eye. He did not look as if he had been crossed in love, or had received any of the scars of passion such as might account for his wish to become a Trappist. He had seen something of the world. He had been to Chili, among other countries, and the war there had ruined his prospects, so he told me. I concluded, from what he said, that on his return to France he had sought a temporary refuge with the Trappists, and that he preferred to remain under the shelter that he had found there rather than run the risk of worse in the struggle for life outside. Becoming more confidential, he told me that what was most difficult to be borne by those in his position was the rule of absolute submission and obedience.

I had not been at the table long, when this postulant glided out of the room, saying:

'I will see if there is a way of getting another bottle of beer.'

Presently he returned with a bottle under his arm, and then I learnt that the abbot had given orders that I was to pass the night *dans la chambre de Monseigneur*. The prospect of sleeping in the bishop's bed furnished me with a conscientious reason for not drawing the cork from the second bottle of monastic barley-brew; but my companion, who was more or less in religion, did not give me a chance of refusing, for he drew it himself and filled two glasses.

'*Nous allons trinquer*,' said he.

We clinked glasses, and talked with greater freedom, although the postulant still spoke under his breath—it was a habit that he had fallen into. We were interrupted by a scuffling outside, and by the opening of the door. A couple of monks in brown frocks were on the threshold. A small gray-bearded brother with a bent back held in one hand a pewter plate and in the other a little basin of the same metal. He was the *frère cuisinier*, who had returned from *salve*, and he had come to offer me some vegetable soup and some more macaroni, both of which I declined. Not a word did these Trappists say, but they carried on with the postulant a conversation in dumb show as to what my requirements would be on the morrow. They stroked their noses, rubbed their fingers together, and grimaced so expressively all on my account that I was much amused, and would have liked to laugh outright; but I durst not in such company.

When they had left I took a stroll outside, for as yet I felt no inclination to go to bed, notwithstanding that a bishop had slept upon the same mattress that was waiting for me. Keeping within the convent bounds, where no woman is allowed to set her foot—that troublesome foot whose imprint may be found on most of the paths that lead to a Trappist monastery in the obscure forest of human motives—wandering beyond the buildings, but still within the enclosure, I came to a bit of waste land covered with heather and gorse that overlooked the wooded wilderness towards the west, as a headland bluff overlooks the sea.

The sun had set, and the wild spirits of the storm had drawn a translucent drapery of vapour from the dark thundercloud hovering overhead to where the fringe of the forest broke the blood-stained bar upon the horizon's verge, and this luminous orange-coloured curtain was crossed every moment upwards and downwards by silvery shafts of lightning. Such an effect of sunset combined with storm was like a new revelation of nature, and the sublimity of the spectacle would have held me fast to the patch of wild heath if the rain had not begun to fall in splashes. The long summer day was over, and the night came forth in trouble and with gushing tears. The roar of the thunder grew louder, and the flash of the lightning brightened every minute.

I returned to the monastery, and found the postulant quite anxious to have done with me, and to put me into the bishop's room. He was sleepy—everybody gets sleepy in these country places at about nine o'clock, irrespective of canonical hours, whereas I grow livelier, like a night-bird, as the dusk deepens. All the monks must have been in their cells snoring with the clear conscience which is the gift of the day that has been well filled up when I reluctantly entered the only room in the place that had any pretension to comfort, but which to me was like a prison. I was making an effort to acquire the virtue of resignation, when the postulant spoilt the mood by speaking again of beer. Had he picked up in his wanderings the notion that an Englishman could not live unless he were kept well supplied with beer, or had he formed an exaggerated idea of the seductiveness of the strange but innocent liquor that the Trappists brewed? Whatever his thoughts may have been, he darted away in spite of my endeavour to stop him, and presently reappeared with another black bottle. I knew that he had not obtained it without diplomacy, and that he had made my unquenchable thirst the excuse; but by this time I had perceived that his solicitude was not wholly unselfish. He muttered something about 'charity' as he filled a glass for me, notwithstanding my refusal; then vanished with the bottle. He had promised to wake me at two o'clock for matins.

When left alone, I made an inspection of the bishop's room. It was spacious enough for fifty people to dance in, and the furniture would not have been greatly in the way. The stones which made the floor had no carpet, not even the *descente de lit*, which in France is considered indispensable even when the floor is of wood. In the corner was a low wooden bedstead with dingy curtains suspended from a rafter, and a paillasse of maize-leaves with a thin wool mattress above it. Coarse hempen sheets and a coloured coverlet completed the bedding. By the side against the wall was a broad *prie-Dieu*, with

a lithograph just above it of the Holy Child bearing
the cross. A plain table in the centre without a
cloth, a *secrétaire* with high crucifix attached, another
bare table with washing-basin, jug, and folded towel,
with a few chairs and several religious prints, made
up the furniture.

This room was on the ground-floor, and looked
out upon a long covered terrace, with the farmyard
immediately beyond. I opened the sashes—I had
already prevailed upon the postulant not to fasten
the shutters—and, having blown out the candle, I
lit my pipe. I suppose if I had had any sense of
propriety I should have refrained from smoking in
the bishop's room; but what was I to do, a prisoner
there at nine o'clock in the evening, and not a bit
sleepy? If it had been a fine evening, I do not
think I could have resisted the temptation to jump
out of the window and to stroll back to the patch of
imprisoned moor. First a cat and then a great dog
came sneaking along, and I tried to get on friendly
terms with them from the window; but they, too,
seemed to have renounced the world, with all its
pomps and vanities, to conform to the Trappist rule,
for each of them looked at me with pity and reproach out of the corner of the eye, and described a
wide semicircle, at the risk of getting wet, in order
not to be drawn into conversation. But the storm,
at all events, had not been silenced; the thunder
growled and groaned, and every half-minute the
lightning lit up all the stones and puddles of the

great farmyard, beyond which my vision was cut off by the roofs of the outbuildings.

Notwithstanding the unpleasantness of being shut up, I felt that if the management of the weather had been left to me I could not have arranged things better for my first night in a Trappist monastery. Here I was in the midst of the desolation of the Double under the same roof with men who were driven into this shelter by the desolation of their souls. Tempest-tossed by the conflict of the spirit and the flesh, wounded, perhaps, by secret griefs and humiliations, strong, perchance, in the eyes of others, while never sure of themselves from one hour to another, putting out upon the same sea again and again only to be thrown back upon the same desert shore, they at length settled down here, and they must have done so with the calm conviction that they had found the medicine to suit their kind of sickness in a life of incessant punishment of self and labour for others.

It was about eleven when I felt tired enough to lie down. I had not been in this position long when something bit me. I thought I knew the enemy, but I dared not whisper its name even to myself, for I was overcome by its condescension. From a bishop to me was a fall in the social scale that ought to have made the most voracious insect tremble on the edge of the precipice. Maybe it did tremble before it yielded to temptation and forgot its dignity.

The storm continued all night with intervals of calm. A little before two o'clock the bell was rung for matins. The clang of the metal must have been heard clear and shrill far over the Double, even when the storm seemed to be rending the black sails of the clouds asunder. The postulant fetched me, as he had promised, and he led me through a labyrinth of passages to the church. Although the building was almost in darkness, I could see that it was in the Pointed style, and that it was marked by a cold elegance befitting its special purpose. The nave was divided near the middle by a Gothic screen of wood artistically carved, although the ornamental motive had been kept in subjection. The half that adjoined the sanctuary was somewhat higher than the other, and here the Trappist fathers had their stalls. The brothers' stalls were in the lower part. I was led to a place below the screen. The office had already commenced; the monotonous plain-chant by deep-toned voices had reached me in the corridors. Perhaps it was half an hour later when the chanting ceased. The lamps were darkened in the stalls above the screen—in the lower part there was but one very small light suspended from the vault—then the monks knelt each upon the narrow piece of wood affixed to his stall for this purpose, and for half an hour with heads bent down they prayed in silence, while the thunder groaned outside, and the lightning flashed through the clerestory windows. To the Trappists, who day after day, year after year, at the same hour had been going through the same part of their unchanging discipline, heedless whether the stars shone overhead or the lightning glittered, there was nothing in all this to draw their minds from the circle of devotional routine : I alone felt as if I was going down into my grave. The gray light that was now making the ribs of the vaulting dimly visible was like the dawn of eternity breaking through the brief night called Death, which is not perhaps so dark as it seems. At three o'clock the chill and awful silence was broken by the white-robed prior, who rose from his low posture like a dead man in his shroud, and began to chant in another tone and measure from what had gone before. It had in it the sadness of the wind that I heard moaning in the pine-tops on the moor before the storm broke. The voice was strong and clear, but so solemn that it was almost unearthly ; and it seemed in some strange way to mingle with the purity of the cold dawn that comes when all the passions of the world are still, but which makes the leaves tremble at the crime and trouble of another day.

When the prior stood up, the brothers left to begin their manual labour, each one in his allotted place. The fathers remained in their stalls until after the four o'clock mass, and then they, too, fell to work until six o'clock—the hour of prime. I soon followed the brothers, although not so far as the fields, the cheese-rooms, and farm-buildings. I returned to my room; but as I had to pass on the upper side of the screen on leaving the church, I looked at the two rows of white figures standing in their stalls. It may have been the effect of the mingled daylight and lamplight: whatever the reason, I thought during those few seconds that I had never before seen such a collection of strange and startling faces. They were those of sombre men who had walked through hell like Dante, and who bore upon their calm and corpse-like features the deep-cut traces of the flame and horror.

I took up my old place by the window, and watched in the twilight of morning an aged brother, with frock hitched up above his naked ankles and his feet in great *sabots*, fetch sack after sack of what I supposed to be bran, and carry it away on his shoulders. He passed close to me, and looked at me with an expression which I interpreted to mean: 'You must be a lunatic to stare at me instead of going to bed you, who have Monseigneur's soft bed, and are at liberty to sleep.' But no word passed between us. At length I did go to bed again, and slept.

I was awakened by a noise in my room, and on opening my eyes I saw a long figure in white two or three yards from me, and I realized that a Trappist father was watching me. Then, when he perceived that I was awake, he glided from the room without saying a word. Had I spoken, he would have replied, and explained what he wanted; but I had not recovered sufficiently from my surprise to remember the rule until he was gone. I now called to mind that the postulant had told me over-night that a certain father would show me round the monastery after prime. This, then, was he, and I was doubtless keeping him waiting, for it was seven o'clock. A few minutes later he returned. I was then at my ablutions.

Now, although I have grown pretty well accustomed to go through this daily duty with the aid of salad-bowls and slop-basins while living in the French provinces, I think it good for the mind to keep up the illusion of a thorough wash even when this is practically impossible. When, therefore, the Trappist stalked again into my room without giving me warning, his costume, simple as it was, was surpassed by the simplicity of mine. I told him that I would be with him in two or three minutes, and he retired with a slow and stately nod. I tried very hard to keep my word, for I expected every moment to see the door open again. When I opened it myself, I found the father pacing slowly in the passage. Knowing that there is not much to be had in a Trappist monastery without asking, I opened the conversation by making some delicate allusions to breakfast. The truth is that the bread-and-cheese supper was nothing to me now but an unsatisfactory recollection, and, with the sense of vacuum that distressed me, I was unwilling to follow the monk upon the promised round, lest I should die of inanition on the way. He asked me what I would like to eat, and I said, 'Anything that is near at hand.' Had I suggested that a chop or a steak would be suitable after so light a dinner, I should not have had it; but I might have received a large measure of silent reprobation for my bad taste in asking for it, and also for having reminded a Trappist of such vanities of the past.

The father—he was becoming fatherly indeed—went to a cupboard of the *salle à manger* already described, and brought out what I had left of the bread and cheese set before me the previous evening. Having placed this on the table, with a bottle of beer—the postulant had led me to hope for coffee and milk, but there was evidently no escape from malt liquor here—he withdrew to a little office close by where he was wont to perform the daily duty of keeping the cheese accounts of the monastery. I felt sure that when he had reckoned up a few figures he would be coming round to tear me away from the bread and cheese, so I endeavoured to hasten the consumption with as much speed as I could decently put on. I was right in my conjecture. I had not been seated five minutes, when he came back and wandered half round the table.

'*J'aurai fini dans un petit moment, mon père,*' said I, as I cut off another piece of cheese. By-the-bye, nobody should call a Trappist '*monsieur,*' because the monk has ceased to have even a name of his own other than his religious one, and has become a father or brother to everybody. He returned to his accounts; but he had not gone very deeply into them when he saw me standing at the door of his little den. He left his books at once, and we walked side by side where he chose to lead me. He was a rather tall man, with a face that was an enigma. The features were so like those of the late Mr. Charles Bradlaugh, that if the English Freethinker had disappeared mysteriously I might have strongly suspected him of having turned Trappist.

This father volunteered no information whatever; it had all to be drawn out of him. He spoke in a low voice, and, as it appeared to me, with something of the hesitation of a man who is recalling his mother tongue after many years of disuse. His face was large and heavy; but there was a keen light in his eyes which at times was that of gaiety well kept under. He soon let me see that even a Trappist may give out an occasional flash of humour. I was questioning him respecting the help that the monastery gave to the poor, and he told me that in addition to thirty or forty persons living in the locality who received regular assistance every day, about the same number of wanderers stopped at the gate and waited for the bread and cheese which was never refused them.

'Men looking for work?' I asked innocently.

'Yes,' replied the monk, without moving a muscle of his stolid face; 'and who pray to God that He will not give them any.'

It was evident that no sentimental illusions respecting the begging class were entertained by the community. The monk confirmed what people in the country had already told me of the help afforded by the Trappists to peasant agriculturists in difficulties. The sick were, moreover, supplied with medicines gratuitously from the small pharmacy attached to the monastery. I did not ask the question, but I concluded that at least one of the fathers had a medical diploma. The medicine that was chiefly wanted in the Double when the Trappists settled there was quinine. The demand upon it was very heavy years ago, but by removing to a great extent the cause of the fever-breeding miasma, the monks have been able to economize the drug.

Talking about these matters, we reached the refectory. A great cold room with whitewashed walls, and five long narrow tables with benches on each side, stretching from end to end, was the place where the monks took their very frugal meals. The tables were laid for the first meal. There were no cloths, and it is almost needless to add that there were no napkins, although these are considered so essential in France that even in the most wretched auberge one is usually laid before the guest. Trappists, however, have little need of them. At each place were a wooden spoon and fork, a plate, a jug of water, and another jug—a smaller one—of beer, and a porringer for soup, which is the chief of the Trappists' diet. Very thin soup it is, the ingredients being water, chopped vegetables, bread, and a little oil or butter. Until a few years ago no oily matter, whether vegetable or animal, was allowed in the soup, nor was it permissible, except in case of sickness, to have more than one meal a day; but the necessity of relaxing the rule a little was realized. Now, during the six summer months of the year, there are two meals a day, namely, at eleven and six; but in winter there is still only one that is called a meal, and this is at four. There is, however, a *goûter*—just something to keep the stomach from collapsing—at ten in the morning. No flesh, nor fish, nor animal product, except cheese and butter, is eaten by these Trappists unless they fall ill, and then they have meat or anything else that they may need to make them well. There is, however, very little sickness amongst them. The living of each Trappist probably costs no more than sixpence a day to the community. Assuming that the money brought into the common fund by those who have a private fortune—the fathers, as a rule, are men of some independent means—covers the establishment expenses and the taxation imposed by the State, there must remain a considerable profit on the work of each individual, whether he labours in the fields or in the dairy and cheese rooms, or concerns himself with the sales and the accounts, or, like the porter at the gate, tests with an instrument the richness of the milk that is brought in by the peasants, lest they who have been befriended by the monks in sickness and penury should steal from them in return. To devote this surplus, obtained by a life of sacrifice compared to which the material misery of the beggars whom they relieve is luxury, to the lessening of human suffering, to the encouragement of the family, offering the hand of charity to the worthy and to the unworthy—expecting no honour from all this, not even gratitude—is a life that makes that of the theoretical philanthropists and humanitarian philosophers look rather barren. Let every man who lives up to an unselfish ideal have full credit for it, whether he be a Trappist or a Buddhist.

At one end of the refectory, below the line of tables, was a small wooden bench for a single person. The monk pointed to it with half a smile upon his face.

'What is it?' I asked.

'The stool of penitence,' he replied.

Here the monk who had brought upon himself some disciplinary correction sat by order of the abbot in view of everybody, and had the extra mortification of watching the others eat, while he, the penitent, had nothing to put between his teeth. I wondered if my cicerone had ever been perched there, but I was not on such terms of familiarity with him that I could ask the question.

From the refectory we went to the dormitory, an oblong room with a passage down the middle, and cells on each side—about fifty altogether. They were very narrow, and were separated by lath and plaster partitions, only carried to the height of about six feet. These partitions, which had been whitewashed over, looked very fragile and dilapidated, and altogether the appearance of this great dormitory was wretched in the extreme. A glance into the interior of two or three of the cells deepened this impression. In each was a small wooden bedstead about a foot and a half high, with nothing upon it but a very thin paillasse, a black blanket (the colour of the wool), and a little bolster. Upon a nail hung a small cat-o'-nine-tails of knotted whipcord.

'How often do you administer to yourselves the discipline?' I asked.

'Every Friday,' said the monk.

To other questions that I put to him he replied that about ten members of the community were priests, and that fathers and brothers used the dormitory in common. There was no distinction between the two classes as regards the vows that were taken.

We passed into the cloisters, which were very plain, without any attempt at architectural ornament; but the garden that filled the centre of the quadrangle was carefully kept, and the many flowers there were evidently watered and otherwise tended by hands that were gentle to them. Then I asked if it was true that the members of the community, when they passed one another in their ordinary occupations, were allowed to break the rule of silence only to say, 'Remember death!'

'No,' replied the monk, 'it is a legend that originated with Chateaubriand.'

We reached the chapter-house, a plain room with benches along the walls and a case containing a small collection of books. I saw nothing of interest here excepting a genealogical tree of the order of Reformed Cistercians, called Trappists, showing its descent from the Abbey of Citeaux, and a portrait of Père Dom Sébastien, Abbot-General of the Trappists, who was a pontifical zouave before he put on the monastic habit.

I asked to see the cemetery, and was led to an uncultivated spot a little beyond the block of convent buildings. A small grassy enclosure, with a wooden paling round it, was the monks' burying-place. About twelve had died in the twenty-five years of the monastery's existence, but most of the graves looked recent. This was explained to me by the father, who actually smiled as he said:

'We who came here at the commencement are getting old now, and are following one another to the cemetery rather quickly.'

Wearers of the white frock and wearers of the brown frock were lying in perfect equality side by side as they happened to die, each having a small cross of white wood standing in the grass of his grave. I read: ' N. Raphaël, monachus——, natus ——, professus——, obiit——.' The dates I took no note of. With the exception of the name and the dates, the inscription on each cross was the same. And the name, it need scarcely be said, was the one taken in religion.

'Do you know one another's family names?' I asked of the living monk by my side, who appeared to have lapsed into meditation, thinking, perhaps, how far his place would be from the last on the line.

'As a rule we do not. There are only two or three monks here whose names I know.'

Lastly, I was taken to the farm buildings, where there were about fifty cows and one hundred pigs. A young brother, a novice, was busy, with his frock hitched up, cleaning out the pigsties. He was piously plying the shovel, but his face had not yet acquired an expression of perfect resignation. He was young, however, and perhaps he had been brought up in better society than that of pigs.

I was invited with much kindness and courtesy to stay until after the eleven o'clock meal; but, grateful as I felt to the Trappists for their bread and cheese and home-brewed beer, which had enabled me to sustain life for more than twelve hours, I was quite content with what I had received in that way. My curiosity being also satisfied, I gladly went forth into the wicked world again after exchanging a cordial farewell with the genial porter, who, when he caught sight of me returning to his lodge, looked sharply to see if the jar of beer was safe, and his mind being made easy on the point, he begged me to let him pour me out a glass. Then he gazed at me with round eyes of surprise and reproach when I declined the offer.

It was only a little past eight when I left the monastery. 'Ah,' I thought, as I felt the gentle glow of the early sunshine and breathed the fresh air of the wide world, 'there is time enough for me to become a Trappist.'

I continued on the road to Montpont. It was a sad and silent land over which I passed, with frequent crosses by the wayside, telling of the influence of the monks. The words, '*O crux, ave !*' met me amidst the heather and on the margin of lonely pools. I was now in the most forlorn part of the Double, where all around the eye rested upon forest, swamp, and moor. Not that I found it dismal : I drew delight from the lonesomeness, and revelled in the wildness of all things. Sunshine and flowers made the desert beautiful. The waysides were red with thyme or purple with heather, and the blooming lysimachia was like a belt of gold around the reedy pools. After walking some miles over this country, patches of maize, potatoes, and vines told me I was nearing a village. At length I came to one, and it was called St. Barthélemy. It was on the top of a bare chalky hill, and commanded an extensive view of the wasteful Double. It had a windblown, naked appearance, like many villages near the sea, although the ocean was still far from here. Moreover, there was a strange quietude—the stillness of a fever-stricken spot. The men and women looked undersized and prematurely old, and the children were pale and thin. Although the village was on a hill, the evil influence of the marshes reached it. I was told, however, that it had become much less unhealthy of late years. On the highest spot was a poor and plain little church, with a paddock-like cemetery on one side of it.

Although the hour was still early, I stopped for a meal at St. Barthélemy, for it seemed to me that I had been fasting a day or more. Choosing the only inn that looked promising, I sat down in a large room, where there were two long tables and a bed in one corner. The shutters of the windows were carefully closed to keep out the flies, and all the light that entered came through the chinks and cracks. In the South, people prefer to eat in semi-darkness rather than be tormented by flies. The only other person in the house was a young woman, and she was very uncouth. She may have held me in suspicion, for not a word would she say beyond what was rigorously necessary ; but, as she cooked much better than I had expected, I thought no ill of her. She gave me, after an *omelette au cerfeuil*, a *fricassée* of chicken, with very fair wine of the district, red and white. Dessert and coffee followed, and the charge was not much over a shilling.

As I left the village, I noticed upon a low building these words in large letters, '*Dépôt de Sangsues*,' and concluded that catching leeches in the pools about here was a local industry. On inquiring, however, I was told that such was not the case, but that a man here had had a quantity of leeches sent from Bordeaux to supply the district.

'But what is the meaning of this great liking for leeches?' I asked.

'Well,' replied my informant, 'I should tell you that the people about here always used to be bled when they had anything the matter with them. But the doctors will do it no longer, consequently we do it ourselves.'

The sad-looking peasants, with pale dark faces, whom I saw reaping their meagre wheat on the outskirts of the village, seemed, like many more I had met since I left Riberac, to be in much greater need of blood than leeches. Women, wearing straw-bonnets of the coal-scuttle shape, were reaping with men in the noonday heat. Upon all the burden of life appeared to press very heavily. The chalky soil produced miserable crops of wheat, maize, and potatoes that yielded no just return for the labour expended. The luxuriance of the young vines, planted where the old ones had perished from the phylloxera, showed that the hillsides here are better suited for wine-growing than for anything else.

As I went on, the country became more sombre from the increasing number of pines bordering the road and mingling with the distant forest. Very weird pines these were, chiefly covered with closely-packed dead foliage, with a living tuft of dark green at the end of each branchlet. A living death seemed to be their lot, and they moaned without moving as the light wind passed on its way.

But the descent towards the valley of the Isle had now begun. Huts built of brick and mud and wood became frequent, with hedges of quince bordering the gardens or little fields. Quite unexpectedly the river shone beneath me, and by following its course downward I soon came to a large block of scarcely connected buildings with high Mansard roofs. This was a monastery of the Carthusians. I did not recognise it at once as the conventual establishment well known in the district as the Chartreuse de Vauclaire, nor did I show any better understanding as regards a certain human form hoeing in a field beside the road with back towards me.

Wishing for information, I hailed this fellow-being as 'Madame!' The figure straightened itself immediately and turned towards me a head covered with a broad-brimmed straw hat, such as women wear in the fields; but the face ended in a long, grizzly beard. Then I noticed that what I had taken for a brown stuff dress was a monk's frock.

It was a Carthusian Brother whom I had addressed as 'Madame!' As he gave no sign to indicate what his feelings were with regard to this mistake, I thought it better not to make excuses, but asked him if I was on the road to Montpont

Learning that I was, I went on, and having reached the convent, which I now recognised for what it was, I pulled the bell of the porter's lodge. I was at once admitted to the presence of a tall and meagre Carthusian father, with a long, coal-black beard and very dark eyes, with a fixed expression that expressed nothing that I could be sure about. What I fancied that I read in them was doubtfulness as to my motives, and the necessity of being cautious.

By far the greater number of visitors who call here ask for food. I wished to see the monastery. After a little hesitation, this father, who before I left him was so communicative as to tell me he was a Spaniard, made a sign to me to follow him. He showed me the church—which contains some interesting carvings—the cloisters, and the cemetery; but every bit of information had to be drawn from him as if it were a tooth. This was the kind of conversation that passed between us :

'Are there many monks here?'
'Not a small number.'
'Do you make cheese?'
'Yes.'
'For sale?'
'No.'
'Do you make the *liqueur*?'
'Oh no.'

He would have allowed me to leave with the impression that the Carthusians of Vauclaire did nothing beyond observing the canonical hours ; but I learnt from the peasants of the country that, like the Trappists, they laboured industriously in clearing and draining the desert.

My walk across the Double ended at Montpont, a small agricultural centre on the banks of the Isle, offering no charm to the traveller, unless he be a commercial one. It was a little fortified town of some importance in the Middle Ages. In 1370 the Bretons in garrison at Périgueux besieged it, and it was surrendered without a struggle by the baron, Guillaume de Montpont, an English partisan. The Duke of Lancaster then hurried up and besieged the place with one hundred men-at-arms and five hundred archers. For eleven weeks the little band of Bretons held out, but a breach having been made in the wall, Montpont again fell into the power of the English.

THE DRONNE AT COUTRAS.

A CANOE VOYAGE ON THE DRONNE.

BEFORE starting upon a long-thought-of voyage down the Dronne, I resolved to make the canoe look as beautiful as possible, so that it might produce a favourable impression upon the natives of the regions through which it was going to pass. I had learnt from experience that when one can take the edge off suspicion by giving one's self or one's belongings a respectable appearance, that does not cost much, it is well to do it.

Therefore I sent the bare-footed Hélie, who always helped me when I had any dirty work on hand, to buy some paint. Having first puttied up all the cracks and crevices, we laid the paint on, and as the colour chosen was a very pale green, the effect was anything but vulgar. When the boat was put on the water again it looked like a floating willow-leaf of rather uncommon size.

Now, between the river Isle, where I was, and the Dronne, where I wished to be, there was an obstacle in the shape of some twelve miles of hilly country. A light cart was accordingly hired to convey the canoe and ourselves (I was accompanied on this adventure by an English boy named Hugh, sixteen years old, and just let loose from school) to the point at which I had decided to commence the voyage down-stream. We left at five in the morning, when the sun was gilding the yellow tufts and the motionless long leaves of the maize-field. When we were fairly off—the boat, in which we were seated, stretching many feet in the rear of the very small cart—the most anxious member of the party was the horse, for he had never carried such a queer load as this before, and the novelty of the sensation caused by the weight far behind completely upset his notions of propriety. His conduct was especially strange while going up-hill, for then he would stop short from time to time and make an effort to look round, as if uncertain whether it was all a hideous dream, or whether he was really growing out behind in the form of a crocodile.

The peasants whom we met on the road stood still and gazed with eyes and mouths wide open until we were out of sight. They had never seen people travelling in a boat before on dry land. When they heard we were English all was explained: '*Ces diables d'Anglais sont capables de tout.*'

While crossing the country in this fashion we passed a spot on the highroad where a man was getting ready to thresh his wheat. He had prepared the place by spreading over it a layer of cow-dung, and levelling it with his bare feet until it was quite smooth and hard. It is in this way that the threshing-floors are usually made.

'You see that *type?*' said the young man who was driving, and who balanced himself on the edge of a board.

'Yes.'

'Well, he owns more land than any other peasant about here, and is rich, and yet, rather than turn a bit of his ground into a threshing-floor, he brings his corn where you see him and threshes it upon the road.'

I said to myself that this man was not the first to discover that one way to get on is to trespass as much as possible upon the rights of that easy-going neighbour called the Public.

The hills between the two valleys were, for the

most part, wooded with natural forest, with a dense undergrowth of heather and gorse. As soon as we began to descend towards the Dronne, the great southern broom, six or eight feet high, was seen in splendid flower upon the roadside banks. We found the Dronne at the village of Tocane St. Apre, and we launched the boat below the mill about half a mile farther down-stream. Then, having put on board a knapsack containing clothes, a valise filled chiefly with provisions, several bottles of wine, one of rum (a safer spirit in France than some others), and another of black coffee, made very strong, so that it should last a long time, we took our first lunch in the boat, in the cool shade of some old alders.

The wine had been already heated by the sun during the journey, but the means of cooling it somewhat was near at hand. We hitched a couple of bottles to the roots of the alders, with their necks just out of the water. The young peasant who had driven us was invited to share our meal, and the horse was left at the mill with a good feed of oats to comfort him and help him to forget all the horrible suspicions that the boat had caused him. The meal was simple enough, for we had brought no luxurious fare with us; but the feeling of freedom and new adventure, the low song of the stream running over the gravel in the shallows, the peace and beauty of the little cove under the alders, made it more delightful than a sumptuous one with other surroundings.

Everything went as smoothly as the deep water where the boat was chained, until the spirit-lamp was lighted for warming the coffee. Then it was discovered that the little saucepan had been forgotten. This was trying, for when you have grown used to coffee after lunch you do not feel happy without it, so long as there is a chance of getting it. It is exasperating when you have the coffee ready made, but cannot warm it for want of a small utensil. The peasant went to the mill to borrow a saucepan, and he brought back one that was just what we wanted; at least, we thought so until the coffee began to run out through a hole in the bottom. In vain we tried to stop the leak with putty, which was brought in case the boat should spring one; but after awhile it stopped itself—quite miraculously. Thus good fortune came to our aid at the outset, and it looked like a fair omen of a prosperous voyage.

We did not linger too long over this meal, for I had not come prepared to pass the night either in the boat or on the grass, and I hoped to reach Riberac in the evening. The bottles were put away in the locker, and what was not eaten was returned to the valise. Then we parted company with the young peasant, whose private opinion was that we should not go very far. But he was mistaken; we went a long way, after encountering many serious obstacles, as will be seen by-and-by.

The chain being pulled in, the boat glided off

like the willow-leaf to which I have already compared it. I sat on my piece of sliding board about the middle, and Hugh sat on his piece of wood—which was the top of the locker—in the stern. We both used long double-bladed paddles. In a few seconds we were in the current, and in a few more were aground. Although the canoe was flat-bottomed, it needed at least three inches of water to float comfortably with us and the cargo. We were in a forest of reeds that hid the outer world from us, and we had left the true current for another that led us to the shallows. But this little difficulty was quickly overcome, and I soon convinced myself that, notwithstanding the dearth of water after the long drought, it was quite possible to descend the Dronne from St. Apre in a boat such as mine.

Now, as there was no wager to make me hurry, and my main purpose in giving myself all the trouble that lay before me was to see things, I put my paddle down, and leaving Hugh to work off some of his youthful ardour for navigation, I gave myself up for awhile to the spell of this most charming stream. Its breadth and its depth were constantly changing, and in a truly remarkable manner. Now it was scarcely wider than a brook might be, and was nearly over-arched by its alders and willows; now it widened out and sped in many a flashing runnel through a broad jungle of reeds where the blistering rays of the sun beat down with tropical ardour; then it slept in pools full of long green streamers that waved slowly like an Undine's hair. Here and there all about stood the waxen flowers of sagittaria above the barbed floating leaves, cool and darkly green. Close to the banks the tall and delicately branching water-plantains, on which great grasshoppers often hang their shed skins, were flecked with pale-pink blooms—flowers of biscuit-porcelain on hair-like stems.

The splashing of a water-wheel roused me from my idle humour. We had reached—much too quickly—our first mill-dam. It was a very primitive sort of dam, formed of stakes and planks, but chiefly of brambles, dead wood and reeds that had floated down and lodged there. Then began the tugging, pushing, and lifting, to be continued at irregular intervals for several days. The canoe was less than three feet wide in the middle, but it was more than six yards long, and this length, although it secured steadiness and greatly reduced the risk of capsizing in strong rapids or sinister eddies, brought the weight up to about 170 lb., without reckoning the baggage, which was turned out upon the grass or on the stones at each weir. After passing the first obstacle, we floated into one of those long deep pools which lend a peculiar charm to the Dronne. Usually covered in summer with white or yellow lilies—seldom the two species together—these and other plants that rejoice in the cool liquid depths show their scalloped or feathery forms with perfect distinctness far below the surface of the limpid water.

Here, O idle water-wanderer, let your boat glide with the scarcely moving current, and gaze upon the leafy groves of the sub-aqueous wilderness lit up by the rays of the sun, and watch the fish moving singly or in shoals at various depths—the bearded barbel, the spotted trout, the shimmering bream, and the bronzen tench. Watch, too, the speckled water-snakes gliding upon the gravel or lurking like the ancient serpent in mimic gardens of Eden. Mark all the varied life and wondrous beauty of nature there. Above all, do not hurry, for little is seen by those who hasten on.

At a weir of sticks and stones forming a rather wide dam, overgrown by tall hemp-agrimony now in flower, we met with our first difficulty. There was no overflow to help us, for in this time of drought the mill-wheel needed all the stream to turn it ; so the boat had to be lifted over the stakes and stones. Into the water we had to go, and boots and socks, being now put aside, were not worn again for five days, except when we went ashore in the evening, and had to make an effort to look respectable.

The dam being passed, the boat shot down a rapid current ; then, as the bed widened out and the water stilled, we were hidden from the world by reeds, through which we had to force a way while the sun smote us and frizzled us. Countless dragon-flies flashed their brilliant colours as they whirled and darted, green frogs plunged at our approach

from their diving-boards of matted rush, or quirked
defiance from the banks where they were safe; and
now and again a startled kingfisher showed us the
blue gleam of a wing above the brown maces of
the bulrushes and the high-hanging tassels of the
sedges.

The bell of an unseen church a long way off
sounded the mid-day angelus, and told that we had
not drifted so far as it appeared from the peopled
world. Leaving the reeds, we passed again into the
shade of alders that stretched their gnarled, fantastic
roots far over the babbling or dreaming water, and
thence again amongst the sunny reeds. And so the
hours went by, and there were no villages, or even
houses, to be seen, but the little rough mills beside
the slowly toiling wheel, which in most cases seemed
to be the only living thing there. Once, however,
there was a naked child, very brown, and as round
as a spider between the hips and the waist, playing
upon a flowery bank above the mother, who wore a
brilliant-coloured kerchief on her head, and who
knelt beside the water as she rinsed the little elf's
shirt. I thought the picture pretty enough to make
a note of it. This caused some contemptuous
surprise to my companion in the back of the boat—
not yet alive to the innocent cunning of the artist
and writer, for he asked me, in the descriptive
language of the British schoolboy:

'Are you going to stick down *that*?'

On we went, turning and turning, gliding into

nooks that seemed each more charming than the other, and having a constant succession of delightful surprises, interrupted only by the mill-dams, which were distressingly frequent.

The hot hours stole away or passed into the mellowness of evening, and the marsh-mallows that fringed the stream were looking coolly white when we drew near to Riberac. The water widened and deepened, and we met a pleasure-boat, vast and gaudy, recalling some picture of Queen Elizabeth's barge on the Thames. Under an awning sat a bevy of ladies in bright raiment, pleasant to look at, and in front of them were several young men valiantly rowing, or, rather, digging their short sculls into the water, as if they were trying to knock the brains out of some fluvial monsters endeavouring to capture the youth and loveliness under the awning.

Having reached that part of the river which was nearest Riberac, I had to find a place where the boat could be left, and where it would be safe from the enterprise of boys—a bad invention in all countries. It is just, however, to the French boy to say that he is not quite so fiendish out of doors as the English one ; but he makes things even by his conduct at home, where he conscientiously devotes his animal spirits to the destruction of his too-indulgent parents.

My difficulty was solved by a kind butcher, whose garden ran down to the water. He let me chain the boat to one of his trees, and he took our fowl, which was intended for lunch next day, and put it into his meat-safe—an excellent service, for the drainage of his slaughter-house, emptying into the river by the side of the boat, was enough to make even a live fowl lose its freshness in a single night. We were soon settled in a comfortable inn that prided itself, not without reason, upon its *cuisine*. Here we had a *friture* of gudgeons from the Dronne, which is famous throughout a wide region for the quality of these and other fish.

The next morning I bought a saucepan, a melon, and grapes—which were already ripe, although the date was the 9th August. Thus laden, we returned to the boat and to the kindly butcher, who gave us our fowl wrapped up, not in a newspaper as we had left it, but in a sheet of spotless white paper. Having refilled our bottles, some with water, others with wine, we parted from our hospitable acquaintance with pleasant words, and were afloat again before the hour of eight. We had a serious wetting at the first weir, but were dry again before we stopped to lunch. This time we landed, and chose our spot in a beautiful little meadow, where an alder cast its shade upon the bank. It was far from all habitations, but had the case been otherwise, there would have been no danger of our being disturbed by a voice from behind saying: 'You have no right to land here,' or, 'You are trespassing in this field.'

Now, this little meadow was, except where the

river ran by it, enclosed by a high hedge, just as one in England might be, and although it was some four hundred miles south of Paris, and the season had been exceptionally dry, the grass was brightly green. Just below us was the clear river, fringed with sedges, sprinkled all over with yellow lilies; beyond this were other meadows, and then rose towards the cloudless sky the line of wooded hills. There was a great quietude that nothing broke, save the splash of a rising fish and the chorus of grasshoppers in the sunny herbage. Here we stayed a good hour and warmed our coffee tranquilly in the new saucepan, which afterwards proved very useful for baling purposes. Then I smoked the pipe of peace, and felt tempted to tarry in this pleasant place; but Hugh roused me to action by talking of fishing.

A few minutes later we were again on our voyage. Not far below was another mill-dam of sticks and stones, and when this was passed the river widened so that it flowed round a little island covered with alders and purple loosestrife, and girt by a broad belt of white water-lilies. At the next weir, which was troublesome, we were helped by the miller and his brother, while a pretty young woman of about twenty, who stood with bare feet, short skirt, uncovered stays, open chemise, and a linen sun-bonnet of the pattern known in England, looked on with a fat baby in her arms. These helpful people refilled our water-bottles, and watched us with interest until we were out of sight.

Reeds again—innumerable reeds—through which we had to drag the canoe, for we had somehow lost the current. Arrow-head and prickly bur-reed, great rushes and sedges—a joy to the marsh botanist by the variety of their species—stood against us in serried phalanxes, saying: 'Union is strength; we are weak when alone, but altogether we will give you some work that you will remember.' And they did so before we left them behind. Now, above the lily-spotted water, deep and clear, showed a little cluster of houses on a low cliff, and below these, close to the river, an old pigeon-house with pointed roof.

To finish the picture, a narrow wooden bridge supported by poles stretching downward at all angles, like the legs of an ungainly insect, had been thrown across the stream. And here a great flock of geese, horrified at so unwonted an apparition as the pale green boat and the paddles in fantastic movement, were holding a hasty council of war, which we broke up before they came to a decision.

The flow of water in the river had been perceptibly increased by tributaries, and now, after each mill, the current was strong enough to take us down for a mile or two at a quick rate. The little boat danced gaily in the rapids. The great heat of the day had gone, and the light was waning, when we mistook an arm of the river for the main stream, and found ourselves at length in a little gully, very dim with overarching foliage, and where the sound of rushing water grew momentarily louder.

It was all one to Hugh whether he got turned out or not, but I had lived long enough not to like the vision of a roll in the stream at the end of the day, with baggage swamped, if not lost. Therefore I chained up the boat, and went to examine the rapids. I found the stream in great turmoil, where it rushed over hidden rocks, and in the centre was a wave about three feet high, that rose like a curve of clear green glass, but turned white with anger, and broke into furious foam, as it fell into the basin below. Having ascertained that the rock was sufficiently under water, I decided that we would take our chance in the current after turning out the baggage.

We kept right in the centre. It was an exciting moment as we touched the wave. The canoe made a bound upwards, then plunged into the boiling torrent below. A moment more and we were out of all risk. So swift was the passage that scarcely a gallon of water was taken in. Having put the baggage back, we continued our voyage towards the unknown, for I knew not whither this stream was going to take us. About a mile or two farther down, however, it joined the river, which here seemed very wide. It was marvellous to find that the brook of yesterday had grown to this; a circumstance to be explained, however, by the number of springs that rise in its bed.

The scene was beyond all description beautiful. The wooded banks, the calm water, the islands of reeds and sedges, the pure white lilies that scented the air and murmured softly as the boat brushed their snowy petals, were all stained with the blood of the dying sun. For a moment I saw the upper rim of the red disc between the trunks of two trees far away that seemed to grow taller and more sombre; then came the twilight with its purple tones.

The colours faded, darkness crept over the valley, and the water, losing its transparency, looked unfathomably deep, and mirrored with tenfold power all the fantastic gloom of the leaning alders, and the weird forms of the hoary willows. And there was no light or sound from any town or village, nor even from a lonely cottage. I had expected to reach at sundown the little town of Aubeterre, in the department of the Charente, but all ideas of distance based upon a map are absurdly within the mark when one follows the course of a winding river, and the information of the inhabitants is equally misleading, for they always calculate distances by the road.

When we reached the next weir there was very little light left, so, without attempting to pass it, we paddled down to the mill. It was kept by three brothers, who treated us with much kindness and attention. I learnt that we were not far from the village of Nabinaud in the Charente, where there was a small inn at which it would be possible to pass the night.

Aubeterre was still some miles off by water, and there were weirs to overcome. Tired out, with legs and feet scraped and scratched by stones and stumps, and smarting still more from sun-scorch, we were glad enough to find a sufficient reason for getting out of the boat here.

One of the brothers carried politeness so far—I saw from the importance of the mill that remuneration was not to be thought of—as to walk about a mile uphill in order to show the inn and to see us settled in it. Then he left, for I could not prevail upon him to sit down and chink glasses. It was but a cottage-inn on the open hillside, and I doubt if the simple-minded people who kept it would have accepted us for the night but for the introduction. Husband and wife gave up their room to us, and where they went themselves I could not guess, unless it was to the loft or fowl-house. They were surprised, almost overcome, by the invasion, the like of which had never happened to them before; but they showed plenty of goodwill.

All that could be produced in the way of dinner was an omelet, some fried ham, very fat and salt, and some *grillons*—a name given to the residue that is left by pork-fat when it has been slowly boiled down to make lard. The people of Guyenne think much of their *grillons* or *fritons*. I remember a jovial-faced innkeeper of the South telling me that he and several members of his family went to Paris in a party to see the Exhibition of 1889, and that they took with them *grillons* enough to keep them going for a week, with the help of bread and wine, which they were compelled to buy of the

Parisians. Had they done all that their provincial ideas of prudence dictated, they would have taken with them everything that was necessary to the sustenance of the body during their absence from home.

The best part of our meal must not be forgotten; it was salad, fresh-plucked from the little garden enclosed by a paling, well mixed with nut-oil, wine-vinegar, and salt. Then for dessert there was abundance of grapes and peaches.

The little room in which we slept, or, to speak more correctly, where I tried to sleep, had no ornament except the Sunday clothes of the innkeeper and his wife hanging against the walls. Next to it was the pigsty, as the inmates took care to let me know by their grunting. Had I wished to escape in the night without paying the bill, nothing would have been easier, for the window looked upon a field that was about two feet below the sill.

I opened this window wide to feel the cool air, and long after Hugh went to sleep, with the willingness of his sixteen years, I sat listening to the crickets and watching the quiet fields and sky, which were lit up every few seconds by the lightning flash of an approaching storm—still too far away, however, to blur even with a cloudy line the tranquil brilliancy of the stars.

Leaving the window open, I lay down upon the outer edge of the bed, but to no purpose. In the first place, I am never happy on the edge of a narrow bed, and then sleep and I were on bad terms that night. The lightning, growing stronger, showed my host's best trousers hanging against the whitewashed wall, and from the pigsty came indignant snorts in answer to the deepening moan of the thunder; but the crickets of the house sang after their fashion of the hearth and home, and those outside of the great joy of idleness in the summer fields. From a bit of hedge or old wall came now and then the clear note of a fairy-bell rung by a goblin toad.

I lit the candle again, and elfish moths, with specks of burning charcoal for eyes, dashed at me or whirled and spun about the flame. One was a most delicately-beautiful small creature, with long white wings stained with pink. Thus I spent the night, looking at the sights and listening to the sounds of nature; which is better than to lie with closed eyes quarrelling with one's own brain.

We left with a boy carrying a basket of grapes and peaches, also wine to refill the empty bottles in the boat. On my way down the hill, I stopped at the ruin of a mediæval castle that belonged to Poltrot de Méré, the assassin of the Duc de Guise. All this country of the Angoumois, even more than Périgord, is full of the history of the religious wars of the sixteenth century. The whole of the southwestern region of France might be termed the classic ground of atrocities committed in the name of religion. Simon de Montfort's Crusaders and the Albigenses, after them the Huguenots and the

Leaguers, have so thickly sown this land with the seed of blood, to bear witness through all time to their merciless savagery, that the unprejudiced mind, looking here for traces of a grand struggle of ideals, will find little or nothing but the records of revolting brutality.

There is nothing left of Poltrot de Méré's stronghold but a few fragments of wall much overgrown with ivy and brambles. In order to get a close view of these I had to ask permission of the owner of the land—an elderly man, who looked at me with a troubled eye, and while he wished to be polite, considered it his duty to question me concerning my 'quality' and motives. I knew what was in his mind: a foreigner, a spy perchance, was going about the country, taking notes of fortified places.

It was true that this fortress, nearly hidden by vegetation, was no longer in a state to withstand a long siege, but who could tell what importance it might have in the eyes of a foreign Power traditionally credited with a large appetite for other people's property? However, he was not an ill-natured man, and when I had talked to him a bit, he moved his hand towards the ruin with quite a noble gesture, and told me that I was free to do there anything I liked. Had I been a snake-catcher, I might have done a good deal there.

We were afloat again before the sun had begun to warm an apple's ruddy cheek; but already the white lips of the water-lilies were wide-parted, as

the boat slid past or through their colonies upon the
reedy river. We glided under brambled banks,
overtrailed with the wild vine; then the current
took us round and about many an islet of reeds and
rushes where the common *phragmites* stood ten or
twelve feet high; and now by other banks all
tangled with willow-herb, marsh-mallow, and loosestrife. Over the clear water, and the wildernesses
of reeds and flowers, lay the mild splendour of the
morning sunshine. But the blissful minutes passed
too quickly; all the tones brightened to brilliancy,
and by ten o'clock the rays were striking down
again with torrid ardour.

We had lunched amongst the reeds under a
clump of alders, and were paddling on again, when
the massive walls and tower of a vast fortress of old
time appeared upon the top of a steep hill, rising
above all other hills that were visible, and at the
foot of the castle rock were many red roofs of houses
that seemed to be nestled pleasantly in a spacious
grove of trees. Above all was the dazzling blue of
the sky. A truly southern picture, flaming with
shadeless colour, and glittering with intense whiteness. We were reaching Aubeterre.

We beached the canoe beside a meadow, opposite
a spot where about twenty women were washing
clothes, their noses very near the water. They were
mightily surprised to see us suddenly arrive in our
swift boat. All the heads came up together, and
the rest went down.

We walked into a riverside inn, and there I made friends with the innkeeper over one or two bottles of beer—there was an innocent liquor so called on sale at Aubeterre. The *aubergiste* was rather down on his luck, for some mill at which he had been employed had gone wrong financially, and the wheels thought it no longer worth while to turn round. He therefore undertook to show us the way to everything that ought to be seen at Aubeterre.

He led us up a steep winding road where the sun smote furiously, where there was no shade, and where the dust was so hot that it might have roasted an egg, if the person waiting for it was in no great hurry. We had gone a very little way, when Hugh proposed to return and mount guard over the boat, for whose safety he had become unreasonably anxious. On reaching the steep little town there was more shade, because the streets were narrow, but the rough pitching of cobble-stones was very bad for feet so sore as ours, and so swollen that the boots into which we managed to force them before leaving the river were now several sizes too small.

We stopped at the parish church, but not so long as I should have, had I been a lonely wayfarer without anybody to guide me. It is a delightful example of a Romanesque style that is found much repeated in Périgord, Angoumois, and the Bordelais. The great interest lies in the façade, which dates from the eleventh century. Here we have a large central portal, and on each side of it, what the architectural design supposes to be a smaller one, but which in reality is only a sham doorway. The slender columns of the jambs, and the archivolts filled in with little figures, sacred, fantastic, and grotesque, are there, as in connection with the central arch; but all this has only an ornamental purpose. The spectator who is at all interested in ecclesiastical architecture will examine with much delight the elaborate mouldings and the strangely-suggestive forms of men, beasts, birds, shapes fantastic and chimerical, which ornament these Romanesque doorways.

But this church has not the interest of singularity which belongs to another at Aubeterre—that of St. John. It is, or was, truly a church, and yet it is not an edifice. Like one at St. Emilion, it is monolithic in the sense that those who made it worked upon the solid rock with pick, hammer, and chisel; in which way they quarried out a great nave with a rough apse terminating in the very bowels of the hill. On one side of the nave, enough has been left of the rock to form four immense polygonal piers, whose upper part is lost to sight in the gloom, until the eye grows somewhat reconciled to the glimmer of day, which, stealing in through openings in the cliff, is drowned in darkness before it reaches the hollow of the apse. On the opposite side is a high gallery cut in the rock in imitation of the triforium gallery. The row of piers separates the church proper from what was for centuries the cemetery of Aubeterre: a vast burrow made by the living for the reception of the dead, where they were plunged out of the sunlight teeming with earthly illusion and phantasy, to await the breaking of the great dawn.

Not a spring violet nor a gaudy flower of summer gave to the air the perfume, or to the earth the colour of sweet life, to soothe and lighten the dreariness of the dead: such thoughts in the Middle Ages would have been almost pagan. Then the darkness of death was like the darkness of night here in this necropolis hewn in the side of the ancient rock, whose very substance is made up chiefly of other and older forms of life. Moreover, the hope that was then so firmly fixed beyond the grave was the hope of rest—everlasting repose—after so much tossing and battling upon the sea of life. The palmer dying of weariness by the wayside, and the Crusader of his wounds upon the blood-soaked sand, could imagine no more blessed reward from the '*dols sire Jhésu*' for all their sacrifice of sleep, and other pain endured for their souls' sake, than a 'bed in paradise.' To me it seemed that had I lived seven centuries ago, I should, when dying, have been so weak as to beg my friends not to lay my body in the awful gloom of this sepulchral cavern, there to remain until the end of time. But the mediæval mind, having better faith, appeared to be moved by no such solicitude for the lifeless body.

If there are ghostly people who haunt the earth, and have their meeting-places for unholy revel, what a playground this must be for them at the witching hour! It is enough to make one's hair stand on end to think of what may go on there when the sinking moon looks haggard, and the owls hoot from the abandoned halls open to the sky of the great ruin above. The burying went on within the rock until thirty years ago, and the skulls that grin there in the light of the visitor's candle, and all the other bones that have been dug up and thrown in heaps, would fill several waggons. It was with no regret that I went out into the hot and brilliant air, and left for ever these gloomy vaults, with their dismal human relics and that penetrating odour of the earth that once moved and spoke, which dwells in every ancient charnel-house.

Now we climbed to the top of the calcareous and chalky hill and made the round of the castle wall. We could not enter, because by ill-luck the owner had gone away, and had not left the keys with anybody. This was especially disappointing to me, because my imagination had been worked upon by the stories I had heard of the subterranean passages leading from this fifteenth-century stronghold far under the hill, and which had not been thoroughly explored since the castle was abandoned. The innkeeper assured me that during an exploration that was being made in one of them the candles went out, and that nobody had attempted again to reach the end of the mysterious gallery.

I may observe here that people in this part of France have such a strong horror of passages underground, which they commonly believe to be inhabited by snakes and toads—an abomination to them—that it is just possible the candles of which the *aubergiste* spoke may have been put out by the superior brilliancy of the meridional imagination.

The time spent in this interesting little town that lies quite off all beaten tracks made the prospect of arriving that night at St. Aulaye, the next place by the river, look rather doubtful. We re-started, however, with the knowledge that we had still several hours of daylight before us. The voyage now became more exciting, and likewise more fatiguing. Mills were numerous, and the weirs changed completely in character. The simple dam of sticks and stones, with a drop of only two or three feet on the lower side, disappeared, and in its place we had a high well-built weir, with a fall of eight or ten feet. Fortunately, there was generally enough water running over to help us, and not enough to threaten shipwreck. The manœuvre, however, had to be quite altered. The boat had to be thrust or drawn forward until it hung several feet over the edge of the weir, then a quick push sent it down stern first into the water, while I held the chain, which was fastened to the other end. Then Hugh, saucepan in hand, let himself down by the chain, sometimes in a cascade, and baled out the water taken in. Finally, when all the traps had been collected from the dry places where they had been laid and were handed down, I had to get into the boat and bring the chain with me. It was a movement that had to be learnt before it could be done gracefully and surely, and at the second weir of this kind, where there was a considerable rush of water, in stepping on board I lost my balance, and rolled into the river. It was, however, not the first bath that I had received in my clothes since starting upon this expedition, and the inconvenience of being wet to the skin was now one that troubled neither of us much. We were dry again in two hours, if no similar misadventure happened in the meantime.

It was an afternoon full of misfortune. We lost the spirit-lamp and the best dinner knife, and, what was far more precious to me, the most companionable of sticks—one that had walked with me hundreds of miles. It was once a young oak growing upon the stony *causse*. A friendly baker hardened it over the embers of his oven, and a cunning blacksmith put a beautiful spike at one end of it, which became the terror of dogs throughout Guyenne.

Evening stole quietly upon us with a stormy yellow glow; then little clouds turned crimson overhead. Onward went the boat through the reeds in the rosy light, onward over the purpling water. It was nearly night when we caught sight of the houses of St. Aulaye upon a hill.

Presently the wailing of water was heard, by which we knew that another weir was near. Instead of trying to pass it, we went on down the mill-stream, my intention being to leave the canoe with the miller and walk to the town.

Now the gentle miller, after accepting the custody of the boat, held a rapid consultation with his wife on the threshold of his dwelling, and as we were moving off to look for a hostelry, he limped up to me—he had a leg that seemed as stiff as a post—and said:

'If *ces messieurs* would like to stop here to-night, we will do our best for them. We have little to offer, for we do not keep an inn, and are only simple people; but *ces messieurs* are tired perhaps, and would rather stay near their boat.'

Although it was dark, I quite realized what a disreputable figure I made, with my bare red feet, muddy flannels, and my straw hat, which, after taking many baths and being dried as often by the sun, had come to have the shape of almost everything but a hat. I had, therefore, grave doubts of my ability to inspire any respectable innkeeper with confidence, and I resolved at once to accept the offer that had been so unexpectedly made.

The spot where we were to pass the night was decidedly sombre, for there were trees around that cast a dark shadow, and there was the incessant cry of unseen, troubled water; but from the open door of the low house that adjoined the mill there flashed a warm light, and, as we entered, there was the sight, which is ever grateful to the tired wanderer, of freshly-piled sticks blazing upon the hearth. The room was large, and the flickering oil-lamp would have left it mostly in shadow had it not been helped by the flame of the fire. The walls were dark from smoke and long usage, for this was a very old mill. There was no sign of plenty, save the chunks of fat bacon which hung from the grimy rafters. There were several children, and one of them, almost a young woman, went out with a basket to buy us some meat. We had not a very choice meal, but it was a solid one. It commenced with a big tureen of country soup, made of all things, but chiefly of bread, and which Hugh, with his ideas newly-shaped in English moulds, described as 'stodgey.' Then came an omelet, a piece of veal, and a dish of gudgeons. I am sorry to add that these most amusing little bearded fish were dropped all alive into the boiling nut-oil.

Although our bedroom was immediately overhead, we had to pass through the mill to reach it, and the journey was a roundabout one. The lame miller was our guide, and on our way we learnt the cause of his lameness. About a year before he had been caught up by some of his machinery and mangled in a frightful manner. We came to a brick wall plastered over, and a little below a shaft that ran through it was a ragged hole nearly three feet in diameter.

Said the miller : ' You see that hole?'

' Yes.'

' You wouldn't think a man's body could make that? Mine did : and all those dark splashes on the plaster are the marks of my blood !'

The poor fellow had been brought within a hair's-breadth of death, and the long months during which he could do nothing but lie down or sit in a heap after his accident had, he said, nearly ruined him.

This night, although we had but one room, we had two beds. I lingered at the open window, and watched the swiftly-running mill-stream a few feet below. It had an evil sound. Then I felt the bad power that lies in water ; above all, its treachery. Had not this small stream, by lending its strength to a wheel that turned other wheels, taken up a man as if he were a feather, and dashed him through a wall? When the morning light and sunshine returned, the chant of the running water was as soothing as the song of birds.

We contrived, after infinite torture, to put on our boots again, and then walked up the hill to the village-like town. Besides the church of mixed Romanesque and Gothic, there was nothing worth seeing there, unless the spectacle of a woman holding up a rabbit by the hind-legs, while her daughter, a tender-hearted damsel of about sixteen, whacked it behind the ears with a fire-shovel, may be thought improving to the mind. At a shop where we bought some things, Hugh was deeply offended by a woman who insisted that some rather small bathing-drawers were large enough for him, and especially for speaking of him as the *petit garçon*. He talked about her 'cheek' all the way back to the boat. It was on returning that I noticed the picturesque charm of our mill, with the old Gothic bridge adjoining it, a weather-beaten, time-worn stone cross rising from the parapet. Fresh provisions having been put on board the boat, we wished our friends of the mill good-bye. They and their children, with about a dozen neighbours and their children, assembled upon the bank to see us off. A long line of dancing rapids lay in front of us, so that we were really able to astonish the people by the speed at which we went away where any boat of the Dronne would have quickly gone aground. In a few minutes the strong current had carried us a mile, and then, looking back, we saw the little crowd still gazing at us. A turn of the stream, and they had lost sight of us for ever.

Under the next mill-dam was some deep water free from reeds and weeds. On the banks were tall trees; behind us was the rocky weir, over which the stream fell in a thousand little rivulets and runnels, and less than a hundred yards in front rose the seemingly impenetrable reedy forest. The spot so enclosed had a quiet beauty that would have been holy in days gone by when the mind of man peopled such solitudes with fluvial deities. Here the desire to swim became irresistible. What a swim it was! The water was only cold enough to be refreshing, while its transparency was such that even where it was eight or ten feet deep every detail could be seen along the gravelly bottom, where the gudgeons gambolled. After the bath we paddled until we saw a very shady meadow-corner close to the water. Here we spread out upon the grass eggs that had been boiled for us at the mill, bread, cheese, grapes, and pears, and what other provisions we had. Now and again the wind carried to us the sound of water turning some hidden, lazy wheel. Those who would prefer a well-served lunch in a comfortable room to our simple meal in the meadow-corner under the rustling leaves should never go on a voyage down the Dronne.

Some time in the afternoon we came to a broad weir that was rather difficult to pass, for there was no water running over, and a dense vegetation had sprung up during the summer between the rough stones. The miller saw us from the other end of his dam, which was a rather long way off, for these weirs do not cross at right angles with the banks, but start at a very obtuse one at a point far above the mill. After a little hesitation, inspired by doubtfulness as to what manner of beings we were, he came towards us over the stones and through the water-plants with a bog-trotting movement which we, who had scraped most of the skin off our own bare ankles, quite understood.

He was a rough but good fellow, and he lent us a helping hand, which was needed, for every time we lifted the boat now it seemed heavier than it was before. The hard work was telling upon us. The sound of voices caused another head to appear on the scene. It came up from the other side of the weir, and it was a cunning old head, with sharp little eyes under bushy gray brows, overhanging like penthouses. Presently the body followed the head, and the old man began to talk to the miller in patois, but failing, apparently, to make any impression upon him, he addressed me in very bad French.

'Why give yourselves the devil's trouble,' said he, 'in pulling the boat over here, when there is a beautiful place at the other end of the *barrage*, where you can go down with the current? The water is a bit jumpy, but there is nothing to fear.'

For a moment I hesitated, but I saw the miller shake his head; and this decided me to cross at the spot where we were. The old man looked on with an expression that was not benevolent, and when the boat was ready to be dropped on the other side, the motive of his anxiety to send us down a waterfall came out. He had spread a long net here in amongst the reeds, and he did not wish us to spoil his fishing.

When we got below the mill we saw the water that was not wanted for the wheel, tumbling in fury down a steep, narrow channel, in which were set various poles and cross-beams. And it was down this villainous *diversoir* that the old rascal would have sent us, knowing that we should have come to grief there. The boat would almost certainly have struck some obstacle and been overturned by the current.

Sometimes people rushed from the fields where they were working to the banks to watch us. Dark men, with bare chests, and as hairy as monkeys; women, likewise a good deal bare, with heads covered by great sun-bonnets, and children burnt by the sun to the colour of young Arabs, stood and gazed speechless with astonishment. Who were we in this strange-looking boat that went so fast, and whence had we come? They knew that we must have come a long, long way; but, how did we do it? How did we get over the *barrages?* These were the thoughts that puzzled them. No boat had ever been known to treat the obstacles of the Dronne in this jaunty fashion before.

Several more weirs were passed; one with great difficulty, for the canoe had to be dragged and jolted thirty or forty yards through the corner of a wood. Then the evening fell again when we were following the windings of a swift current that ran now to the right and now to the left of what seemed to be a broad marsh covered with reeds and sedges. Sometimes the current carried us into banks gloomy with drooping alders, or densely fringed with brambles. When I heard squeals behind, I knew that Hugh was diving through a blackberry-bush, or a hanging garden of briars.

I was sorry for him; but my business was to keep the canoe's head in the centre of the current, and leave the stern to follow as it might. At every sudden turning Hugh became exceedingly watchful; but in spite of his steering the stern would often swing round into the bank, and then there was nothing for him to do but to duck his head as low as he could, and try to leave as little as possible of his ears upon the brambles. Before the end of this day he gave signs of restlessness and discontent.

Our stopping-place to-night was to be La Roche Chalais, a rather important village, just within the department of the Dordogne. We still seemed to be far from it, notwithstanding all the haste we had made. While the air and water were glowing with the last flush of twilight, myriads of swallows, already on their passage from the north, spotted the clear sky, and settled down upon the alders to pass the night. At our approach they rose again, and filled the solitude with the whirr of their wings. We likewise disturbed from the alders great multitudes of sparrows that had become gregarious. They stayed in the trees until the boat was about twenty yards from them, and then rose with the noise of a storm-wind beating the leaves. One of the charms of this waterfaring is, that you never know what surprise the angle of a river may bring. Very tired, and rather down at heart, we turned a bend and saw in front of us a clear placid reach, on which the reds and purples were serenely dying, and at a distance of about half a mile, a fine bridge with the large central arch forming with its reflection in the water a perfect ellipse.

On the left of the bridge was a wooded cliff, the edges of the trees vaguely passing into one another and the purple mist, and above them all, against the warmly-fading sky was the spire of a church. That, said I, can be no other than the church of La Roche Chalais; and so it turned out.

There was a large mill below the bridge, where we met with much politeness, and where our boat was taken charge of. Here we were told there was a good hotel at La Roche, and we set off to find it. But how did we set off? With bare feet, carrying our boots in our hands, and looking the veriest scarecrows after our four days of amphibious life. We had tried to put on our boots, but vainly, for they had been flooded. Now, this was the chief cause of the unpleasantness that soon befell us, for no pilgrims ever had more disgraceful-looking feet than ours. Fortunately it was nearly dark, and the people whom we met did not examine us very attentively. Moreover, they saw bare feet on the road and in the street every day of their lives during the summer.

At the inn, however, our appearance made an instantaneously bad impression. It was the most important hotel in a considerable district. It lay in the beat of many commercial travellers—men who never go about with bare feet, or in dirty flannel and battered straw hats, but are always dressed beautifully. We walked straight into the house, with that perfect composure which the French say is distinctly British, and sudden consternation fell upon the people there. Two elderly ladies, sister hotel-keepers—one of whom had a rather strongly-marked moustache, for which, of course, poor woman, she was not responsible—came out of the kitchen, and stood in the passage fronting us. It was not to welcome us to their hostelry, but to prevent us penetrating any farther, that they took up this position.

'Mesdames,' said I, 'we want rooms, if you please, to-night, and also dinner.'

'Monsieur,' replied the lady with the moustache, 'I am sorry, but—but—all our rooms are occupied.'

'You are afraid of us, madame?'

'Yes, monsieur, I am.'

This I thought very frank indeed; and I was turning over in my mind what I had better say next, when she continued:

'We never take travellers without baggage.'

'But,' said I, holding out my knapsack in one hand, and my boots in the other, 'I have baggage.'

Perceiving that the expression did not change, I added:

'I have also a boat.'

'A boat!'

'Yes, a boat.'

'Where is it?'

'On the river. I have left it at the mill just below here. We have come from St. Apre.'

'St. Apre! And where are you going?'

'To Coutras, I hope.'

By this time several persons who had collected in the passage and the kitchen were grinning from ear to ear. I felt that all eyes were fixed upon my red feet, and not liking the situation, I resolved to end it.

'As you are afraid, I will give you my card.' So saying, I pushed my way into the *salle à manger*, and pulled out a card, which, marvellous to say, I had managed to keep dry. Now, the card itself conveyed nothing of importance to anybody. It was the manner of saying, 'I will give you my card,' together with the movement that meant, 'I am here, and I intend to stop,' that broke down the resolution of the two women to turn us from their door.

Their confidence gradually came, and they gave us a very good dinner, notwithstanding the lateness of the hour. We had comfortable beds, too, and the next morning we got our feet into our boots. We bought our provisions for the day at the inn, and to avoid the curiosity of the natives, we escaped by a back way, and hobbled down to the boat through a rocky field.

The stream was strong for a few miles below the mill at La Roche. The canoe went down by itself fast enough, but the water had to be watched carefully, for the bed was strewn with rocks. Sometimes we shot over blocks of limestone that were only three or four inches below the surface. We could not be sure from one minute to another that our rapid flight would not meet with a sudden check. In this excitement of uncertainty there was true pleasure. We chose our first spot for bathing where the current was strong, and had our second swim in a wide and beautiful pool, where the table-like rocks, smooth and polished, could be seen ten or twelve feet below the surface. Then having spread out our provisions once more on the river bank in a nook that seemed to be far from village, or even homestead, we had an unpleasant surprise. About a dozen boys, on their way home from some hidden school, suddenly appeared round a wooded corner, and after being brought to a momentary standstill by their own astonishment, made straight towards us. Having examined the canoe with much curiosity, they sat down in a half-circle just behind us, with minds evidently made up to wait and see us off. They watched us through our meal with much interest, and made jokes in patois at our expense. They were not, however, so boldly bad as many boys, and there was no sufficient reason to drive them away. Moreover, they may have had a better right to be there than we. The field may have belonged to the father of one of them. I suggested to them that their mothers might be anxious, if not angry, on account of their loitering; but they were not to be moved by any such reminders. They had made up their minds to see us off, and this they did, to their great delight and entertainment.

The river was charming, with its myriads of white water-lilies and forests of reeds. Once it spread out into a lake, in which was a little island covered with tall bulrushes and purple loosestrife. But although there was so much pleasure for the eye, the afternoon was one of suffering. We were blistering from the heat of the sun, and our bottles being emptied, we were tormented with thirst. It was true that there was plenty of water always within reach; but it had already run past a good many villages and small towns, and, moreover, it was tepid. After leaving La Roche Chalais the river had on its left bank the department of the Dordogne, and on its right the Charente Inférieure. Rather late in the afternoon we entered the Gironde, and soon afterwards heard the familiar sound of women beating linen with their *battoirs* by the side of the water. We came upon a crowd of them, and learnt from them that the village of Les Eglisottes was close by. Having obtained here both water and white wine, we were able to continue the voyage in better spirits.

This fifth and last day on the Dronne was the most trying of all. The distance may not have been more than twenty-five miles, but we were very jaded. There were few weirs, but some of them were not easy to pass. Then the boat from time to time had to be dragged a long way through reeds, where there was not enough water to float it. For eight or nine hours the sun raged above us; but the cool evening came at length—about the time that we passed the last mill. The river was broad and deep, and I thought that we could not be far from Coutras; but long reaches succeeded one another, and the great forests of the Double on the left seemed as if they would never end.

The river is now running—or, rather, creeping, for it has lost its current—under densely-wooded hills, and the water is deeply dyed with interflowing tints of green and gold. These fade, and in the gathering darkness without a moon the silent Dronne grows very sombre. The boat must have received an exceptionally hard knock at the last weir, for we feel the water rising about our feet. The wonder is that our frail craft has taken its five days' bumping over stumps and stones so well. It would be very annoying if it were to sink with us now that we are so near the end of our voyage. But is the end so near? We scan the distance in front of us in search of twinkling lights, but the only twinkle comes from a brightening star. We see the long wan line of water, marked with awful shadows near the banks, from which, too, half-submerged trees, long since dead, lift strange arms or stretch out long necks and goblin heads that seem to mock and jibe at us in this fashion: 'Ha! ha!

you are going down! We'll drag you under!' And the interminable black forest stretches away, away, always in front, until it is lost in the dusky sky.

Ah, there is a sound at length to break the monotonous dip, dip of the paddles, and it is a sweet sound too. It is the angelus; there is no mistaking it. It is very faint, but it puts fresh strength into our arms, and revives the hope that this river will lead us somewhere.

It led us to Coutras. There at about nine o'clock we beached the half water-logged canoe not far above the spot to which the tide rises from the broad Atlantic. We felt that we had had quite enough waterfaring to satisfy us for the present. We had voyaged about eighty miles, and passed about forty weirs.

BY THE LOWER DORDOGNE.

A STREET AT
ST. ÉMILION.

THE nooks and corners where great men of the past spent their lives quietly and thoughtfully often lie far enough from the beaten ways to provide the romantic tramp with a motive that he may need to excuse his singularity in faring on foot over a tract of country which lacks the kind of picturesqueness that would mark it out as a territory to be annexed by the tourist sooner or later. Having found myself, almost unexpectedly, in the district of Michel de Montaigne, after crossing the Double, I reckoned that less than a day's quiet walking would bring me to the village of St. Michel-Bonnefare — better known in the region as St. Michel-Montaigne (pronounced there Montagne, as the name was originally spelt), close to the castle or manor-house where the contemplative Périgourdin gentleman was born, and where he wrote his ' Essays ' in a tower, of which he has left a detailed description. Then there was another lure : the battle-field of Castillon, a few miles farther south, where the heroic Talbot was slain, and where the cannon that fired the fatal stone announced the end of the feudal ages. We may travel over the whole world of literature without going beyond our house and garden. Even the blind may read, and thus bring back to themselves the life of the past; but how the indolent mind is helped when spurred by the eye's impressions! The eye awakens ideas that might otherwise sleep on for ever, by looking at scenes filled with the living interest of a Montaigne or a Talbot.

I might have got to within four miles or thereabouts of the Castle of Montaigne, by using the railroad that runs up the valley of the Lower Dordogne, but I preferred to start on foot from Montpont. This manner of travelling is very old-fashioned, but it will always possess a certain charm for two classes of people : habitual vagabonds who beg and are freely accused of stealing, and the literary, artistic, antiquarian, or scientific vagabonds who take to tramping by fits and starts. The latter class, being quite incomprehensible to the rustic mind in Guyenne, are regarded by it with almost as much suspicion as the other.

I started at the hour of seven in the morning, which the French—earlier risers than the English—think a late one for beginning the work of a summer day in the provinces. I will not say that the plain on which I now tramped for some miles was uninteresting, because all nature is interesting if we are only in the right mood to observe and be instructed; but to me it was dull, for I had been spoilt by much rambling in up and down country full of strong contrasts. Here I saw on each side of me wide expanses of field, with scarcely a hedge or tree, all dotted with grazing cattle. Not a few of the animals were in the charge of muscular, aggressive dogs, that interpreted their duty too largely, and made themselves a nuisance. At intervals were patches of maize or pumpkins, or a bit of vineyard with a house hard by facing the road—a low ground-floor house solidly built, but its plainness unrelieved by the grace of a vine-trellis or a climbing flower. By-and-by the land became somewhat hilly, and the pasturage changed gradually to open wood and heath, where the gorse was already gilding its summer green, and the bracken stood palm-like in purple deserts of heather. Then the ideas began to warm in the sunny silence, and I fear that I rejoiced in the sterility of the soil which had preserved the charm of free and untormented nature.

When I reached the village-like town of Villefranche, I perceived a movement of men and women like that of bees around a hive. I chanced to arrive on the day of the local fair, when everybody expects to make some money, from the peasant proprietor or the *métayer* who brings in his corn or cattle, to the small shopkeeper who lives upon the agriculturist. I felt disposed to lunch at the grandest hotel in Villefranche, and a good woman whom I consulted on the subject led me through throngs of bartering peasants and cattle-dealers, forests of horns, and by the upturned jaws of braying asses, until she stopped before an inn. There all was bustle and commotion. A swarm of women had been called in to help in anticipation of the crush, and they got in one another's way, walked upon the cats' tails, and raised the tumult of a boxing-booth with the rattle of their tongues. All this was in the kitchen; but there was a side-room in which a long table had been laid for the guests. I took a place at this rustic *table-d'hôte*, and I had on each side of me and in front of me men in blouses who talked in patois or in French, as the mood suited them. I had already perceived that, as I drew nearer to Bordeaux, the Southern dialect became more and more a jargon, in which there were not only many French words, but French phrases. These men in blouses were rough sons of the soil, but I soon gathered that some of them were very well off. In provincial France dress counts for very little as a sign of fortune's favour. There were men at the table whose burly forms and full-coloured faces were just what one would expect to see at a market dinner in an English country town; but their epicurean style of dealing lightly with each dish, so that the charm of variety might not be spoilt by a too hasty satisfaction of hunger, and the unanimity with which they asked for coffee at the close, marked a strong difference in habits and manners. Their politeness to me was almost excessive. As soon as the most jovial member of the company—who had undertaken the carving—had cut up a piece of meat or a fowl, the dish was invariably passed from his end of the table to mine, where I sat alone.

Before leaving Villefranche, a low, square tower enticed me to the parish church. The building was originally Romanesque, but the pointed style must have been grafted upon the other so long ago as the English period. Outside the walls, some steps led me into a little chapel half underground. It was a barrel-vaulted crypt, sternly simple, and lighted only by one very narrow Romanesque window in the apse, just above a rough stone altar of ancient pattern, with a statue of the dead Christ on the ground beneath the slab. In the semi-darkness, the flame of a solitary candle shone without smoke or motion, as if it had been there for centuries, and like all the rest had grown very old.

I had climbed to the ruined Castle of Gurçons, where sloes and blackberries were waiting for the birds in the feudal court strewn with stones. I had left the village of Montpeyroux, with the sound of flails weakening on the wind, and late in the afternoon was drawing near to the Castle of Montaigne, when a small wayside auberge tempted me from the hot road. The woman who waited upon me had a fat body and a hard, firmly inquisitive face—a combination to be distrusted. Having settled down again to her knitting, she inquired of me where I was going, and when I told her that I was on my way to the Château de Montaigne, she asked me if I had any work to do there. I evaded this question, not knowing, or not wishing to know, exactly what she meant. She reflected a few minutes, then, looking at me over her knitting-needles, she said:

'Are you a tiler or a plasterer?'

Now, this was a question that I was quite unprepared for. I had often been set down as a pedlar. I had been suspected of being a travelling musician, and also a colporteur for the Salvation Army; in fact, of being almost everything but a tiler or plasterer. But this shrewd woman had evidently come to the conclusion that, if I did not work upon the housetops, I must perforce be an artist of the trowel. I assured her that I was as incapable of fixing a tile as of making a ceiling; whereupon she said:

'I beg your pardon. I thought you were a workman.'

As I left, I saw by the vivacity with which she scratched the back of her head with a knitting-needle that she was writhing mentally with the torture of unsatisfied curiosity; and I took a malignant pleasure in her suffering. The white flannel that I was wearing was the most agreeable reason I could think of for being associated with plaster, but my resemblance to a tiler continued to perplex me as I trudged along the road.

I now left the broad highway, and took a narrower road that went for some distance through woods up the side of a long hill. The shadows were gathering under the trees, and I was beginning to fear that I should reach the castle too late to carry out my pilgrimage that night, when I saw above me, upon a knoll resting upon rocky buttresses, a modern mansion against a background of trees. This was the very pleasant country residence built by M. Magne, Minister of Finance under the Second Empire, upon the site of the castle of Montaigne, which the author of the 'Essays,' with a better sense of certain distinctions than that which is observed nowadays, preferred to speak of as his *manoir*. This manor-house still preserved its fifteenth and sixteenth century character, when a fire breaking out destroyed everything but the walls, and gave M. Magne a plausible excuse for the demolition. A part that was spared by the fire, and was therefore suffered to remain intact, was the almost isolated tower, to which Montaigne withdrew for the sake of quiet and meditation, and which is so well known to all readers of his 'Essays.' Had this also disappeared, I should have had no motive for wandering down the long avenue at nearly the end of the day.

I met with a courteous reception at the mansion, and obtained immediate permission to visit the retreat of the sixteenth-century moralist who looked with such clear eyes upon human life.

The tower and its gateway belong to the period when feudalism had lost its vitality, and life was troubled by the vague perception of new motives and principles. Montaigne tells us that his family

THE CHÂTEAU DE MONTAIGNE AFTER THE FIRE.

had occupied the manor a hundred years when he entered into possession, and the style of the fragment that is left bears out this statement: it appears to belong to the middle part of the fifteenth century. Already manorial houses, crenated and often moated, but, like this one at Montaigne, defensive rather for show than the reality, were scattered over France. Speaking generally, they belonged to the small nobility who fell under the category of the *arrière-ban* in time of war. In this tower Montaigne had his chapel, his bedroom—to which he retired when the yearning for solitude was strong—and his library. The chapel is on the ground-floor, and is very much what it was in Montaigne's time. It is small, but there was room enough to accommodate his household, which was never a large one. Its little cupola connects it with the local style of architecture, to which the high-swelling name of Byzantino-Périgourdin has been given. A small stone altar occupies the apsidal end, and here, as in two or three other places, the arms of Montaigne will be noted with interest by those who have read in the essays: '*Je porte d'azur semé de trèfles d'or, à une patte de lyon de mesme armée de gueules, mise en face.*'

A man is often a sceptic on the surface and a believer underneath. Pascal has called Montaigne '*un pur pyrrhonien*'; but Pascal himself has been accused of scepticism. Living in an age when the crimes daily committed in the name of religion might so easily have inspired a hater of violence like Montaigne with a horror of creeds, he was no philosopher of the God-denying sort. Moreover, notwithstanding his doubting moods and his fondness of the words '*Que sais-je?*' he upheld the practice of religion in his own home, and died a Christian.

He shared, however, the eccentricity of Louis XI. in keeping himself out of sight when he attended the religious services in his chapel. In the vaulting near the entrance is a small opening communicating with a narrow passage, by means of which Montaigne could leave his bedroom and hear mass without showing himself; but in order to do so he had to grope along his rabbit's burrow almost on hands and knees. To reach his bedroom from the ground, he climbed up the spiral staircase as the visitor does to-day. The steps are much worn in places, and the boots of the essayist must have had something to do with this, for he probably used the tower more than any other man. The room, nearly circular in shape, with brick floor and small windows, looks to modern eyes more like a prison than a bed-chamber befitting a nobleman. But independently of the great difference in the ideas of home comfort which prevailed in the upper ranks of sixteenth-century society, compared to those of the same class to-day, Montaigne, like all men with large minds, loved simplicity. His father, who rode the hobby-horse of frugal and severe training to an extent that might have proved disastrous to his son Michel, had not the boy been singularly well endowed by nature to correspond to his parent's wishes, had nurtured him in the scorn of luxury by methods which would be considered very crotchety nowadays. But this could not have been 'my chamber' in which King Henry of Navarre slept, in 1584, when he paid a visit to Montaigne at his fortified house. There was a better one in that part of the building which has disappeared. Montaigne tells, with his quaint humour, that he was in the habit of retiring to his bedroom in the tower so that he might rule there undisturbed, and have a corner apart from what he curiously terms the 'conjugal, filial, and civil community.' And he expresses pity for the man who is not able to 'hide himself' in the same way when the humour leads him to do so.

It was in the room above, however, where he enjoyed to the full the pleasures of contemplation and quietude. Here, he tells us, he had installed his library, in what had previously been regarded as the most useless part of his mansion. The position had certain advantages. 'I can see beneath me my garden and my poultry-yard, and can look into the principal parts of my house.' It appears from this that he was so much 'in the clouds,' that he did not occasionally find satisfaction from peeping through windows to see what others were doing. It is in this way that the old writers reveal themselves, and they keep themselves in sympathy with mankind by not affecting to be above the little weaknesses common to humanity. Here Montaigne spent the greater part of his time, except in winter, when he often found the library too draughty to be comfortable. It was in this room that he wrote his essays, and chiefly thought them out while pacing up and down the floor, which even then was so uneven that the only flat bit was where he had placed his table and chair. In common with some other celebrated writers, he found that his thoughts went to sleep when he sat down. 'My mind does not work unless the legs make it move. Those who study without a book are all in the same state.'

Montaigne was no despiser of books; on the contrary, he was a great reader, and one of the most scholarly men of his age; but he had his fits of reading like other people, and the intervals between them were sometimes long. Without a doubt, these intervals were the most productive periods. The educational system to which he was subjected as a child was enough to disgust him with books, and to separate him for ever from them as soon as he had obtained his freedom. He was crammed with Latin, as a goose that has to be fattened is crammed with maize in his own Périgord. He was not allowed to speak even to his mother in French or in Périgourdin. Such was the will of his father, who must have been a rather difficult man to live with, and one whom a woman of spirit in this century would kill or cure with curtain lectures if his interference with her in the nursery should outrage the instincts of maternity. The very small boy was handed over to tutors, whose instructions were to make Latin his first language, and even his mother and servants were compelled to pick up enough Latin words to carry on some sort of conversation with him.

In the printers' preface to one of the earliest editions of the 'Essays,' it is said: '*Somme, ils se latinisèrent tant qu'il en regorgea jusque à leurs villages tout autour, où ont pris pied par usage plusieurs appellations latines d'artisans et d'outils.*' It is just possible that some of these Latin terms may have lingered in the district to the present day; but it would need a great deal of patience to find them, and to distinguish them from the patois of the people. Montaigne was more than six years old before he was allowed to say a word in French or in the dialect of Périgord—that of Arnaud and Bertrand de Born. He finished his austere education at the then celebrated College of Guyenne, at Bordeaux, where, according to local authorities, he had among his teachers the Scotch poet, George Buchanan.

'When young,' writes Montaigne, 'I studied for show; afterwards to grow wiser; now I study for diversion.' He liked to have his books around him even when he did not read them. Numerous reading-desks were distributed over the brick floor of this circular room, and upon them he placed his favourite volumes. He therefore read standing, according to the very general custom of his time, which was doubtless better than our own, of making our backs crooked by sitting and bending over our books. According to his own admission, he had a bad memory, therefore he must have been in frequent need of referring to his tomes for the quotations from ancient authors, which he was so fond of bringing into his text, and which make a writer at this end of the nineteenth century smile at the thought of how all the quills would rise upon that fretful and pampered porcupine, the reading public of to-day, if Latin and Greek were ladled out to it after Montaigne's fashion.

The room is bare, with the exception of the wreck of an armchair of uncertain history; but upon the forty-seven beams crossing the ceiling are fifty-four inscriptions in Latin and Greek, written, or rather painted, with a brush by Montaigne. Their interest has suffered a little from the restoration which some of them have undergone; but there they are, the crystals of thought picked up by the hermit of the tower in his wanderings along the highways and byways of ancient literature, and which he fastened, as it were, to the beams over his head, just where the peasants to-day hang their dry sausages, their bacon, and strings of garlic. Many persons copy sentences out of their favourite books, with the intention of tasting their savour again and again; but if they do not lose them, they are generally too busy or too indolent afterwards to look for them. Montaigne, however, had his favourite texts always before his eyes.

The curious visitor intent upon a discovery will be sure to find in these the philosophical scaffolding of the 'Essays;' but I, who examine such things somewhat superficially, would rather believe that Montaigne inscribed them upon the rough wood because they expressed in a few words much that he had already thought or felt. By the extracts that a man makes for his private satisfaction from the authors who please him, the bent of his intellect and cast of character can be very accurately judged. If other testimony were wanting, these sentences would prove the gravely philosophical temper of Montaigne's mind, notwithstanding the flippant confessions of frailty which he mingles sometimes so incongruously with the reflections of a sage. Most of the extracts are from Latin and Greek authors, but not a few are from the Books of Ecclesiastes and Ecclesiasticus and the Epistles of St. Paul. Here one sees written by the hand of the sixteenth century thinker the noble words of Terence :

> ' Homo sum, humani a me nihil alienum puto.'

Then one catches sight of this line by the sagacious Horace :

> ' Quid aeternis minorem consiliis animum fatigas ?'

Looking at another piece of timber, one slowly spells out the words :

> ' O miseras hominum mentes ! O pectora cæca !'

And so one follows the track of Montaigne's mind from rafter to rafter.

Had I been left alone here while the evening shadows gathered in the tower, I might soon have seen the figure of a man in trunk-hose, doublet, and ruff, with pointed beard and pensive eyes, moving noiselessly between rows of spectral desks covered by spectral books; but, as it was, even in the most shadowy corner I could not detect the faintest outline of a ghost. Nobody knows what has become of all the volumes which were here, and which were said to have numbered a thousand. They were given by Montaigne's only surviving child, his daughter Léonore, to the Abbé de Roquefort, but what became of them afterwards is a mystery. There is a small room adjoining the library, the one that Montaigne mentions as having a fireplace. The hearth where he sat and warmed himself has scarcely changed. Here on the walls may be seen traces of paintings. They are supposed to be the work of a travelling artist, to whom Montaigne gave food and shelter in exchange for his labour. It would appear from this that he was careful not to ruin himself by the encouragement of art. Montaigne, however, had a good nature, although he may not have cared to spend money on bad pictures. He has told us of his efforts to reclaim little beggars, and to make them respectable members of society. Before the present château was built, the old kitchen could be seen where he warmed and fed the young mendicants, who, having been refreshed and comforted, returned to their old ways, '*les gueux ayant leurs magnificences et leurs voluptés comme les riches.*'

The village of St. Michel is close to the château, but is of much more ancient origin, as its church plainly shows. The venerable Romanesque doorway was to me more beautiful because of the purple spots of snapdragon, that shone in the clear dimness of the twilight like little coloured lamps about the crevices of the old stones. It is uncertain whether Montaigne was christened here or in the family chapel. It was a strange christening wherever it took place, for we are told that he was 'held over the font' by persons of most humble condition, his father's motive in this matter being, according to the printers of the early edition of the 'Essays' already referred to, 'to attach him to those who might have need of him rather than to those of whom he might have need.' It was Papessu, another village in the neighbourhood, to which he was sent as a nurseling, and where, in obedience to the injunctions of his Spartan father, he was treated like one of the peasant family with whom he was placed. He was reared from his cradle in frugality and philosophy, and, considering what an unpleasant childhood he must have passed, it is truly wonderful that he fulfilled parental expectations, and did not turn out a hard drinker and a brawling cavalier.

There is a tradition in Périgord which some local writers have accepted as fact, that the Montaigne family was of English origin. It is not easy to ascertain the ground on which it rests. The patronymic was Eyquem, and the *chevalier-seigneur*, who settled in Périgord and took the territorial title of Montagne or Montaigne, came from the Bordelais.

That is about all that is really known of the family. If the Eyquem had borne a prominent part against the French kings in the long wars which had not ended a hundred years before the birth of the moralist, this would have been sufficient to account for their being described as English.

Speaking of the peasants of his district, Montaigne tells us that their dress was 'more distant from ours than that of a man who is only clothed with his skin.' From this we have a right to suppose that their appearance was original, if not picturesque. To-day it is neither one nor the other. With the exception of the kerchief tied round the back of the head, after the fashion of the Périgourdine or the Bordelaise, by some of the women, these peasants wear nothing to distinguish them from those who have entirely abandoned a local costume.

'I was in no way pleased with the villagers of St. Michel-Montaigne, nor did they seem to be agreeably impressed by me. Those to whom I spoke did not conceal their surprise that I had been allowed to see over the castle. I think they must have set me down for something less respectable than a plasterer, and I began to think quite seriously that I was neglecting my appearance. Then I thought of the knapsack, which was really getting to look, from long usage, as if the time had come for placing it in the way of a deserving *chiffonnier*, but I could not make up my mind to buy another. I was anxious to pass the night in the village, for

I hoped that the inhabitants had preserved some traditions of Montaigne; but there was only a small and very dirty-looking auberge that had any pretension to lodge man and beast, and here the hostess rejected my overtures with vivacity. Consequently, I was compelled to trudge on, and as I left the place I shook the dust from off my feet at the inhabitants. There was plenty of it, but I am afraid it did them little harm.

The road, now descending towards the Dordogne, passed through great vineyards, and there was enough light for the clustered bunches of grapes to be seen on every vine. Under the calm sky, still full of the heat of the summer day, and glowing duskily, the wide, sloping land offered up all its myriads of broad, motionless leaves and its wealth of fruit to the god of wine. O gentle peace of the summer night that has still the bloom of the sun upon its dusky cheek—peace untroubled by any sound save the joyous shrilling of the cricket that has climbed upon the darkening leaf—why do I hurry onward upon the dusty road, instead of sitting upon a bank amid the fragrant thyme and agrimony, and letting the mind lay in great store of your sweetness against the cold and dismal nights to come?

I reached the village of La Mothe by the Dordogne, and while I was casting about for an inn that looked comfortable, and also hospitable, I met a pretty little brunette with a rich southern colour in her cheeks, charmingly coifed *à la bordelaise*, and tripping jauntily along with a coffee-pot in her hand. It was pleasant to look at a nice face again after all the ill-favoured visages that had risen up against me during the second half of the day, and so I stopped this pretty girl and asked her to tell me which was the best hotel in the place. She would not answer the question, but she mentioned a hotel which she said was as good as any. Thither I went, and found a comfortable little inn, where I was well received. I had not been there long when the little brunette entered. She was the ' daughter of the house.' I now understood that her hesitation was conscientious.

The hostess was a small, sprightly woman with a smiling face, which, together with her bright-coloured coif gracefully hanging to her black hair, made up such a head as puts one in a good temper for a whole evening. She was so highly civilized that she actually asked me if I would like to wash my hands. I expected that she was going to lead me to one of those little cisterns—' fountains ' in French—attached to the wall, that one sees throughout Guyenne, and which have come down almost unchanged in form, as well as the roller-towels that often go with them, from the feudal castles of the twelfth century ; but I was wrong. She led me to a bucket. Filling a large ladle with water, she fixed it lengthwise, and the handle being a tube, the water ran slowly out from the end. I quite understood that I had to wash my hands with the trickling water, for I had often done it before. These ladles with hollow handles are also used for sprinkling the floors, which are never washed in Southern France. The sprinkling lays the dust, cools the air, and depresses the fleas for at least a quarter of an hour.

After I had dealt with a well-cooked little dinner, plentifully bedewed with a pleasant but not insidious wine grown upon the sunny slopes above the Dordogne, I made the discovery that the best room in the house was occupied by the dark-eyed damsel, except when a guest came along who managed to ingratiate himself with her mother, and then the daughter had to turn out. The room was not exactly luxurious, for it contained little besides the bed, a table, and a chair, but it was bright and clean; and when I had confided myself to the strong hempen sheets that had still half a century of wear in them, and had passed the first quarter of an hour, which is always critical, without being made aware by scouts and skirmishers of the advance of a hostile force, I was very thankful that I was not received with open arms in the village of St. Michel-Montaigne.

The next morning I met the Dordogne again after a long separation. It was now a great river flowing quietly through a vine-covered plain. The rapids had all been left far away, but it had begun to feel the tide, and this to a river is like the first shock of death. It struggles for awhile with destiny, and a sadder sound than the cry which it made when it came forth from the rock or the little lake is heard in the quiet evening or the more solemn night. Although it is flowing back to its true source, the river shrinks from the vast and mysterious ocean as we shrink ourselves from the immense unknown.

But at this hour of eight in the morning, with a sun so bright and a sky so blue, only the broad and serene beauty of the water makes itself felt. As the river goes curving over the vine-covered land, its stillness is almost that of a lake, and it mirrors nothing but the sky, save the trees and flowers of its banks. The moments are precious, for the tender loveliness of the landscape will wane as the light gains strength.

On each side of the Dordogne, between the water and the vineyards, which stretch away with scarcely a break across the plain and up the sides of the distant hills, is a strip of rough field. The sunshine of four months, with hardly a shower to moisten the earth, has made flowers scarce, but on this long curving bend of coarse meadow the grass has kept something of its greenness, and the season of blossoming stays by the beautiful stream. There is a wanton tangling and mingling of the waste-loving flowers, such as the yellow toad-flax, the bristling viper's bugloss, the thorny ononis that spreads a hue of pink as it creeps along the ground, sky-blue chicory on wiry stems, large milk-white blooms of *datura*, and purple heads of *centaurea calcitrapa*, whose spines are avoided like those of a hedgehog by people who walk with bare feet. Upon the banks, the high hemp-agrimony and purple loosestrife, with here and there an evening primrose, flaunt their masses of colour over the water or the pebbly shore.

From a distant church tower that rises above the wilderness of vines a clear-voiced bell calls through the morning air, *Sanctus! sanctus! sanctus!* by which all know who care to think of it that the priest standing at the altar there has come to the most solemn part of his mass.

Wandering on, indifferent to the flight of time, upon these pleasant banks, which, but for a bullock-cart that came jolting and creaking along by the edge of the vines, I might have thought quite abandoned by all other humanity, I saw afar off a little cluster of white houses that seemed to be floating on the blue water. I knew that this could be nothing else but Castillon, and that the effect of floating houses was an illusion caused by a bend of the river. And so I was nearing at length that place where the destinies of France and England, so long interwoven, became again distinct, and where the English nationality, which five-and-twenty years before was in imminent danger of absorption as the fruit of victory, was decisively saved from this fate by a defeat for which all England then in her blindness mourned. The loss of Guyenne made an alien dynasty national, and by stopping the outflow of the Anglo-Saxon race upon the Continent, preserved its energies for the fulfilment of a very different destiny from that which had almost begun when a peasant-girl dropped her distaff and took up the sword.

On reaching Castillon I had one of those disappointments to which a traveller should always be prepared after being taught so often by experience that distance idealizes a scene. How much less romantic the town looked now than when I saw it floating, as it seemed, upon the sky-blue water in a haze of gold-dust fired by the slanting rays! It was then like the Castillon of some troubadour's song; now it was a mean-looking little sun-baked town modernized to downright plainness, with no remnant of its ramparts remaining save a sombre old Gothic gateway near the river, and no ecclesiastical architecture deserving notice. Its site, however, is the same as that which it occupied in the Middle Ages, namely, close to the Dordogne, upon a ridge of rising land running up towards the hills which close the valley on the north. On the eastern side this ridge for some distance is so steep as to be almost escarped, but it is covered with grass or vines; on the opposite side it is now only a little above the plain. The battle was fought, not under the walls of the town, but somewhat to the north-east of it in the open country.

Talbot's mistake lay in the confidence with which he attacked an entrenched army much stronger than his own, and especially in his contempt for Messire Jean Bureau's guns. The old leader now belonged to a dying epoch, and his great faith in British and Gascon archers may well have led him to undervalue the power of artillery, notwithstanding that it was used with terrible effect by Edward III. at Crécy more than a hundred years before. The French had profited by that lesson, and at Castillon they turned the tables on their tenacious adversaries.

It may be well to briefly recall the circumstances under which this momentous battle was fought. One after another the English had been compelled to surrender to the victorious armies of Charles VII. their fortresses in Poitou, Angoumois, Guyenne and Gascony; so that of their immense province of Aquitaine, which at one time stretched from the Loire to the Pyrenees, they possessed nothing. Even Bordeaux, after remaining faithful to England for 200 years, was a French city at the middle of the fifteenth century. It would probably have remained so without any fresh appeal to arms if Charles VII. had treated the inhabitants with the same justice, and accorded them the same liberties which they enjoyed while they were the subjects of the English kings. It is a truly remarkable fact that, although these kings were so intimately connected with France by blood and ambition, they had borrowed enough of the genius of the Anglo-Saxon race for establishing foreign possessions upon the solid basis of reciprocal interest to make their administrative policy in Aquitaine incomparably better by its equity, the facilities which it afforded for local government, the assertion of individual rights, and the growth of communal prosperity, than that of the French kings and the great nobles who, while owing homage to the crown, were virtually sovereigns.

At no time was there much dissatisfaction with the rule of the English sovereigns and their seneschals in Western Aquitaine. It was only in the wilder parts of the country, such as the Quercy and the Rouergue, where Celtic blood was, and still is, almost pure, and where the people were very difficult to govern—Cæsar had found that out before Henry Plantagenet, Becket, and John Chandos—that there were frequent revolts, entailing as a fatal consequence in those feudal ages barbaric repression. Throughout the flourishing Bordelais the people became firmly and thoroughly attached to the English cause, not less than the Alsatians and Lorrainers became attached to that of France in later times — although there is no historical parallel between the origin of the two connections. Bordeaux was like another London when the Black Prince held his splendid but profligate court there. Commercial interest had doubtless something to do with this fidelity of the Bordelais, for the wealthy

English soon learnt to appreciate the delicate flavour of the wines grown upon the chalky hillsides by the Garonne and the Dordogne, and 500 years ago ships came from London and Bristol to Bordeaux and returned laden with pipes and hogsheads; but a sagacious and — the times being considered — a large-minded and generous system of government gave to the people that feeling of security which was then so rare, and which was the beginning of all patriotic sentiment. French writers who have studied this subject frankly admit that we have here the true explanation of the strong attachment of the Bordelais and the Gascons to the English cause. As an illustration, it may not be amiss to translate the following passages from 'Les Anglais en Guyenne,' by M. D. Brissaud:

'The Aquitanians had reason to thank the English Government for not having treated them as foreigners, like the inhabitants of a conquered province, as the people of Ireland, for example, had been treated, and for having confined its action to the development of judicial institutions, of which the germ was found in the feudal system of France. . . . The kings of England not only refrained from setting themselves in opposition to the local justice of the *arrière-fiefs;* we have seen them, and we shall see them again in the history of the communal movement, favour the extension of trial by peers, while accommodating at the same time their administrative system to the spontaneous manifestations of opinion in a continental country. They even took care in the composition of the courts that the Aquitanians should not feel the supremacy of the foreigner. With rare exceptions, the *personnel* of the courts of justice was recruited from among the inhabitants of the province—a precious advantage at a time when the predominance of provincial feeling caused those magistrates who were sent from the North of France into the South by the Capetian royalty to be regarded as foreigners and enemies. The consequence of this choice by England of Aquitanians in preference to English in the composition of the courts was that under Philippe le Bel or Philippe de Valois Guyenne had a right to consider itself in possession of a milder and more impartial system of justice than other provinces of the South already attached like Languedoc to the crown of France.'

When, therefore, the Bordelais fell under French rule, the exactions of Charles and the cynicism with which he broke faith, together with the stagnation in the wine trade, caused the people to wish very heartily that the English would return and try their luck again with the sword. A revolt was secretly planned, in which many of the powerful barons of Aquitaine leagued themselves with the burghers of Bordeaux, for the nobles were as dissatisfied with the new state of things as the commoners. The Earl of Shrewsbury, notwithstanding his great age, came over from England with a very small following, and placed himself at the head of the insurrection. The name of Talbot was sufficient to fire the Bordelais and the Gascons with enthusiasm and confidence. As the news of his landing in the Médoc spread, men rushed to arms and raised the old battle-cries of the English in Aquitaine. Bordeaux opened its gates immediately to the veteran leader, and the example was quickly followed by Libourne, Castillon, St. Émilion, and other strong places in the district. This was in the month of October, 1452. It was not until May of the following year that Charles VII. decided to risk the fortunes of war with the two armies which he had mustered — one on the Garonne, and the other on the Charente. By that time the whole of Western Guyenne was again English. The plan of campaign followed was the one laid out by the long-headed Jean Bureau, a man of figures and calculations—a small Moltke of the fifteenth century. He had been the King's treasurer, his *argentier;* then the Bastard of Orleans made him Mayor of Bordeaux, and now, because he had a taste for guns, he was Grand Master of the Artillery. He advised Charles that the best course to adopt in order to spoil the English scheme would be to take possession of the roads leading to Bordeaux, and thus cut off communication with the interior. Now, Castillon was an important strategical point, commanding one of the principal gates of the Bordelais, and it was resolved to make a vigorous effort to snatch this fortress, which was but weakly garrisoned, from the hands of the English. The army, which was under the nominal command of the Comte de Penthièvre, but whose ruling spirit was Jean Bureau, accordingly marched on Castillon, and the King's army moved in the same direction. Talbot, having tidings of the enemy's plans, hurried eastward with all the forces he could muster to the relief of the garrison. His main object, however, was probably to prevent a junction of the two armies. He was confident of being able to defeat both if he could engage them separately.

The French army came down the valley of the Dordogne, and drew near to Castillon when Talbot was still far away. The plan of the leaders was not to attack the town until their camp had been well fortified with earthworks and palisades, for it was felt that they could not be too cautious when an adversary like Talbot was in the country, and possibly near at hand. The entrenched camp was laid out and ordered with a military science in advance of the age. The position, moreover, was very judiciously chosen, considering the impossibility in which the French were placed of selecting high ground. The camp was in a fork formed by the Dordogne and its small tributary, the Lidoire, which flows in a south-westerly direction, and falls into the broad river a mile or two above Castillon. Bureau was given ample time to raise his ramparts, dig his moats, fix his palisades, and set up his park of artillery, on which he laid so much store. Then were detached 800 archers—Angévins and Berrichons—who took up their quarters at an abbey that then existed a little to the north of the town, at the foot of a wooded hill. The fortress was therefore threatened on two sides.

On July 16 Talbot arrived on the scene, and at the first brush obtained a signal advantage by taking the French completely by surprise. On the march from Libourne he did not trust himself to the broad valley, which, being highly cultivated then as it is now, offered no cover, but followed the line of hills to the north of it, on which much of the ancient forest still clung. Thus he managed to conceal his advance until his men broke suddenly upon the unsuspecting archers of Anjou and Berry, and slaughtered them with that thoroughness which was characteristic of mediæval warfare. Talbot belonged to an age that gave no quarter and expected none. A man down was a man lost, unless he had extraordinary luck. The massacre of these archers put the English army—which, after the drafts made on various garrisons, was now said to be about 6,000 strong—in good spirits. Not many of the fugitives reached the camp. Talbot did not follow up this advantage by attempting an immediate attack upon the fortified position in the plain. He gave his men a rest after their toilsome march over rough ground, and put off the decisive battle until the morrow. In the meantime, he placed himself in communication with the garrison of Castillon, and arranged that a sortie in force should take place on the signal being given for the great tug-of-war. He made the abbey his headquarters, and it has been recorded that the casks of wine found in the cellars of the dispossessed monks were speedily drained.

The momentous day of July 17 broke, and Talbot was waiting to hear mass before risking upon the die of a battle the English cause in Aquitaine, so wonderfully and bloodlessly redeemed in a few months. One of the last of the mediæval knights, the ardour of his loyalty was tinged with mysticism, and any cause that he had espoused would have become holy in his eyes. He therefore raised those aged eyes now to the God of battles as he knelt in the quiet sanctuary, impatient though he was to see the vineyards and the meadows redden again with the blood that he had been shedding with the zeal of a Crusader for more than half a century. His chaplain was laying the altar, when a sudden movement of armed men disturbed the kneeling octogenarian from his devotions. Tidings were brought that the French camp was breaking up in disorder, and that the enemy was about to escape. At this news the blood of the old warrior began to rush through his veins, and without waiting for the mass, he had his armour brought to him. Clad in iron and mounted upon his white horse, accompanied by his son, the Lord Lisle—Shakespeare's John Talbot—he rode down into the plain. The enemy was not in disorder, but was waiting behind the entrenchments for the expected onslaught.

Talbot gave the order for the attack, and his thousand knights and esquires charged down upon the camp. When they were well within range of Bureau's artillery, the 'three hundred cast-iron pieces mounted on wheels, which they called *bombardes*,'* broke into a roar, and the stone balls worked terrible havoc upon horses and riders. The ground was quickly strewn with heavily armoured men, who lay there as helpless as turned turtles, and who were ridden over by those in the rear. The mediæval cavalry was shattered or thrown into hopeless confusion by the new artillery. The infantry met with no better success in moving to the assault of the hastily raised ramparts bristling with guns. The English army was demoralized by this unexpected reception. In vain did Talbot ride again and again into the thickest of the fray—the besieged had now assumed the offensive. Even his grand old figure and his rallying cry failed to turn back the tide of disaster. It has been written that in his wrath he struck those of his own party who endeavoured to draw him out of the danger to which he was constantly exposing himself. He felt that at his age it was not worth while to survive defeat, in order that he might die in his bed with a mind tortured by gnawing regret a few months or years later.

* Chroniques de Jean Tarde.

But although he resolved not to save himself, he urged his son to flee. On this point there is too much agreement between English and French chroniclers for it to be possible to doubt that Shakespeare's well-known scene between the old and the young Talbot, in the first part of 'King Henry VI.,' was founded on fact. Moreover, what was more natural than that the father, when he saw the evil turn that things were taking, should have said to his son:

> 'Therefore, dear boy, mount on my swiftest horse,
> And I'll direct thee how thou shalt escape
> By sudden flight. Come, dally not ; be gone'?

What more natural, too, than that the son of such a father should have replied in words which, although less rythmical, would have been in substance these?—

> 'Is my name Talbot? and am I your son?
> And shall I fly? . . . .
> The world will say he is not Talbot's blood,
> That basely fled when noble Talbot stood.'

To the fact that the battle of Castillon was fought in Périgord, although the town is in the Bordelais, we doubtless owe the interesting description that Jean Tarde has left us of the memorable struggle. His narrative, so far as it relates to the incident between Talbot and his son, is in the main the same as Shakespeare's; but being told in the plain prose of a simple annalist, it lacks the rhetorical and romantic embellishments which the British poet thought fit to add. In the following translation of the most interesting part of Tarde's description of the battle, an effort has been made to preserve the style of the writer :

'The English troops entered courageously by the passage where the artillery awaited them, which (passage) alone could give them access to the French army. He who commanded the artillery took his time, and at the first discharge laid low three or four hundred. This massacre, coming unexpectedly, troubled the whole English army, and threw it into disorder, which pained Talbot to see; and fearing the defeat of his men, he told the Sieur de l'Isle, his son, to withdraw and reserve himself for a more fortunate occasion ; who replied that he could not retire from the combat in which he saw his father running the risk of his life. To this Talbot rejoined, " I have in my life given so many proofs of my valour and military virtue, that I cannot die to-day without honour, and I cannot flee without making a breach in the reputation I have acquired by so much labour; but to you, my son, who are bearing here your first arms, flight cannot bring any infamy nor death much glory."* But without giving heed to this counsel, the young lord, full of generous courage,

---

* 'J'ay pendant ma vie donné tant de tesmoignages de ma valeur et vertu militaire que je ne puys meshuy mourir sans honneur et ne puys fuir sans fère brèche à la réputation que j'ay acquise par tant de travaux ; mais vous mon filz qui portés icy vos premières armes, la fuitte ne vous peut apporter aucune infamie, ny la mort beaucoup de gloire.'

reassured his men, made them fall again into rank, and having ranged them with their bucklers fixed in tortoise fashion, sped on to the attack of his enemies in their camp; for they had not dared to leave their trenches. The French, seeing themselves pressed in this way, entered into the battle. Great was the *mêlée*. The artillery of the French continued all the while to fire upon the English troops, and so well that a stone striking Talbot broke his thigh. The English seeing their chief on the ground, believing him dead, and recognising that the French were the stronger in artillery and in the number of men, lost courage, fell into disorder, and only thought of saving themselves. The French, on the contrary, took heart and fought with fury. The battle was bloody. Talbot, his son the Sieur de l'Isle, another bastard son, and a son-in-law, were killed with the greater part of the English nobility, and the whole army was cut to pieces. Talbot's body was buried on the spot where it was found, and upon his grave was built a small chapel that still exists, but open to the sky and half ruined.'

Jean Tarde concludes his narrative of the battle with these remarks:

'The English army being thus defeated, Castillon surrendered, and the King in person besieged Bordeaux, which surrendered on October 18. Following its example, all the other towns of Guyenne again submitted to him. Thus ended the domination of the English in Guyenne, of which (province) they were completely dispossessed, and which at once returned to the sceptre and crown of France, after remaining for three hundred years in the claws of the English leopards.'

There are some patent inaccuracies in Tarde's account—the statement, to wit, that Talbot was buried on the spot where he fell, whereas his body was carried from the field and taken to England. The ecclesiastical chronicler must have accepted the story in circulation among the common people, which is repeated to this day by the peasants around Castillon, who even point out a mound which they call 'Talbot's grave.' Shakespeare does not fall into this error, although he brings Jeanne d'Arc upon the battlefield, notwithstanding that she was burnt twenty-two years before the death of Talbot.

According to the version accepted by French historians, Talbot was overthrown by a cannon-shot, and was afterwards despatched on the ground by a soldier who ran his sword through the hero's throat. His body was carried into the French camp, where it remained all night, and it was so disfigured that his herald could hardly recognise it. Many of the fugitives were drowned or were killed by the archers while attempting to swim across the Dordogne. Four thousand English, or English partisans, were said to have been slain on this fatal day, and only a small remnant of the army managed to retreat within the walls of Castillon. The French then besieged the town, and the bombardment was so furious that the garrison was soon willing to surrender on the best terms that could be obtained. Bordeaux was not besieged until St. Émilion, Libourne, Fronsac, Bazas, Cadillac, and other strongholds of the Bordelais had capitulated.

After this rather long journey into the past, I must return to my wayfaring upon the battlefield of Castillon, over which more than four centuries have crept since the events occurred which gave it so dramatic a celebrity.

Scorched by the now blazing sun, I took the shadeless road leading out of the town towards the north-east, and after walking about a mile between vineyards, I came to the commemorative monument of the battle raised in 1888 by the Union Patriotique de France. It is a low obelisk, with no ornament save a mediæval sword carved upon it, with point turned upwards. Facing the road is the following inscription :

'*Dans cette plaine le* 17 *Juillet,* 1453, *fut remporté la victoire qui délivra du joug de l'Angleterre les provinces meridionals de la France et termina la guerre de cent ans.*'

The abbey where the French archers were surprised and slain must have been near this spot, but it was down in the valley by the Lidoire where Talbot fell. There is no trace of a chapel such as that of which Tarde speaks, nor any other mark to show the place. But the little stream is there as of old, and the beautiful Dordogne that drank the mingled blood of the two armies which its tributary poured into it flows serenely and blue as it did then under the same summer sky.

An Englishman who now wanders over the battle-field of Castillon can hardly realize how his country grieved at the defeat of Talbot far away here amidst the southern vines. To-day it seems so absurd, so contrary to the policy of common-sense, that England, then so thinly populated, should have striven so hard and so long in order to be a Continental power; when now, with her dense population, half subsisting upon foreign supplies, she blesses that accident of nature which caused the bridge of rocks that connected her with the mainland to disappear beneath the sea. Surely if history teaches anything, it teaches the vanity of politics.

From Castillon I bent my course to St. Émilion on the road to Libourne; the Dordogne, which here twists like a snake in agony, being left somewhat to the south. The whole country, hill and plain, was clad with vineyards, but I soon grew weary of looking at the numberless short vines fastened to stakes in one broad blaze of unchanging sunshine. Even the hanging clusters of grapes wearied the eye by endless repetition.

By-and-by, out of all this sameness rose a hill in that abrupt manner which strikes a peculiar character into this southern landscape, and upon the hill were jutting rocks and a broken mass of strangely-jumbled masonry—roofs rising out of roofs, gables crushing gables, feudal towers, great walls, and one tall heaven-pointing spire. This was St. Émilion, respected in the Middle Ages as a strong fortress of the Bordelais, and now so famous for its wine that the locality has long ceased to produce more than an insignificant part of that which is put into bottles bearing the name of a saint who drank nothing stronger than water. Only the wine that is grown upon the sides of the hill is really St. Émilion; it changes as soon as the vineyards reach the plain. It is then a *vin de plaine*, and is no more like the other than if it had been grown fifty miles away.

Celtic remains point to the conclusion that, long before the foundation of the first monastery, which was the beginning of the mediæval town, the Gauls had an *oppidum* on this hill. St. Émilion became a fortified town in the reign of King John, who signed a charter here, and it may be said to have been thoroughly gained over to the English cause by Edward I., who granted numerous privileges to the burghers. For a short time the place fell into the power of Philippe IV., but it was in its collegial church in May, 1303, that the duchy of Aquitaine was ceremoniously restored by the Seneschal of Gascony to the King of England, represented on this occasion by the Earl of Lincoln. To reward the inhabitants for their fidelity, and to compensate them in some sort for the trials which they had endured in consequence, St. Émilion was made a royal English borough, and enjoyed the special favour and protection of the sovereign.

It was in this fourteenth century that it rose to the height of its importance and prosperity. We can gather to-day from the ruins of its religious buildings and fortifications what that importance must have been. Besides the monastery dating from the age of Charlemagne, whose monks early in the twelfth century were placed under the rule of St. Augustin, two great religious establishments were those of the Minor Friars or Cordeliers, and the Preaching Friars or Dominicans. Of the vast convent of these last nothing remains but a very stately and noble fragment of the church wall, standing isolated on the top of the hill.

During the Hundred Years' War St. Émilion was besieged and taken by Du Guesclin; but although the burghers were often compelled to dissemble in order to save their throats, they were always ready to welcome an English army. They were among the first to follow the example of the men of Bordeaux, who raised the English flag for the last time in 1452.

During the religious wars of the sixteenth century St. Émilion suffered grievously from the fury and bestiality of the vile ruffians of both camps. The excesses of the Norman barbarians when they burnt and pillaged the town in the ninth century were mild in comparison with those of the sixteenth-century Christians.

There are few spots more fascinating to the artist and archæologist than this ruinous old stronghold of the English kings. One might ramble a long time over the cobble stones of its steep narrow streets, and about the ruined ramparts draped with green pellitory and the spurred valerian's purple flowers, with a mind held in continual tension by the picturesque. At every angle there is a fresh surprise. The monolithic church, made by excavating the calcareous rock, which crops out and forms a kind of table near the top of the crescent-shaped hill, is said to have been mainly the work of monks in the ninth century. There is no other resembling it, with the exception of the one at Aubeterre, the idea of which was probably borrowed here. Steps lead down into the nave, where there is an odour of ancient death, and where the light darting through windows pierced in the face of the cliff reveals on each side a row of huge rectangular piers supporting round-headed arches, all forming part of the rock. These separate the nave from the aisles, of which there are three, the one farthest from the centre having been used chiefly for burial. All about are numerous tomb recesses. The piers and their arches are covered with green or black lichen, which adds not a little to the gloom and dismalness of this subterranean church.

Ornamental details of the exterior, such as the

doorway with its bas-relief of the Last Judgment, are of a much later period than the rude excavations of the interior. From the platform of rock immedi-

MONOLITHIC CHURCH AND DETACHED TOWER AT ST. ÉMILION.

ately above the vast crypt rise a Gothic tower and spire dating from the twelfth century. This structure, which lends so much character to St. Émilion, appears to belong to the church beneath; but such is not the case. Although separated, it is a part of the collegial, now parish, church, which is higher up the hill, just within the line of the ramparts. It is said to have been built by the English, but the Romanesque lateral doorway would be strong evidence of the contrary if there were no other. English influence, however, may have played some part in the extensive rebuilding which was carried out in the fourteenth century. The east end, scarcely forming an apse, and pierced in the centre with a high broad window with a narrower window on each side, suggests this, as do also the very massive columns of the choir.

Close to the monolithic church is the cavern where the hermit Émilion is supposed to have dwelt. In order to see it, I had to find a little girl who kept the key, and who led the way down the steps with a lighted candle. St. Émilion might have looked far before finding a more unpleasant place to live in than this cavern. It might be safely guaranteed to kill in a very short time any man with a modern constitution, unless he were miraculously preserved from rheumatism and other evils of the flesh. The damp oozes perpetually from the slimy rock, and the air is like that of a well. Indeed, there is a little well here called St. Émilion's Fountain. The spring is intermittent; every two or three minutes the water is seen to rise with one or more bubbles. It never fails, no matter how prolonged the drought may be.

The little girl pointed out to me a great number of pins lying upon the sandy bottom of the basin. I asked her how they came there, and she said that they were dropped into the water by people—chiefly young girls—who wished to know when they would be married. If two pins that had been dropped in together crossed one another upon the bottom, it was a sign that the person who let them fall would be married within a year. As I could distinguish none that were crossed, I concluded that all who had made the experiment here were condemned to celibacy. This form of superstition—doubtless of Celtic origin wherever met with—is much more frequent in Brittany than in Guyenne.

Close to the 'grotto' is an old charnel-house quarried in the rock with a dome-shaped roof, at the top of which is a round hole that lets the light of heaven into the awful pit. This opening formerly served another purpose. There was a cemetery above, and as the bones were turned up from the shallow soil to make room for others still clothed with their flesh, they were thrown down the orifice. For those who did not wish to be disturbed after death, the charnel-house was the securer place of burial. Here, as in the underground church, one sees numerous recesses in the wall which were made for tombs. Those who feel the need of sombre ideas will be as likely to find the incentive to them here as anywhere. Oh, what ghostly places are these old southern towns, with their heaps of ruins, their churches as dim as sepulchres, their crypts and charnel-houses filled with bones!

Fellow-wanderer, come and see with me the convent of the Cordeliers. There are no monks

CONVENT OF THE CORDELIERS: THE CLOISTERS.

here now. Since the Revolution their habitation has been open to all the winds of heaven, and the shadow of the wild fig-tree falls where that of their own forms once fell as they stood in the stalls of their chapel choir. In the cloisters, the ivy and the pellitory and the little cranesbill have crept with the moss and the lichen from stone to stone, and in the centre of the quadrangle stands a great walnut-tree that spreads its branches and long leaves over all the grassy ground. Birds that cannot be seen sing aloft under the flaming sky; but here in the shadow of the arcades and the dark foliage nothing moves except the snail and the lazy toad at evening amidst the damp weeds. The stones that we see here in this ruined convent bear testimony to the eternal restlessness of man's desire to give some fresh artistic form to his religious aspiration. Some were carved in the Romanesque period, others in the Gothic, others in the Renaissance. Witnesses of the human mind in different ages, all are crumbling and growing green together, sharing a common fate.

Among the many holes and corners full of curious interest at St. Émilion, but which have to be searched for by the visitor, is the cave where during the Reign of Terror seven of the Girondins sought refuge, and where they remained hidden from their persecutors several months, notwithstanding the unflagging efforts made to discover their retreat. Their enemies were convinced that they were somewhere in the town, or, rather, underneath the town, for the rock on which it rests is honeycombed with quarries. These Girondins were Guadet, Salles, Barbaroux, Pétion, Buzot, Louvet, and Valady. Guadet was a native of St. Émilion, and he had a relative there named Madame Bouquey. She and her husband were a brave and noble-minded couple at a time when the craven-hearted—always the accomplices of tyrants—were in the ascendancy everywhere. They sheltered Guadet and his companions in a cave under their garden. The fugitives had first thought of hiding in the old quarries, but they realized that they would be much safer in the cave.

Hearing that the 'Grotte des Girondins' was in the garden of the school, now kept by Christian Brothers, thither I went. A little boy in a long black blouse, with a leather belt round his waist, having obtained the permission, pulled open a trapdoor in the garden, and, candle in hand, led the way down a flight of steps into a cavern, about the same size as St. Émilion's, but much dryer and more comfortable. On one side of it was an opening, which was made perceptible by a very faint glimmer of daylight. I found that this opening was in the side of a well. The water was still far below, and the surface of the earth was about fifteen feet above. The trap-door entrance—so the Brothers assured me—did not exist in the last century, and the only entrance to the cave was by the well. It was, therefore, an admirable hiding-place, for the lateral opening was not distinguishable from above, and anybody looking down and seeing the water at the bottom would have thought it quite unnecessary to search any further there. The Girondins were let down by the rope, or they let themselves down. As time went on, the position of Monsieur and Madame Bouquey, on whom strong suspicion rested, became more and more difficult ; and when the fugitives were informed that commissioners were on their way to St. Émilion, they resolved that, rather than expose their benefactors to further peril, they would make an attempt to escape in different directions. Louvet got to Paris, and was the only one of the seven who did not come by a violent death. Guadet and Salles were captured at St. Émilion, and were executed, as a matter of course. Barbaroux was also taken, after making an unsuccessful attempt to blow out his brains, and he, too, was guillotined at Bordeaux. Buzot and Pétion stabbed themselves in a field between St. Émilion and Castillon, where their bodies were found half eaten by wolves. The seventh, Valady, was brought to the scaffold at Périgueux. Monsieur and Madame Bouquey met the same fate. And it is with this page of modern history that the quiet little garden of the Brothers' school, its well and hidden cavern, are so tragically associated.

Near a ruinous *donjon*, called the Château du Roi, and attributed to Louis VIII., now much overgrown with herbs and shrubs, I stood on a bastion of the town wall, overlooking the crescent-shaped hollow, covered with houses, bits of fortification older than the outer wall, ruined convents—a chaos of lichen-tinted stones and tiles gilded by the warm yet tenderly softened sunshine of early evening. And as I gazed, I longed the more to be able to carry away a picture of that scene, with all its tones and tints, that would last in the memory, as I also wished to draw out of it all the meaning of what I felt. I left with a sense of failure, of weakness, of confused impressions, which was to me like a gnawing weevil of the mind, on the road to Libourne.

Vines, vines, nothing but vines, gradually shading down to the darkness of the night that covers them. Then, when the dusky gauze of the cloudless night is drawn all over it, the broad leafy land sleeps under the sparkling stars.

Here at Libourne I am in a town of whose English origin there can be no doubt. It was one of the thirteenth-century *bastides* founded in Guyenne by Edward I. These *bastides* were at the outset intended as places of refuge for serfs and other non-belligerents of the rural districts in time of war. Their character was that of free or open towns, and most of the burgs that still bear the name of Villefranche in the South of France were originally *bastides*. Not a few of them keep the name of *La bastide*, in combination with some other to this day. They are to be found all over Guyenne and a great part of Languedoc. They were often fortified with a wall, a palisade, and a moat. Their strong peculiarity, however, the one that has been preserved in spite of all the changes that centuries have brought, was the rectilinear and geometrical manner in which they were laid out. In contrast to the typical mediæval town that grew up slowly around some abbey, or at the foot of some strong castle that protected it, and in the building of which, if any method was observed, it was that of making the streets as crooked as possible, to assist the defenders in stopping the inward rush of an enemy, the streets of the *bastide* were all drawn at right angles to each other. Consequently, however old the houses may be, such towns have somewhat of a modern air. For the same reason, one of the chief attributes of the picturesque—an accidental meeting of various motives—is absent. To the inhabitants of these free towns a certain quantity of land was apportioned in equal parts, for which a fixed rent was paid to the king or other feudal lord.

I have said that the *bastides* were not picturesque. In their early days they must have been quite hideous; but time, that plays havoc with human beings, lends to such of their works as may offer to it the resistance of a long, hard struggle an interest which becomes at length a beauty. There is usually to be found in these towns the thirteenth-century *place*, or square, which formed, as it were, the heart of the commune. Along each of the four sides is a Gothic arcade, on which the first and all the higher storeys of the houses rest. Thus, there is a broad pavement completely vaulted over on each side of the quadrilateral, where people can walk, sheltered from the sun or rain. These old squares, wherever they are found, are now always picturesque.

Libourne, from being a small *bastide*, grew to such importance, on account of its position on the right bank of the Dordogne and the wine trade that it was able to carry on by water, that it rivalled Bordeaux before the close of the English domination, and the question of making it the capital and the seat of the Prince of Wales and Aquitaine was seriously pondered. To-day it preserves all the plainness of its line-and-rule origin; but it has a few redeeming features, such as one side of its ancient square, with broad pavement under Gothic arches, a picturesque town-hall of the sixteenth century, and a curious mediæval tower, with machicolated embattlements, now capped with a very tall and pointed roof, and known as the Tour de l'Horloge. It is a remnant of the fourteenth-century ramparts.

The people of Libourne were steadfast partisans of the English to the last, and after 1453 they did not seek to distinguish themselves by their resignation to the rule of the French kings. When in 1542 the insurrection against the salt-tax, commencing at La Rochelle, spread over Saintonge and the whole of Western Guyenne, the Libournais threw themselves heartily into the movement. When the time of repression came they were made to smart sorely for their turbulent spirit. The Place de l'Hôtel de Ville, of which one side remains very much as it was then, bristled with gibbets, and

150 persons were hanged in a single day. The man who had rung the tocsin that called together the insurgents was suspended by the neck to the

TOUR DE L'HORLOGE AT LIBOURNE.

hammer of the bell, as a warning to others not to ring it again unless they had a better motive.

Standing by the broad river, a little above the

point where the Isle is falling into it, carrying down all manner of craft with the tide, I see at a distance of a couple of miles or so towards the west the hill that is known in history as Le Tertre de Fronsac. There Charlemagne built a castle, of which nothing now remains. The hill owes its modern celebrity entirely to its wine. It is not everybody who knows the virtue of the genuine Fronsac, especially that which was yielded by the old vines before the phylloxera destroyed them, but most people are familiar with the brand. But for this, the *tertre* would long since have ceased to be famous, notwithstanding Charlemagne.

The hill has a strange appearance, for it rises abruptly from the river bank in the midst of the plain. It did not tempt me to walk to it in the scorching heat, but as a steamboat was going there, I paid two sous and went on board. I had never been in such a cockle-shell of a steamer before. It rocked and tumbled like a coracle, and spat and fumed and snorted like a veritable devil composed of an engine, a couple of paddle-wheels, and a few boards. Helped by the tide that was pouring out, it went down stream at a rate that was almost exciting, and in a few minutes I was landed at the bottom of the famous hill. I made a conscientious attempt to reach the top, but was stopped just where it began to grow interesting by a notice-board that warned me, if I ventured any farther, I should be prosecuted and heavily fined. Such things are not often seen in France. Vineyards are generally open, but here they were fiercely protected with walls and fences and notice-boards. The land was evidently very precious. I had wandered into truly civilized country, where land and manners were too highly cultivated to please me, and I again regretted the rocky wastefulness that I had left behind me.

THE HILL OF FRONSAC.

I turned back, and wandering about the village, which is a straggling one, looked for the church, hoping that this at least would show something of interest. Not being able to find it, I asked a man to tell me the way to it, and he, stopping, said :

'*L'église pour aller prier dedans ?*'

What does he mean by asking me that ? I thought. Could there be a church at Fronsac that was not used for praying ?

'Yes, that is the kind of church I am looking for.'

'Very good,' rejoined the man. 'Now I know what you want I can inform you. I put that question to you because there are some people here called Léglise.'

It was to the church *pour prier dedans* that I went, not to Mr. Church. Originally Romanesque, it has been pulled about and changed almost as much as the Tertre de Fronsac, which I am sure I shall never wish to climb again.

BY THE GARONNE.

I HAVE reached—I need not say how—the southeastern corner of the Bordelais, and am now at Bazas in very hot September weather. I am not only as warm as a lizard of the dusty roadside likes to be, but am hungry and thirsty. I therefore cast about for an inn that looks both cool and capable of giving a fair meal to a tired wanderer. My choice rests with one that swings the sign of the White Horse; for, to tell the truth, I have somewhat of a superstitious belief in the luck that this emblem brings to the traveller. I place it immediately after the Golden Lion, my favourite beast on a signboard, although it deceived me once. The deception, however, befell in the Bordelais, where the inhabitants are far from being the most pleasant to be found in France; therefore I judged this *Lion d'Or* charitably, and took account of all that might have frustrated its good intentions.

Having made up my mind to trust myself to the White Horse, I entered a large *salle-à-manger*, which, after the glare of the mid-day sunshine, seemed as dark as a cellar that is lighted by a small air-hole. The shutters had been closed against the heat and the flies, but the rays that broke through had the ardour and brilliancy cast by molten metal in a smelting-house, and the sight very quickly accepted with relief the lessened light of the room. There was one other person present, and, although the table was long enough to accommodate fifty, my plate was set immediately opposite his. He was a young negro gentleman, with such a shining ebony skin that he was almost refreshing to eyes that had just left the dazzling whiteness of the outer world. He gave me the impression of being a rather conceited African, but this may have been because my dress compared so unfavourably with his. He was the son of a merchant at St. Louis in Senegal, and was just like a Frenchman in all but his colour. I asked him if he found the weather we were having sufficiently warm, and he replied:

'*Regardez comme je sue!*'

True enough, the beads of perspiration glistened upon his forehead like black pearls. What is the use, I thought, of being an African if one cannot keep dry in a temperature of 95° Fahrenheit?

I soon left my dark acquaintance, and went forth

to roam about Bazas, which, like so many little old towns of Southern France, is in the early hours of a summer afternoon as quiet and deserted as a cemetery. The stones are so heated that a cat that begins to cross the road lazily, stopping to stretch or examine something in the gutter, will suddenly start off at a rush as if a devil had been cast into it.

The interest of Bazas to the traveller lies mainly in its church, which was formerly a cathedral. Its broad and imposing façade, encrusted with ornament, chiefly in the florid Gothic of the fifteenth century, but disfigured by a hideous eighteenth-century *fronton* that crowns the gable, stands at the top of a broad and rather steep *place*, of which some of the houses are of the fifteenth and sixteenth centuries. The tower built against the northern end of the front carries a lofty and graceful crocketed spire. Until the Revolution, this west front, ornamented as it was with nearly three hundred statues, was considered the most elaborately decorated in the South of France. Even now, although so many of the niches are vacant, it is exceedingly rich in sculpture. The central doorway is so lofty that it occupies more than half the height of the original façade, and the doorway on each side of it is only a little lower. The central tympanum is divided into five compartments filled with figures in relief. The uppermost panel represents the Last Judgment. The interior admirably combines grandeur and lightness. The nave (without transept) is very long and lofty, and, together with its clerestory, is

BAZAS.

beautifully proportioned. Finally, the effect of a delightful vista is obtained by the wide sanctuary, with its lofty and airy arcade separating it from the *pourtour*.

All the old part of the town is built upon a rocky hill, and it is still almost surrounded by ruinous ramparts. The church is just within the wall on the side where the rock is precipitous. Looking upward from the bottom of the narrow valley, the view of the ramparts high overhead, tapestried with ivy and other plants, and above these the tabernacle work, the crocketed pinnacles and spire, and the fantastic far-stretching gargoyles of the venerable cathedral, makes one feel that joy of the eye and the spirit which is the wanderer's reward for all the sun-scorch and other petty tribulations he may have to endure in searching for the picturesque.

From Bazas I made my way to Villandraut, a neighbouring town of about 1,000 inhabitants. I had left the vines, and was now in the *landes* of the Gironde. I was surrounded by pines, gorse, and bracken, which last was as brown as if it had been baked in an oven. Ten summers had nearly passed since I undertook my long walk through the great pine forests of the Landes. I had wandered on and on, and was again drawing near to them. Already the country wore much the same appearance as that farther south, although less wild and desolate. I expected to have a return of the old feelings when I found myself again in the midst of the pines that said so much to me years ago; but somehow the old spirit would not come back, and

I felt little besides the heat and the weariness of the way.

Villandraut, ordinarily a very dull place, was exceedingly animated when I walked into it. A fair was being held there, and a fair in a village or rural town is always a reason for being gay, and often an excuse for worse. There was some local colour here. All the young girls wore the Bordelaise coiffure, the handkerchief being generally of white, yellow, green, or crimson silk. Just clinging to the back of a young head, no coif is more graceful or picturesque than this. There was much dancing. Cheeks flushed and dark eyes flashed as the brilliant coifs and light-coloured dresses whirled round and round. I found more feminine beauty in this south-eastern corner of the Bordelais than I had seen for a very long time among the French peasants. The young women here are well and delicately formed, and have an erect and graceful carriage. They are coquettes from their childhood. They have fine eyes and luxuriant tresses, and the face often shows richness of colour. A few *blondes* are seen among the *brunes;* but whether fair or dark they have all the same exuberance of nature. The teeth are rarely good after early youth. The cause of this blemish is said to be the water, which, passing through a sandy soil, contains little or no lime.

My motive in coming to this place was to see the ruined castle of Villandraut, the gloomy stronghold built at the commencement of the fourteenth century by Bertrand de Goth (or Got), Archbishop of Bordeaux, who afterwards as Pope Clement V. took the momentous step of transferring the Papal See from Rome to Avignon. I found it a little outside the burg, but near enough to be used by many of the peasants who had come into the fair as a convenient place for putting up their carts and stabling their animals. Each of the towers had been turned into a stable for horses and oxen, and scattered over the weedy space within the walls were vehicles of all sorts and sizes.

The plan of the castle is a vast oblong, with a high cylindrical tower at each angle, and two additional towers on the side of the town. The deep and wide moat that still surrounds it, except where it has been filled up in front of the gateway from which the drawbridge was once raised and lowered, is like a ravine that is choked with brambles and shrubs. The exterior view is very striking. It is impossible to approach this ruin without being impressed by its mournful grandeur. From all these piled-up stones which the wild plants strive to cover, there comes the sentiment of pride in death. A very slow but a certain death it is. One after another the stones will continue to fall as they have been falling for centuries, and will be put to fresh uses. How many houses and pigsties at Villandraut have been built with materials taken from the castle? Nobody knows exactly, but everybody in the place has a shrewd suspicion on the subject. I climbed up the dilapidated spiral staircase of one of the

INTERIOR OF THE CHÂTEAU DE VILLANDRAUT.

towers, and after passing through two guard-rooms with Gothic vaulting, where the wind, now blowing up for storm, moaned through the loopholes, I came out upon the *chemin de ronde*, quite overgrown with shrubs and ivy. All around stretched the pine forest, with tints of violet and the purple rose deepening in the misty distance.

This bastille on the edge of the sandy desert was a queer sort of fold for a shepherd to build. To judge the past, however, by the present is one of the most mischievous of errors. Nothing is easier than to criticise the actions of men in a bygone age, and nothing is more difficult than to do justice to their motives. The militant bishop is intolerable now even, when he is nothing more formidable than a controversialist. It may have been necessary, however, in the Middle Ages for him to make himself dreaded as well as respected, like the judges of Israel. This Clement V., at any rate, must have believed in the need of the Church to be able to defend itself behind strong walls.

From Villandraut I turned towards the Garonne. A furious storm was now raging southward, and after nightfall the lightning flashes kept the whole forest seemingly ablaze. The hour was late when I reached the town of Langon by the river, and at the inn where I put up I met with a cold dinner as well as a cold reception.

When the sun came again I took the road to St. Macaire, and this soon crossed the Garonne. The broad blue river was very beautiful in the early morning sunshine, and a mild lustre lay over the

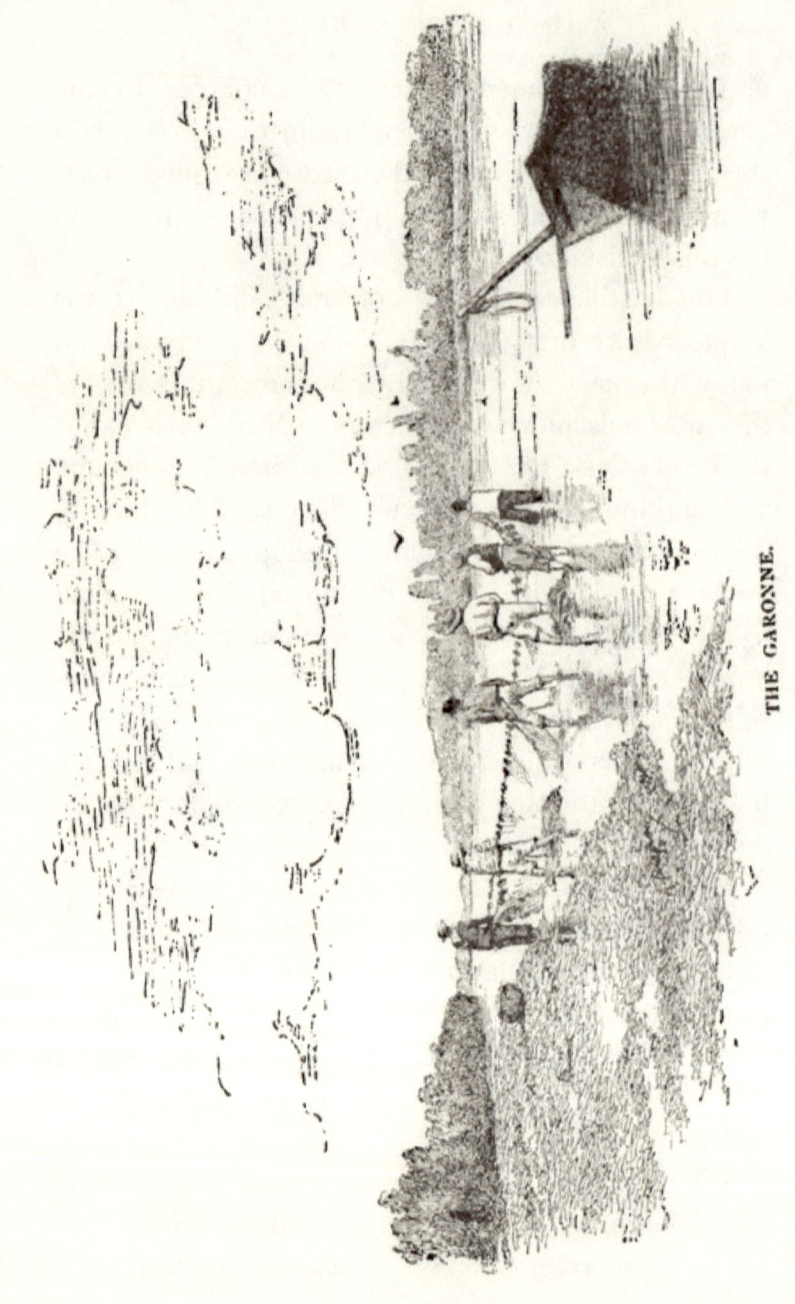
THE GARONNE.

vine-clad plain beyond. The vintagers were getting busy. Bullock-waggons were waiting with the barrels, now empty, that were to bear the grapes to the wine-press, and here and there amidst the green of the motionless leaves was the gleam of a white, yellow, or crimson coif that moved with the head of the woman or girl who wore it.

The morning had not lost its freshness when I reached St. Macaire. This is one of those ruinous old towns of the Bordelais where the traveller, if he were an artist, would find a thrilling subject for his pencil at every street corner, and at the angle of every bastion of crumbling rampart, where the bramble, the ivy, and the wild fig-tree strike their roots between the gaping stones. Proud and strong in the centuries that have been left far behind, St. Macaire is now a little spot of slow life in the midst of a wilderness of ruins. Three walls encircled it, and although these did long service as the quarries wherefrom the inhabitants drew such building stone as they needed, yet have they not been demolished, but tell their whole story still, in spite of wide gaps and breaks—ay, and with a far more soul-moving voice than when they could show to the enemy their crenated parapets without a flaw, when not a stone was wanting to any tower or gateway, and when the twang of the cross-bow might have been heard from every loophole. There are heaps of stones where the lizard runs, where the coiled snake basks untroubled, where the dwarfed fig-tree sprouts when the spring has come, and where the wild cucumber pushes forward its yellow flowers that fear not the flame of summer. The fig-tree may also be seen hanging from high walls, and the vine rambles among blooming or embrowned wallflowers on the top of ruinous gateways, through which the people still enter and leave the town as they did centuries ago.

The spirit of originality that animated the mediæval architects in this part of France, and which has given to so many churches a distinct character, an individual expression, that keeps the interest of the traveller constantly alive, is strongly marked upon the church of St. Macaire. Commenced at the beginning of the twelfth century, its earliest portions show the Pointed style in its infancy, fearful as yet of committing what seemed so like heresy—a departure from the Roman arch; but in the same building a much bolder Gothic asserts itself in the parts that were added in the thirteenth century. The west front and doorway have not the majesty of the style as it was developed chiefly in the North, but they have that venerable air which is not always to be found in the stately and majestic. The low tympanum is crowded with figures belonging to the period when the statuary's art was still swathed in the swaddling clothes of its new infancy, and what with their own uncouthness, and the wear and tear of time, it is no easy matter now to trace in them all the purpose and meaning of the sculptor.

And yet in their blurred and battered state they tell us much more than they would if they had been restored with the best skill and learning of our own time. The age is gone when these bas-reliefs were the religious books of the people. To imitate them is mere æstheticism, and to restore them is often destruction.

A few words must be said of the old market-place of St. Macaire. Thanks to the poverty or the apathy of the commune, three sides have retained all their mediæval character, the interest of which has been refined and deepened by the artistic touch of time, the sentimental ravisher, the slow and gentle destroyer. A Gothic arcade encloses a wide pavement, and each bay, with its vaulting, forms, as it were, the portico of the house, whose first and higher storeys rest upon it. Here those who are interested in civic architecture can see thirteenth and fourteenth century houses still retaining their wide Gothic doorways.

I rested awhile in a café, and chance led me to one that was kept by an Englishman. He recognised my nationality, while I supposed him to be a Frenchman, and he seemed as glad to see me as if I had been an old friend. He told me that when he was a boy his father brought his family from England to Les Eyzies, where he was employed at the iron works. (The smelting furnace has been cold for many a year.) The man who spoke was middle-aged, and although he expressed himself with difficulty in English, and turned his phrases out of French moulds of thought, he had kept a strong accent of the Midland counties. The tenacity with which an accent adheres to the tongue, even when the language to which it belongs has been half lost, is very remarkable. I remember meeting in my roamings an Englishwoman who had married a French cobbler, and who had been buried alive with him in the Haut-Quercy for forty years. She had learnt to speak patois like a native, but it had become a sore trial to her to put her thoughts into English words; nevertheless, when she did bring out those words that had been so long put away in the mind's lumber-room, the accent was as pure Cockney as if she had but lately drifted away from her own Middlesex.

The freshness of the morning was gone, and even in the shade of the café I felt the hot breath of the day. When I was again upon the powdered road between interminable rows of vines, the glare was dazzling; but I was not alone. Groups of people were trudging under the same fiery sky, and upon the same dusty road, and all were moving in the same direction. When I learnt that they were pilgrims on their way to Verdelais, I thought that I might do worse than be a pilgrim, too. I therefore went with the stream, which soon turned up the flanks of the vine-clad hills.

Thus I found myself about noon in a small village, seemingly composed of one wide street lined on both sides with cafés and restaurants. There was also a very conspicuous modern church in a fantastic and debased, but showy, style of architecture. It was densely crowded, and the shine of innumerable candles was seen through the open doors. The whole street was likewise crowded with people, who had come from various parts of the Bordelais, and who seemed determined to spend a happy day in a sense no less material than spiritual. There was a great rush to the restaurants, and there was flagrant overcharging on the part of those who kept them—all speculators on piety.

Perhaps the grandeur of the solitude of Roc-Amadour, the antiquity of the buildings, and the simplicity of the pilgrims had made me a wrong-headed judge of the newer places of pilgrimage. However this may be, after the first glance at Verdelais I wished I had not come. There was no quiet corner here where a wayfarer could sit and refresh himself; in this hurly-burly of eager hunger, and with this infernal clatter of tongues, repose was impossible.

After lunching in the midst of a noisy and vulgar throng, I regained the open country, with the conviction that, should I ever decide to start off upon a serious pilgrimage, the road to Verdelais would not be the one that I would take.

I now turned down towards the valley through the vines, the inevitable vines, and was soon on the banks of the Garonne. Almost facing me upon the opposite hillsides were the famous vineyards of

Sauterne, and I knew that the vintagers were busy there, every woman—women are chiefly employed—with her pair of scissors snipping off the grapes one by one from the gathered bunches, and rejecting all that were not sound. It is a costly method, but the wine pays for it.

A steamer comes panting down the river, and stops near the grove of willows where I have been trying to hide myself from the all-searching, all-burning sun. I go on board and take a delicious rest under an awning for two or three hours, while the vine-covered hills on either side glide backward with their many steeples and towers.

I left the steamer at a place called Castres, some fifteen miles below Bordeaux. My motive for stopping here was to see the castle where Montesquieu was born, and where he spent the greater part of his life. The map told me that it lay some five or six miles from Castres in the direction of the *landes*, and as the day was already far spent, I reckoned upon passing the night at the small town of La Brède, which is very near the castle. The sun's rays were as yet but little calmed as I turned from the broad, blue river.

I had to follow the highway, on which the white dust lay thick. This road was carried up the hills. In the vineyards were crowds of men and women, many of whom had been drawn out of the slums of Bordeaux. Some of them were forlorn-looking beings, whose faces told that they were glad to seize this opportunity of earning for a few days a sure wage. Those who wish to feel the poetic charm of the vintage should not go into the district of Bordeaux to seek it. Here only the legend remains. It is not that the vines are wanting. The Bordelais, except in the sandy and pine-covered region of the *landes*, has again become one immense vineyard ; but whether it be from the struggle to live, or the lust of prosperity, the people fail to impress the traveller with that communicative openness and joyousness of soul which he would like to find in them, if only that he might not have the vexation of convicting himself of laying up for his own fancy another disillusion.

Although the hills were not steep, the long ascent was wearisome in the sultry air that no breath of wind freshened. At length the sun went down in a golden haze, where the vine-leaves spread to the horizon like the sea. Then I descended the other side of the range of hills that follows the line of the river. The vineyards gradually fell away, and scattered pines gave a touch of sadness to the darkening land. By these signs I knew that I was on the outskirts of the *landes* of the Gironde. But the sand was still some miles away, and the country here was well cultivated. A church spire that looked very high in the clear obscure, as I saw it through an opening of trees, led me to La Brède.

Here I thought I should have no difficulty in

finding night quarters, for there was at least one good inn, which in its own estimation was a hotel. But the way in which I was scrutinized when I wearily set down my knapsack on an outside table and took a seat under the plane-trees told me that I was not welcome. Since I had been in the Bordelais I had become rather too familiar with such signs. The hotel-keepers here have but very slight faith in the respectability of travellers who do not come in the usual way—that is to say, by train or omnibus, or something with wheels, though it be but a bicycle. To them the walking traveller, whether he carries a bundle over his shoulder on a stick, or a knapsack on his back (the latter is very rarely seen), is merely a tramp. If he speaks with a foreign accent, he is doubly deserving of suspicion. These people of the Gironde are, perhaps, all the more doubtful of the morality of others because of the little confidence that they are able to place in their own.

My request for a room at this inn was not refused immediately. There was a consultation indoors, the result of which was that I was presently told that every room was already engaged. There was nothing for it but to walk on to the next inn, and hope for better luck there. It would seem as if they had been prepared here for my coming, and had already made up their minds how to act. Two women stood in the doorway, and did not move an inch to make way for me. I had hardly asked the question about the room, when the answer came emphatically 'No.' At the next house to which I went I met with the same answer; but in spite of the unpleasantness of my position, I was almost thankful for it, such a villainous-looking place it was. There now remained but one small auberge at La Brède. If I was denied shelter there, I should have to go to Bordeaux that night, and I was five miles from the nearest railway-station. The prospect had become sombre, and I began to regret that I had allowed the Château de Montesquieu to entice me among these too civilized savages.

The last inn was a little outside the town. A dark man, whose face, even in the feeble light, I could see was deadly pale, was seated outside the door, breathing the freshness that now began to be felt in the evening air. As my previous negotiations had been with women, I was glad to perceive now an innkeeper of the other sex. My experience of the French provinces had taught me that, wherever people are suspicious of strangers whose appearance is not such as they are familiar with, and where the measure of prosperity has been sufficient to produce a cautious disinclination to move out of the daily trodden track, it is far better to deal with men than with women.

The pale-faced man, after looking at me fixedly for a few seconds, said :

'Yes, I have one spare room, and it is at your service.'

I crossed the threshold, and took a seat in the

kitchen and general room. The surroundings were not very cheerful; but no other people would have anything to do with me, and therefore my choice of accommodation had to be what is termed Hobson's. After all, it would not be the first time that I had passed the night in a little roadside inn.

The pale man's wife did not look in a very sweet temper at her husband for having put extra work upon her without consulting her, and there was an exceedingly obnoxious boy of about fourteen who sat upon the corner of a table and, with the assurance of a mounted gendarme, put all sorts of questions to me in a voice that would change suddenly from a bark to a bleat. I was seized with such a longing to knock him off his perch that I presently kept my eyes fixed upon the frying-pan so that I might not be tempted beyond my strength. The father was evidently too weak to contend with his horrible offspring. My interest in the man was at once awakened. He told me that he was from the Lot-et-Garonne, where he owned land, and had been a tobacco-planter, until a disease of the spinal marrow compelled him to seek an occupation that required less exertion. Thus he came to be an innkeeper. He had spent much money upon doctors, who had done him little or no good. The only treatment that had given him any relief was *la pendaison*.

'Hanging!'

'Yes, hanging. I have passed hours hung up by the neck.'

Then he explained the apparatus that is used for stretching the spinal marrow in this manner, and how it differs from the method of hanging that is best known in England. When I learnt what he had undergone in order to get cured, I could understand why he looked so pale and sad. A melancholy Jacques was he, indeed, in appearance, and he was certainly not the most cheerful of hosts whom one might hope to find at the end of a weary day; but I knew that I was in the house of an honest man, who was also brave and patient, while he looked out upon the world through darkening windows.

Before going to bed I had some talk with my host about my adventures at La Brède before I applied to him for a night's lodging. There was actually a sparkle of mirth in his melancholy dark eyes, and his sunken cheeks were puckered up with a sort of smile.

'If you had been dressed in a black coat,' said he, 'like a *commis voyageur*, they would have all found room for you.'

This was my opinion, too. The Bordelais believe in the respectability of no travelling motives under heaven that are not commercial.

My bedroom that night had much the character of an outhouse or fowlhouse. It was on the ground-floor, and the rafters overhead sloped rapidly towards the exterior wall. A small low window opened upon the garden. The walls were whitewashed, but the floors were very black, as all these southern floors are. Upon the single table a heap of raw wool waiting to be spun had been pushed back a little to make room for the doll's washing-basin and towel that had been placed there for me. Besides the bed that had been prepared for me, there was another, which happily was to remain unoccupied that night. The traveller should always be thankful when he has a room, however poor and plain, that for the few hours which he needs for rest he can call his own. If he snores himself, he will sleep through the noise, and have, perhaps, pleasant dreams; but if anybody else snores in the same room, he may lie awake with clenched fists, and be tortured by the foolish desire to throw something.

The next morning I believe I was the earliest visitor who in modern times has troubled the serenity of the Château de la Brède. A mist—one of the first of the falling year—lay white and dense upon the land. It was a fine-weather mist, such as in the opinion of the wine-grower helps to ripen the grapes.

I had entered the park about half a mile beyond the town, and then between two rolling banks of vapour I saw the high walls and higher towers of the castle looming through the grayness. A little later I distinguished the dull water of the very wide moat, and the three connected bridges, which were formerly blank spaces between low

towers, unless the drawbridges happened to be let down.

Over these the visitor must now pass in order to reach the castle. As I was so early, I killed time to my own good by trying to fix some impressions of the vast pile of masonry that stood here in the middle of a little lake. It is an extraordinary block of architectural patchwork, quite without symmetry, and yet the mass is imposing. The ground-plan approaches the circle more than any other geometrical figure, but it is a circle with slices cut off, and composed of angles so irregular as almost to imply a fantastic motive. But the motive was purely utilitarian. The feudal fortress which was built here in the thirteenth century underwent in subsequent ages so many modifications and additions with a view more to the comfort of the dwellers therein than to their protection from enemies, that in course of time little of the mediæval buildings remained besides the great hall, the basement, and the keep. These became jumbled up with late Gothic and Renaissance work.

Jean de Secondat, who purchased the old fortified manor-house out of his savings as *maître d'hôtel* to Antoine de Bourbon and Jeanne d'Albret, was probably responsible for most of the sixteenth-century work that one now sees. When his descendant, Charles de Secondat de Montesquieu, took possession, the building was almost identical with that which exists to-day. It has been exceptionally favoured, for it has remained in the family, and for at least two hundred years it has undergone none of those alterations which in previous times had so changed its appearance. The eye may not be delighted with its symmetry, but the mind has the satisfaction of knowing that this was verily the birthplace and home of him who more than any other man made political science popular.

The present owner of the castle, recognising the duty that the descendant of a great man owes to society, receives with the most liberal courtesy all those who make a pilgrimage to this spot.

The relics of Montesquieu are numerous, and they have been preserved with admirable solicitude. The room where he slept and wrote is almost the same as when he finally left it; with this difference, that time has made everything look dingier. Even the white linen curtains which hung at the window hang there still, and they are by no means so yellow as one might expect them to be. On the plain little table at which he washed himself stand his basin and ewer. The basin would be called to-day a dish, for it is not more than two inches deep. It held quite enough water, however, to serve for the ablutions of a baron a century and a half ago. Much the same notion of what is fit and proper in a washing-basin remains to this day among the French peasantry, and even among the middle class in the provinces the growth of the toilet crockery has been far from rapid since the time of Montesquieu.

The bed in which the political philosopher slept is a broad four-poster, not with slender and finely carved posts, like Fénelon's, but severely simple. Indeed, in none of the furniture of this room is there any indication of the love of the ornamental. On the contrary, everything tells of a mind that set no value upon aught but the strictly needful. Montesquieu's small writing-case, divided into compartments, the borders of the leather covering embellished with dingy, half-obliterated gold ornament, was perhaps the finest bit of property he had before his eyes as he sat and worked there. He always carried it about with him when he travelled. No doubt it went with him to England, and he probably wrote letters to his friend Lord Chesterfield upon it. And here is his travelling trunk. It still looks fit to bear many years' rough usage; and yet, if railway porters had to pull it about, they would not know whether to laugh at its strange appearance or to swear at its weight. It was built for wear, like Noah's ark, and it is entirely covered with leather, elaborately decorated with patterns, composed of the round heads of small nails. The high stone chimney-piece, plain and solid like the character of the man who did so much lasting work in this room, remains, together with the fire-dogs, as it was in his time.

Montesquieu formed the habit when thinking alone of leaning back in his chair before the hearth and resting his feet against one of the jambs of the chimney-piece. The stone was much worn away by his feet; but the marks would pass unobserved if the knowledge of their cause had not been preserved in the family. A bust of Montesquieu made in his life-time shows him with closely-cropped hair, and without a wig. It is a remarkably Cæsar-like head, every feature indicating the decision and positivism of the Roman character—such a one, indeed, as ideally became the author of the 'Considerations.' But how the face is altered when we look at it in another portrait—a painted one, representing the writer in a great wig as President of the Parliament of Guyenne! A head becomes another head if the coiffure be but changed.

A little room adjoining this one was where Montesquieu's secretary worked. He was the drudge of a literary man, who was probably not exempt from the constitutional irritability of those who carry a whirling grindstone within their brains for the sharpening and polishing of thought. The unremembered scribe may have done good service to literature while undergoing his purgatory in this world.

Distributed throughout this suite of apartments on the ground-floor is much furniture of the sixteenth, seventeenth, and eighteenth centuries, most of which was here when Montesquieu was *châtelain*.

A spiral staircase leads to the great hall of the old castle. It has been very carefully preserved, and although the walls are now lined with bookshelves, it keeps the air of baronial grandeur and simplicity. Montesquieu made it his library, and had reading-desks set up all down the middle. His books remain, as well as some of his manuscripts, including that of ' Les Lettres Persanes.' This long hall is covered by a plain barrel-vault, and at the far end is an immense chimney-place, the chimney built out at the base several feet from the line of the wall, and sloping back towards the ceiling. On the plain (not conical) surface of this mediæval chimney are painted figures, said to be of the thirteenth century, but probably later. One can distinguish a king, a cardinal, and a page on horseback. The mediæval fireplates are still in their old place at the back of the vast hearth.

I have little more to add to this story of my wanderings. From La Brède I went to Bordeaux, where I found much to admire that I had not noticed before. The architecture of this city is incomparably richer than that of Paris by the diversity of style and the good fortune that has protected so many of the buildings from the destructive influences of war, fanaticism, and the presumption of those who in all ages would abolish the past if they could, and refashion the world according to their own ideas. The Roman period is only represented by a fragment of the amphitheatre, now called the Palais Gallien. But what a picturesque fragment this is, and how well it introduces the visitor to the study of the Romanesque, the Gothic, and the

Renaissance buildings, of which he will find such characteristic examples here! The interest of the Englishman will be increased by the knowledge that some of the most notable of the Gothic edifices were raised when to his countrymen Bordeaux was a continental London, and a well-known tendency of his will probably lead him to attribute much of

THE GARONNE AT BORDEAUX.

their grave stateliness to the influence of the Anglo-Saxon character.

The people of Bordeaux are supposed to have derived not a little of their keen commercial spirit from the English. If this be so, they may take credit for having in some respects surpassed their teachers. By the gift of persuasiveness and the

THE PALAIS GALLIEN AT BORDEAUX.

abundance of words, by aplomb, combined with astuteness, they are fitted by nature to be the most successful traffickers on earth. But in return for a little work they expect a great deal of enjoyment, and more than most industrious cities is Bordeaux given up to the worship of pleasure.

From Bordeaux I continued down the river until I saw the Dordogne join the Garonne, where both are lost in the Gironde. Here the two beautiful and noble streams, one flowing from the Auvergne mountains, and the other from the Pyrenees, no sooner embrace than they die on the breast of the salt wave. They and their tributaries caused one of the sternest, and yet one of the most smiling, of regions—a country where Nature seems to have the passion of contrast, and where she brings forth all the best fruits of the earth—to be named by the Celts the Land of Waters, and by the Romans Aquitania. A little reflection explains why the English of the Middle Ages, having once possessed it, should have clung to it with such tenacity. Less easy is it to understand why so few of their descendants of to-day feel the peculiar spell that almost every rood of this broad land should cast upon them, apart from the charm of old story and of the picturesque that appeals to all.

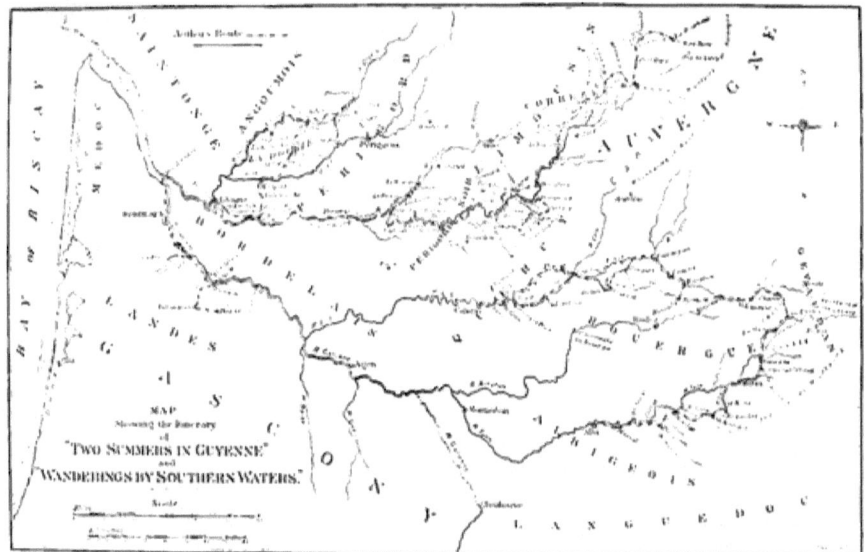

INDEX.

AGRICULTURE in the Corrèze, 52
    in Périgord, 102, 196, 201
Albigenses, The, 298
Ales, 145
Angelus, The, 56, 321
Angling, 31, 123, 211
Architecture:
    Byzantine, 213, 227, 235
    Gothic, 65, 84, 94, 142, 364, 380, 389, 406
    Renaissance, 127, 142, 213, 219, 406
    Roman, 213, 405
    Romanesque, 16, 47, 141, 175, 245, 249, 301, 326, 337, 405
Argentat, 59
Arnaud (Arnaud Daniel, troubadour), 244
Artaud, The (River), 36
Aspic, The, 6, 30
Aubeterre, 300
Aulaye, St., 309
Auvergnats, Descent of the, 147

Barthélemy, St., 275
Bastides, 145, 371
Bazas, 378, 380
Bazile, St., 57
Beaulieu, 64
Beüne, Valley of the, 155
Beynac, 109
Boëtie, Etienne de la, 127
Boleti, 42
Bordeaux, 405
Bordelaises, 383
Born, Bertrand de, 178
Bort, 25

Bourdeilles, 225
Brantôme, 219
    Abbey of, 221
    Pierre de Bourdeilles, 220
Brède (La), 394
Buckwheat, 23
Buisson (Le), 139
Bureau, Jean, 350

Cacolets, 204
Cadouin, Abbey of, 142
Cadurci, The, 73
Cæsar at Uxellodunum, 73
Carthusians of Vauclair, 278
Castillon, 344
    Battle of, 353
Castres (Gironde), 393
Cazoulès, 91
Cemeteries, Rural, 238
Céou, The (River), 123
Cèpes, 42
Chandos, 128
Château d'Aubeterre, 304
    de Beynac, 116
    de Biron, 145
    de Bourdeilles, 225
    des Eyzies, 153
    de Fâges, 133
    de Fénelon, 94
    de Grignols (Talleyrand), 208
    de Gurçons, 326
    de Hautefort, 179
    de Marouette, 233
    de Montaigne, 328
    de Montesquieu, 399
    de Nabinaud, 298
    de Villandraut, 383

Chavannon, Gorge of the, 18
Christy, Mr., 158
Clement V., Pope, 384
Coiffure at Mort-Dore, 2
  in the Bordelais, 383
  in the Corrèze, 16
  in Périgord, 119
Coligny, 221
Condé, Madame de, 73
Court-Mantel, Henry, 80, 178
Coutras, 321
Coux, 137
Crayfish, 121
Cyprien, St., 132

Denis, St., 78
Domme, 103
Dordogne, Valley of the, 1-8, 20-31, 60-65, 88-149, 340-377
Double, The. 246-280
Dovecots, 205
Droit Seigneurial, 205
Dronne, Valley of the, 218-234, 243-245, 281-321

Échourgnac, 250
Églisottes, Les, 319
Eleanor of Aquitaine, 80
Émilion, St., 361-371
English, The, at Bordeaux, 347
  at Castillon, 344
  at Domme, 105
  at Les Eyzies, 177
  at Libourne, 371, 373
  at Martel, 80-82, 84, 86
  at Montpont, 280
  at St. Émilion, 361
  at St. Cyprien, 133
  at Sarlat, 127
  at Tayac, 165
Eyquem. *See* Montaigne
Eyzies, Les, 151

Fage, La, 48
Fénelon, 95
Frogs, 188
Fronsac, 375
Front, St., Cathedral of, 212
Funeral Customs, 13, 14. 160

Gallien, Le Palais, 405
Garonne, Valley of the, 386-408
Gipsies, 165

Gironde, The (River), 408
Girondins. The, 368
Gorge of Hell. The, 164
Goth, Bertrand de, 384
Grand-Brassac, 235
Groléjac, 98
Guyenne, English rule in, 346-349

Hautefort, 179
Huguenots, 65, 208, 220, 229, 298

Ilex, The, 95, 159
Implements, Flint, 158
Isle, Valley of the, 180-217

Jongleur, The modern, 92

Knolles, Robert, 106

Landes (of the Gironde), 382, 394
Langon, 386
Laplau, 47
Leaguers, The, 229, 299
Leopard, The English (Heraldic), 81
Libourne, 373
Limeuil, 149
Lisle, 229
  The Lord, 353, 355
Luxège, The (River), 46

Macaire, St., 388
Madeleine, La, 168
Malaria, 249, 269
Man, Prehistoric, 155, 158, 173
Marcillac, 53
Martel, 79
  Charles, 79
Master and servant, 207
Méré, Poltrot de, 298
Messeix, 10
Métayage, 201
Michel-Bonnefare, St., 337
Miremont, Cavern of, 156
Modières, 145
Mondane, St., 94
Montaigne, Michel, 322, 328-339
Montesquieu. 401
Montpont, 280
Mothe-Montravel, La, 340
Moustier, Le, 173

INDEX

Nabinaud, 295
Neuvic, 40
Normans, The, in Périgord, 215

Orgues de Bort, 25
Oriel, The golden, 190
Owls, 103

Pantaléon, St., 44
Peasant-proprietor, The, 102, 196
Périgord Noir, 97
Périgueux, 212
Plantagenet, Henry, 80
Plateau, Great Central, of France, 11
Plough, Ancient form of, 53
Poaching, 50
Politics, Local, 206
Port-Dieu, 20
Puy d'Issolu, 71

Raymond II., Viscount of Turenne, 64
Religious Customs, 16, 241
Riberac, 244, 290
Roche Canillac, La, 54
Chalais, La, 315
Romance Language, The, 83
Roque-Gageac, La, 107
Rue, The (River), 27

Salignac, François de. *See* Fénelon
Sarlat, 127
Saut de la Saule, Le, 27
Sauterne, The vintage at, 393
Sauve, St., 4
Savennes, 17
Sébastien, Dom, 273
Secondat, Charles de. *See* Montesquieu

Servières, 58
Shroud, The Holy, 143
Siorac, 136
Snail-eaters, 166
Songs of Périgord, 199
Souillac, 88
Spinning-wheels, 51
Superstition, 211, 366

Taillefer, 215
Talbot, 323, 346, 350-360
Tarde, Jean, 105, 129, 143, 355
Tayac, La Roque de, 164
Church of, 175
Tocane St. Apre, 284
Tocsin, The, 241
Tour de Mareuil, 93
de Vésone, 214
Trappists, 246, 248, 250-275
Troglodytes, 155
Truffles, 93, 136
Turenne, 73
Tursac, 168

Uxellodunum, 71

Vauclaire, La Chartreuse de, 278, 279
Vayrac, 70
Verdelais, 391
Vézère, Valley of the, 151-179
Victor, St., 240
Villandraut, 382
Villefranche de Longchapt, 324
Villeinage, 79
Vin de plaine, 361
Vins du pays, 171
Vintage, The, in the Bordelais, 393
Viper, The Red, 6, 30

Wages, 46, 57, 203
Wolves, 97

THE END.

BILLING AND SONS, PRINTERS, GUILDFORD.
J. D. & Co.

www.ingramcontent.com/pod-product-compliance
Lightning Source LLC
Chambersburg PA
CBHW030550300426
44111CB00009B/925